New Frontiers of Educational Research

Series Editors

Zhongying Shi, Beijing, China
Ronghuai Huang, Beijing, China
Zuoyu Zhou, Beijing, China

Editorial Board

Chengwen Hong, Beijing, China
Cynthia Gerstl-Pepin, Vermont, USA
David Osher, Washington, DC, USA
Felix Rauner, Bremen, Germany
Huajun Zhang, Beijing, China
Jonathan Michael Spector, Georgia, USA
Kenneth Zeichner, Washington, USA
Kerry Mallan, Brisbane, Australia
Levin Ben, Toronto, Canada
Liyan Huo, Beijing, China
Mang Li, Beijing, China
Qi Li, Beijing, China
Ronghuai Huang, Beijing, China
Shinohara Kyoaki, Gifu, Japan
Susan Neuman, Michigan, USA
Wei Kan, Beijing, China
Xudong Zhu, Beijing, China
Yan Wu, Beijing, China
Yanyan Li, Beijing, China
Yaqing Mao, Beijing, China
Yong Zhao, Oregon, USA
Zhikui Niu, Beijing, China
Zhiqun Zhao, Beijing, China
Zhongying Shi, Beijing, China
Zuoyu Zhou, Beijing, China

More information about this series at http://www.springer.com/series/10795

Xin Liu · Xiumin Hong · Wanzhen Feng ·
Xiaowei Li · Xinghua Wang · Yuejuan Pan

Research on the Development and Education of 0–3-Year-Old Children in China

Springer

Xin Liu
Faculty of Education
Beijing Normal University
Beijing, China

Xiumin Hong
Faculty of Education
Beijing Normal University
Beijing, China

Wanzhen Feng
Faculty of Education
Beijing Normal University
Beijing, China

Xiaowei Li
Faculty of Education
Beijing Normal University
Beijing, China

Xinghua Wang
Faculty of Education
Beijing Normal University
Beijing, China

Yuejuan Pan
Faculty of Education
Beijing Normal University
Beijing, China

The book is supported by the Fundamental Research Funds for the Central Universities.

ISSN 2195-3473   ISSN 2195-349X (electronic)
New Frontiers of Educational Research
ISBN 978-3-662-59753-8   ISBN 978-3-662-59755-2 (eBook)
https://doi.org/10.1007/978-3-662-59755-2

© Springer-Verlag GmbH Germany, part of Springer Nature 2019
This work is subject to copyright. All rights are reserved by the Publisher, whether the whole or part of the material is concerned, specifically the rights of translation, reprinting, reuse of illustrations, recitation, broadcasting, reproduction on microfilms or in any other physical way, and transmission or information storage and retrieval, electronic adaptation, computer software, or by similar or dissimilar methodology now known or hereafter developed.
The use of general descriptive names, registered names, trademarks, service marks, etc. in this publication does not imply, even in the absence of a specific statement, that such names are exempt from the relevant protective laws and regulations and therefore free for general use.
The publisher, the authors and the editors are safe to assume that the advice and information in this book are believed to be true and accurate at the date of publication. Neither the publisher nor the authors or the editors give a warranty, expressed or implied, with respect to the material contained herein or for any errors or omissions that may have been made. The publisher remains neutral with regard to jurisdictional claims in published maps and institutional affiliations.

This Springer imprint is published by the registered company Springer-Verlag GmbH, DE part of Springer Nature.
The registered company address is: Heidelberger Platz 3, 14197 Berlin, Germany

Preface

The first 3 years is the starting point of children's development and learning, when infants and toddlers experience the most rapid physical, cognitive, language, emotional, and social development of their lives. This period lays the foundation for lifelong health, well-being, and success. In recent years, research on neuroscience, psychology, pedagogy, and other disciplines has confirmed the importance of the development and education of infants and toddlers. Promoting the development of infants and toddlers and improving the quality of their care and education have gradually become one of the focuses of early childhood education in many countries around the world.

Recently, China has attached great importance to the development and education of infants and toddlers. In 2001, the State Council issued the *Outline of Child development in China (2001–2010)*, which first proposed to "develop early education for children aged 0–3." In 2010, the *Outline of National Medium-and Long-Term Program for Education Reform and Development (2010–2020)* stressed that "attention should be paid to the education of infants and toddlers," marking that the education of infants and toddlers was officially incorporated into the national education service system in China.

Scientific research is the forerunner of appropriate education. The promotion and educational guidance for early childhood development should be age-appropriate and follow the rules of infants and toddlers' physical and mental development. Previous research on infants and toddlers' mental development and its influencing factors can provide scientific bases for childcare providers and parents to comprehensively understand the age characteristics and individual differences of infants and toddlers, meet their development needs, create an appropriate environment, and develop appropriate curricula for them.

Although great progress has been made in the research on the development and education of children aged 3–6 in China, there are still few empirical studies on the development and education of infants and toddlers, which has attracted attention gradually in recent years.

This book is based on numerous studies examining the development and education of infants and toddlers conducted by many professors and their graduate students in the Institute of Early Childhood Education at Beijing Normal University. Its contents primarily include the characteristics of the physical and mental development of infants and toddlers in China, family environment and parenting status, the impact of family on infants and toddlers' development, and the impact of national policies on infants and toddlers' families and their development. This book has greatly enriched the basic research on the development and education of infants and toddlers in China.

The book is divided into the following three parts:

Part I (Chaps. 1–6): The Developmental Status of Infants and Toddlers and Its Influencing Factors.

In this part, based on the existing research, comprehensive methods, such as questionnaire, testing, and observation, were used with 2- and 3-year-old children and their parents. An observation and evaluation tool suitable for assessing the physical and mental development of Chinese infants and toddlers aged 2–3 was developed. By using this tool, the developmental status of 145 2- and 3-year-old children from four districts in Beijing was evaluated in a real and natural play situation, and the developmental status and characteristics of 2- and 3-year-old children in five domains—motor, cognition, language, emotion, and social adaptation—were preliminarily investigated, and the factors affecting the development of 2- and 3-year-old children were explored. To some extent, this study has promoted the professional level of infants and toddlers development evaluation in China, and provided an important basis for research on the developmental status and influencing factors of 2- and 3-year-old children in large samples in China in the future.

Part II (Chaps. 7–9): Family Environment and Infants and Toddlers' Development.

In this part, we investigated the characteristics of grandparent–parent co-parenting and its influence on infants' emotional adjustment, and explored the mechanism of infants and toddlers temperament in it. In addition, we also examined the early parenting concept, the current situation of family education environment and the characteristics of learning and development related to infants and toddlers from the perspectives of home literacy environment and family art education, and analyzed and discussed the impact of family education environment on infants and toddlers' early literacy and artistic development. Through the above-related research, we hope to provide targeted advice for families to better prepare suitable parenting environment for infants and toddlers, change inappropriate parenting concepts, and further improve parenting ability.

Part III (Chaps. 10–12): Policies and Challenges.

In this part, we investigated and forecasted the growth trends of 0–3 years old population under the universal two-child policy in Beijing. We also conducted an in-depth investigation and analysis of the characteristics of second-child family rearing and sibling relationship in urban families and the problems faced by them. These basic studies provide us with implications for understanding national conditions, analyzing current situation, and meeting challenges.

Beijing, China   Xin Liu

Acknowledgements

We are very grateful to the following organizations and individuals, without whom this book would not have been published.

First of all, we are appreciative of the support from the leaders of the Faculty of Education of Beijing Normal University. They helped us build a bridge of friendship with Springer. Furthermore, we are grateful to the editors of Springer, for their earnest, careful, and professional work and for their great tolerance of time.

We would like to thank the National Social Science Foundation (Approval No.17ZDA123) for its support for the research of this book.

We would also like to express our gratitude to our graduate students from the Institute of Early Childhood Education for their active participation as well as their conscientious and hardworking in this project. They participated in the development of research tools, data collection, data analysis, and writing of the research paper. Of course, we also believe that through our joint research, they will also gain professional growth in the field of infants and toddlers' development and education, which is also an important result of our research that we expect from this project, namely, the cultivation of future researchers and educators. Here, we would like to express our special gratitude to the graduate students who participated in the writing of this book. They are Ting Liu, Xiaoyu Wei, Guiying Zhong, Zhiying Wang, Liyun Jiang, Xiaoyan Mao, Tiantian Dang, Lihua Long, Jiaqi Yang, Wanting Zhou, Feng Chen, Xuemei Ding, Ruiling Zhu, Shihan Hua, Luqun Liu, Manhua Yang, Siyu Zhou, Xiaoli Yang, Yawen Chen, Yue Zhang, Yingtong Liao, etc.

We are also grateful to Su Li, Li Luo, Xiaoye Liu, Caixia Yang, Yin Yang, Guangling Ju, Jing Li, Xin Gong, Na Lin, Shufang Li, Guangping Zhu, Ping Zhao, and Qi Ding for their participation in the writing of this book.

We would like to express our deepest gratitude to My Gym fund of Beijing Normal University. Mr. Junjun Liu from My Gym provided us with great support in research funding and research sites. We are also grateful to Ms. Ying Feng as well as children and their parents from My Gym who gave support to our research.

We would like to thank teachers, children, and parents from Blue Sky Kindergarten, People's Liberation Army 61 Kindergarten, and Yangzhen Central Kindergarten who participated in our research.

The book is supported by the Fundamental Research Funds for the Central Universities.

Xin Liu

Contents

Part I The Developmental Status of Infants and Toddlers and Its Influencing Factors

1	**Research Contents and Methods of Development in 2- and 3-Year-Old Children**	**3**
1.1	Research Background	3
1.2	Literature Review	4
1.3	Research Purpose and Tasks	6
1.4	Research Subjects	6
	1.4.1 Sampling	6
	1.4.2 Samples	7
1.5	Research Methods	7
	1.5.1 Questionnaire Method	7
	1.5.2 Test Method	8
	1.5.3 Observation Method	9
1.6	Research Tools	9
1.7	Data Processing and Analysis	9
References		12
2	**Analysis of Motor Development in 2- and 3-Year-Old Children**	**13**
2.1	Introduction	13
2.2	Methodology	14
	2.2.1 Subjects	14
	2.2.2 Research Instrument	15
	2.2.3 Research Process	16
2.3	Results and Analysis	18
	2.3.1 Analysis of Status Quo of Motor Development of 2- and 3-Year-Old Children	18

		2.3.2	Difference Analysis of Status Quo of Motor Development of 2- and 3-Year-Old Children	24
	2.4	Conclusion		46
	References			47

3 Analysis on Cognitive Development of 2–3 Years Old Children ... 49

	3.1	Introduction		49
	3.2	Research Methods		50
		3.2.1	Research Object	50
		3.2.2	Specific Research Methods	51
		3.2.3	Research Tools	51
		3.2.4	Research Process	52
		3.2.5	Data Analysis	54
	3.3	Research Results and Analysis		54
		3.3.1	Cognitive Development of Children Aged 2–3 Years Old	54
		3.3.2	Number–Concept Recognition of 2–3 Years Old Children	55
		3.3.3	Three-Dimensional Pattern Matching of 2–3 Years Old Children	55
		3.3.4	Symbolization and Representation of 2–3 Years Old Children	56
		3.3.5	Exploration and Construction of 2–3 Years Old Children	59
		3.3.6	Problem-Solving Capability for 2–3 Years Old Children	60
		3.3.7	Attention and Participation Development of Children Aged 2–3	61
	3.4	Case Studies		63
		3.4.1	Sensible Geng Geng	64
		3.4.2	Negative Luo Luo	65
		3.4.3	Analysis	66
	References			67

4 Status and Analysis of Language Development in 2- and 3-Year-Old Children ... 69

	4.1	Introduction		69
	4.2	Methodology		70
		4.2.1	Subjects	70
		4.2.2	Research Instrument	70
		4.2.3	Research Process	71
	4.3	Results and Analysis		74
		4.3.1	Analysis of Basic Situation of Language Development of 2- and 3-Year-Old Children	74

		4.3.2	Analysis of Difference Between Language Understanding and Language Expression	78
		4.3.3	Analysis of Difference in Language Development Between Children Aged 2–2.5 Years and Children Aged 2.5–3 Years	78
		4.3.4	Relationship Between Other Factors and Children's Language Development Level	83
	4.4	Conclusion		83
		4.4.1	Children Aged 2–3 Years Have a Good Language Development, with no Significant Difference in Language Understanding and Language Expression	83
		4.4.2	There Are Significant Differences in Language Development Level Between Children Aged 2–2.5 Years and Children Aged 2.5–3 Years	83
	References			84
5	**Study on the Developmental Characteristics of Social Adaptation of 2–3-Year-Old Children**			85
	5.1	Introduction		85
	5.2	Research Design		86
		5.2.1	Research Objects	86
		5.2.2	Research Methods	87
		5.2.3	Data Analysis	89
	5.3	Research Results		89
		5.3.1	Overall Analysis on Social Adaptation of Children Aged 2–3	89
		5.3.2	Analysis of Development Features of Children Aged 2–3 in All Dimensions	89
		5.3.3	Age and Gender Differences in Social Adaptive Development of 2–3 Year Old Children	91
	5.4	Analysis and Discussion		92
		5.4.1	The Characteristics of Social Adaptation of 2–3 Years Old	92
		5.4.2	Developmental Characteristics of Social Adaptation of 2–3 Years Old in All Dimensions	93
	5.5	Suggestion		93
		5.5.1	Parents Should Encourage Young Children to Come into Contact with the New Environment and Increase Opportunities for Young Children to Interact with Their Peers	93

		5.5.2	Parents Should Be Good at Guiding Young Children to Establish Good Behavior Standards and Foster Pro-social Behaviors.....................................	94
	References...			94
6	**Analysis of Infants' Emotional Development**...................			97
	6.1	Introduction..		97
	6.2	Methods..		99
		6.2.1	Participants.................................	99
		6.2.2	Measures...................................	100
	6.3	Analysis of Results.................................		105
		6.3.1	Emotional Development of Young Children..........	105
		6.3.2	Characteristics of Young Children's Emotional Development at Different Ages.....................	112
		6.3.3	Characteristics of Emotional Development of Children in Different Gender..................	114
		6.3.4	Correlations Between Emotion Recognition, Emotional Understanding, Emotion Regulation Strategies, and Development of Social Emotions.....	115
	6.4	Discussion...		117
		6.4.1	Overall Analysis of the Emotional Development of Young Children.............................	117
		6.4.2	Age and Gender Differences in Emotional Development of Young Children..................	119
		6.4.3	Correlation Analysis of Emotion Recognition, Emotion Understanding, Emotion Regulation Strategies, and Social Mood Development..........	120
	6.5	Conclusion...		122
	References...			123

Part II Family Environment and Infants and Toddlers' Development

7	**Relationship Between Grandparent–Parent Co-parenting, Infant Temperament, and Emotional Adjustment**...............			127
	7.1	Introduction..		127
	7.2	Methods..		130
		7.2.1	Participants.................................	130
		7.2.2	Measures...................................	130
	7.3	Relationship Among Grandparent–Parent Co-parenting and Infant Temperament and Emotional Adjustment.........		132
		7.3.1	Correlations Among the Study Variables............	132
		7.3.2	Multiple Regression Analyses....................	132

	7.4	Discussions	134
		7.4.1 Relationship Between Grandparent–Parent Co-parenting and Infant Emotional Adjustment	134
		7.4.2 Regulating Effect of Infant Temperament on the Relationship Between Grandparent–Parent Co-parenting on Infant Emotional Adjustment	138
		7.4.3 Implications	139
	7.5	Conclusions	140
	References		140
8	**The Influence of Home Literacy Environment on Print Awareness of Children Aged 2–4 in Urban China**		143
	8.1	Introduction	143
	8.2	Literature Review	144
		8.2.1 Definition and Measurement of Print Awareness	144
		8.2.2 Home Literacy Environment and Early Print Awareness	145
	8.3	Method	147
		8.3.1 Participants	147
		8.3.2 Measurements	148
	8.4	Research Results and Analysis	151
		8.4.1 Analysis on the Basic Conditions and Characteristics of the Development of the 2–4-Year-Old Children's Print Awareness	151
		8.4.2 The Status and Characteristics of the 2–4-Year-Old Children's Home Literacy Environment	157
		8.4.3 Influence of Home Literacy Environment on the Development of Print Awareness in Children Aged 2–4-Year-Old	160
	8.5	Discussions and Suggestions	164
	References		167
9	**Study on the State and Influencing Factors of Family Art Education for Children Aged 0–3 in China**		169
	9.1	Introduction	169
	9.2	Research Design	171
		9.2.1 Research Problems	171
		9.2.2 Participants	171
		9.2.3 Research Methods	171
	9.3	Research Results	172
		9.3.1 The State of Family Art Education for Children Aged 0–3	172
		9.3.2 Influences of Family Background on Family Art Education for Infants	178

	9.4	Discussion	187
	9.5	Conclusion and Suggestion	189
	References		190

Part III Policies and Challenges

10 Growth Prediction of Population Aged 0–3 Under the Universal Two-Child Policy: A Study Case of Beijing 195
- 10.1 Research Background 195
  - 10.1.1 Rollout of Universal Two-Child Policy to Tackle Aging Population Crisis 195
  - 10.1.2 Unknown Population-Changing Trend Under the Influence of Factors 195
  - 10.1.3 Beijing–A Typical Case for the Research on Population Growth and Policy Demands 196
- 10.2 Literature Reviews 199
- 10.3 Research Questions 201
- 10.4 Research Design 201
  - 10.4.1 Research Object: Population Aged 0–3 Years in Beijing 201
  - 10.4.2 Research Method (Population Prediction) 202
- 10.5 Results and Analysis 204
  - 10.5.1 Analysis of Dynamic Trend of Population Aged 0–3 Years During 2016–2026 in Beijing 204
  - 10.5.2 Analysis of the Trend and the Proportion of Total Population Aged 0–3 Years Old During 2016–2026 in Beijing 207
  - 10.5.3 Comparative Analysis of the Prediction of Population Changes Before and After the Two-Child Policy 209
  - 10.5.4 Summary 210
- 10.6 Discussion and Suggestions 211
  - 10.6.1 Increase First and then Decrease of Population Aged 0–3 Years Old During 2016–2026 in Beijing ... 211
  - 10.6.2 Full Understanding of the Reality that Beijing Is in a Low Fertility Level for a Long Time and in the Future 212
  - 10.6.3 Learning the Experience from Low Fertility Countries in Formulating the Social Pro-breeding Policies 213
- References 213

11 Parenting Characteristics and Problems of Urban Two Children Families Amid the Universal Two-Child Policy 215
- 11.1 Introduction 215
- 11.2 Research Methods 217

		11.2.1	Target Groups	217
		11.2.2	Research Methods and Research Tools	221
	11.3	Research Results and Analysis		222
		11.3.1	Analysis on Features of Parenting Before and After the Birth of the Second Child	222
		11.3.2	Influences of Parenting on the First Child in a Family with Two Children	224
		11.3.3	Parents' Difficulties in Raising the Second Children	226
	11.4	Suggestions		228
		11.4.1	More Care About the First Child	228
		11.4.2	Fair Treatment of Two Children and Care About Emotional Changes of the First Child	228
		11.4.3	Emphasis on Guidance of the First Child and Development of Interpersonal Skills	229
		11.4.4	Build Parenting Synergy Through Reasonable Communications	229
		11.4.5	Mother's Age and Health Shall Be Taken into Account Before Having a Second Child	230
		11.4.6	Parents Take into Account Development of Children and Themselves	230
	11.5	Conclusion		230
	References			231
12	A Case Study on Sibling Relationship Characteristics for Urban Families with Two Children			233
	12.1	Introduction		233
	12.2	Research Methods		234
		12.2.1	Target Groups	234
		12.2.2	Research Methods	234
	12.3	Research Results and Analysis		235
		12.3.1	Beginning of Sibling: Sibling Willingness	235
		12.3.2	Sibling Performance	236
		12.3.3	Influences and Roles of Sibling Relationship	239
	12.4	Educational Suggestions		242
		12.4.1	Create More Opportunities for Positive Sibling Interactions	242
		12.4.2	Help Children Learn to Resolve Sibling Conflict and Rivalry, Sibling Right Comparison	242
		12.4.3	Manage Influence Factors to Enhance Sibling Relationship	243
	12.5	Conclusion		243
	References			244

Part I
The Developmental Status of Infants and Toddlers and Its Influencing Factors

Chapter 1
Research Contents and Methods of Development in 2- and 3-Year-Old Children

1.1 Research Background

The period from 0 to 3 year-old is the start of life, the starting point of individual development, a key period for the children's physical growth, development in motor, cognition, language, emotion, and social adaptation, and also the elementary and most fundamental stage of education. In recent years, research on neuroscience, psychology, pedagogy, and other disciplines has confirmed the importance of the development and education of infants and toddlers aged 0–3 years. The early education of infants and toddlers aged 0–3 years has attracted more and more attention from the international community, and various actions have been taken in the world.

For example, the "Head Start" in the USA, which began in 1965, provides healthcare services for women before and during pregnancy and after delivery, and also provides information about infant nutrition and early education for infants and toddlers in and outside the family. Afterward, the U.S. Federal Government constantly increased investment in children's early education and attached special importance to the early intervention project for poor children, so as to promote equal access to education, such as Project Head Start and Early Head Start, which mainly provided services for preschool children of low-income families, including babies and toddlers. New Zealand has been tracking the growth of infants and toddlers since 1972. In 1993, "Puru Kate Plan"—the national plan for development and education of infants and toddlers aged 0–3 was activated. In the report titled *Education for the 21st Century*, the Ministry of Education of New Zealand pointed out that "education must start from birth". The Early Year Foundation Stage (EYFS) of the UK was incorporated into the legal system in 2008.

In recent years, China has also gradually attached importance to the early development and education of infants and toddlers aged 0–3. In 2001, the State Council issued the *Outline of Child development in China (2001–2010)*, which explicitly proposed to "develop early education for children aged 0–3" for the first time. In 2010, in the development tasks of preschool education in the *Outline of National Medium-*

and Long-Term Program for Education Reform and Development (2010–2020), it was stressed that "attention should be paid to the education of infants and toddlers aged 0–3", which marked that the education of infants and toddlers aged 0–3 was officially incorporated into the national education service system. In December 2012, the Ministry of Education also issued a document to carry out the experimental early education for infants and toddlers aged 0–3 in 14 regions, including Shanghai and Beijing. As a result, the early education for infants and toddlers aged 0–3 in China has gradually entered a golden age of vigorous development. It is in such a context that early education guidance services for infants and toddlers aged 0–3 and related institutions emerged and launched the practical exploration of early education for infants and toddlers aged 0–3.

Scientific research is the forerunner of appropriate education, and the promotion and educational guidance for early childhood development should follow the age characteristics and rules of the infants' physical and mental development. Previous research on infants' mental development and its influencing factors can provide scientific bases for childcare and education personnel and parents to comprehensively understand the age characteristics and individual differences of infants, meet the development needs of infants, and create an appropriate childcare and education environment and develop appropriate courses. In order to deeply understand the physical and mental development characteristics and influencing factors of infants and toddlers aged 0–3 in China, it is indispensable to study the evaluation on development of infants and toddlers aged 0–3. The purpose of evaluation on infant development is to understand and analyze the development status of infants and toddlers in time, explore the relevant factors affecting the infant development, and provide a basis for actively promoting education and research suitable for infants and toddlers and promoting the overall development of infants and toddlers.

Although great progress has been made in the research on the development and education of children aged 3–6 in China, there are still few basic studies on the development and education of infants and toddlers aged 0–3, which has gradually attracted attention in recent years. In recent years, Chinese early childhood educators and researchers have realized the important value of evaluation on infant development and made active exploration in this field. However, there is still a big gap between China and foreign countries in the research on evaluation on development of infants and toddlers aged 0–3. Based on the shortcomings of previous studies, this study aims to explore and study a development evaluation tool suitable for infants and toddlers aged 0–3 in China, and further understand and explore the development status and influencing factors of infants and toddlers in China.

1.2 Literature Review

By reviewing the previous evaluation tools and studies on development of infants and toddlers aged 0–3, it can be found that the previous studies in this field mainly have the following deficiencies:

1.2 Literature Review

First, in terms of testing and evaluation subjects, there are many measurement tools for the development of children over 3-year old, but few for the development of infants and toddlers aged 0–3.

Second, in terms of evaluation tools, most of the previous evaluation tools for infants and toddlers aged 0–3 are translated from evaluation scales of foreign countries and promoted after establishing models based on the Chinese people. These evaluation tools better draw lessons from the research achievements of western countries, but because of influence of China's cultural environment, geographical environment, and living environment, the physical and mental development of Chinese infants and toddlers has its uniqueness. Thus, the measurement validity of the scales introduced from foreign countries, which are later revised into Chinese models, is thought-provoking and doubtful. Therefore, there is an urgent need to develop a set of localized testing tools suitable for the development characteristics of Chinese infants and toddlers.

Third, in terms of evaluation domains, most of the previous studies evaluate the development of infants and toddlers in such domains as motor development, cognitive development, language development, emotional development, and social adaptation, but there is limited research on comprehensive evaluation on the development of several major domains of infants and toddlers.

Fourth, in terms of the evaluation subject, the main implementers of the evaluation on infant development in China are still researchers, and the awareness of parents to participate in the evaluation of infant development is very weak. The dynamic development process of interaction between children and environmental systems and the development evaluation content determines the diversification of evaluation subjects, so only information collected through the diversified evaluation subjects can reflect the most authentic development status of infants and toddlers. Therefore, the infant development evaluation should be made from a relational perspective, and pay full attention to the dynamic changes of various relationships, including interactions among parents, teachers, researchers, peers, and individuals. In the infant development evaluation process, parents, infants, and toddlers may participate as subjects. The evaluation information provided by parents may become important resources in the infant development evaluation, because parents have a more authentic and comprehensive understanding of various aspects of the infant development.

Fifth, in terms of evaluation context, the traditional evaluation method attaches importance to the evaluation in the laboratory environment. However, more and more researchers emphasize the evaluation on child development in the real play context, because the real situation is more helpful to induce the highest development level and ability performance of children.

Based on the deficiencies of previous research, this study will expand the research on the infant development evaluation in the following aspects: First, introducing and revising a comprehensive development evaluation tool in the domains of motor, cognition, language, emotion, and social adaptation that are applicable to the evaluation and research of infants and toddlers aged 2–3 in China; second, combining the parents' reports with the infant measurement and observation to objectively evaluate the development status of infants and toddlers in several domains from a multidimensional perspective; third, localizing the play-based evaluation to explore the evaluation tools and methods for the development of 2- and 3-year-old children in multiple domains in the natural context.

1.3 Research Purpose and Tasks

The purpose of this study is to explore and study the development evaluation tools suitable for 2- and 3-year-old children in China, and based on this, to comprehensively understand the development status and influencing factors of 2- and 3-year-old children in several major domains, so as to enhance the professional level of infant development evaluation in China, and provide a basis for the investigations and research on the development status of 2- and 3-year-old children in large samples in China in the future.

Specifically, one of the main tasks of this study is to develop an observation and evaluation tool suitable for the development characteristics of 2- and 3-year-old children in China, so as to provide a suitable evaluation tool for early childhood educators and early intervention workers to comprehensively understand the development process and age characteristics of infants and toddlers in five domains—motor, cognition, language, emotional, and social adaptation in China. This can provide an important basis for the investigations and research on the development status of 2- and 3-year-old children in large samples in China in the future.

Another major task of this study is to test the 2- and 3-year-old children with the help of the developed evaluation tool for infant development, learn and analyze the basic development characteristics and development status of 2- and 3-year-old children in five domains—motor, cognition, language, emotional, and social adaptation, explore the related factors affecting the infant development, so as to provide valuable reference and suggestions for comprehensively and objectively evaluating the quality of early education for 2- and 3-year-old children, and putting forward educational countermeasures for promoting the development of infants and toddlers with target.

1.4 Research Subjects

1.4.1 Sampling

The survey in this study focused on the urban area of Beijing and the surrounding suburbs, and purposive sampling was mainly adopted. In order to improve the representativeness and universality of samples, this study selects samples based on the following three criteria: first, according to the division of Beijing municipal administrative region, four districts were selected, including two in the urban area, one in the

1.4 Research Subjects

Table 1.1 Distribution of infant samples

Category	Sample size	Percentage (%)
Male	69	47.6
Female	76	52.4
30-month-old or younger	27	18.6
30-month-old or older	118	81.4
Total	145	100

suburbs, and one in the outer suburbs. Second, according to the different nature of early childhood education institutions, two kindergartens and three early education agencies were selected. Third, according to the different levels of samples receiving early education, the infants and toddlers and their parents are divided into two groups: infants and toddlers who have received early education and their parents, and those who have not received early education and their parents.

1.4.2 Samples

The samples are from Haidian District and Chaoyang District in the urban area of Beijing, Daxing District in the suburbs, and Shunyi District in the outer suburbs.

The test subjects are 2- and 3-year-old children.

The observation subjects are 2- and 3-year-old children and their parents.

The subjects of questionnaire survey are 2- and 3-year-old children and their parents (Table 1.1).

1.5 Research Methods

In this study, questionnaire, test, and observation methods were employed to collect relevant information and data about infant development.

1.5.1 Questionnaire Method

Questionnaire method is a research method that collects data by asking questions in writing so as to understand the views and opinions of the subjects on a certain phenomenon or problem (Pei 2000).

In this study, the questionnaire method is mainly used in three domains, namely, motor development, emotional development, and social adaptation. It is used to understand the basic family situation of infants and toddlers, and to measure variables such as emotional development, social adaptation, temperament, co-parenting by grandparents and parents, and parent–child interaction. Except the questionnaire for the motor development in which the trained experimenters visit the parents to ask questions about motor development of their infants and toddlers through face-to-face interview, the emotional development, social adaptation, temperament, and co-parenting by grandparents and parents of infants and toddlers are all learned by giving answers in writing.

After contacting the kindergartens, early education agencies, or local street offices, the researchers distributed informed consents to parents of infants and toddlers through their teachers in the kindergartens or early education agencies. With the signature of the parents, the professionally trained experimenters explained the research purpose, method of answering the questionnaire, and the matters needing attention to the teachers. The teachers and the experimenters explained the matters needing attention to fill in the questionnaire to the parents. The parents were required to fill in the questionnaires on the spot or hand them to the teachers or the experimenters within 2 days. Finally, the questionnaires were collected and sorted out by the experimenters.

1.5.2 Test Method

Test method refers to the method of measuring some important characteristics of the evaluated subjects with the help of certain measuring tools so as to collect relevant evaluation information (Zhang 2014).

In this study, the test method is mainly used to measure the motor development, cognitive development, language development, and emotional development of 2- and 3-year-old children. This test takes the form of one-to-one test. Throughout this test, the trained experimenters test the motor ability, cognitive ability, language ability, emotion recognition ability, and emotional comprehension ability of 2- and 3-year-old children according to the test content under the items, testing and scoring requirements, and grades the performance of the infants and toddlers, which is greatly objective.

Based on the Transdisciplinary Play-Based Assessment (TPBA) established by Professor Linder from the University of Denver, USA, this study is aimed to evaluate the development of infants and toddlers in various aspects by observing their performance in play context (Lander 2008). Different from the traditional test method, the test in this study is based on play. The researcher created corresponding play environment for infants and toddlers, and the experimenters assessed the performance of infants and toddlers in play. Infants and toddlers' performances in play are its most natural and real. Researchers evaluated the development level of infants and toddlers by observing their performance in play, and thus the ecological validity was effectively guaranteed.

1.5.3 Observation Method

Observation method is one of the most basic methods to study the rule and characteristics of children's psychological development. Since children's psychological activities have prominent externality, their psychological activities can be learned by observing their external behaviors (Wen 2015). At present, there is a growing opposition to laboratory evaluation on infants and toddlers, and in the evaluation on infants and toddlers, more stress is increasingly laid on the observation-based evaluation in the real situation.

In this study, the observation method is mainly used in the cognitive development, emotional development, and social adaptation of 2- and 3-year-old children to measure their cognitive development level, emotion adjustment ability, social adaptability, parent–child interaction, and other variables of 2- and 3-year-old children in the real situation. By observing the cognitive development level, emotion adjustment ability, environmental adaptation, stranger adaptation, companion adaptation, and parent–child interaction process of 2- and 3-year-old children, the experimenters collect the behavioral variables of infant development in relevant aspects. These results and questionnaire survey results confirm and support each other, ensuring the ecological validity of the study. Specific observation methods vary from domain to domain and will be described in detail in the research methods of the relevant chapter below.

1.6 Research Tools

In this study, the research methods and tools for the five domains—motor development, cognitive development, language development, emotional development, and social adaptation of 2- and 3-year-old children are summarized as follows (Table 1.2).

1.7 Data Processing and Analysis

The data obtained through questionnaire, test, and observation methods were analyzed by SPSS 19.0, Amos 22.0, and other statistical analysis software. The specific analysis methods include descriptive statistical method, independent-samples T-test, one-way analysis of variance, correlation analysis, multiple regression analysis, path analysis, and so on.

* in this book has the same meaning: * means significance at the level of 0.05; ** means significance at the level of 0.01; *** means significance at the level of 0.001.

Table 1.2 Research tools for various domains

Development domain	Research method	Research tool	Sub-domain
Motor development	Questionnaire method	Self-prepared questionnaire	Feeding situation, breast milk stopping time, self-care situation, etc.
	Test method	Self-prepared scale of *Evaluation on motor development of 2- and 3-year-old children*	Fine motor: functional hand skills, object manipulation, object matching, etc.
			Gross motor: body posture, movement, object manipulation, etc.
Cognitive development	Test method	Self-prepared scale of *Evaluation on cognitive development of 2- and 3-year-old children*	Symbol and representation, problem-solving, one-to-one correspondence, working memory, reversal classification and matching, attention and participation, pattern cognition, exploration and construction, etc.
	Observation method	Observation table for *Evaluation on cognitive development of 2- and 3-year-old children*	Symbolization and representation, problem-solving, one-to-one correspondence, working memory, reversal classification and matching, attention and participation, pattern cognition, exploration and construction, etc.
Language development	Test method	Heep Hong Society's Child Development Assessment Form Language Sub-scale	Language expression, language understanding
Emotional development	Questionnaire method	Bayley Scales of Infant Development III Social Emotion Questionnaire	Sensory processing, early social emotional development, etc.
	Test method	Face recognition test	Emotion recognition

(continued)

1.7 Data Processing and Analysis

Table 1.2 (continued)

Development domain	Research method	Research tool	Sub-domain
		Test of Emotion Comprehension (TEC)	Emotion comprehension
	Observation method	Setback situation experiment	Emotion adjustment
Social adaptation	Questionnaire method	Self-prepared parent questionnaire for social adaptation of 2- and 3-year-old children	Environmental adaptation, interpersonal adaptation, etc.
	Observation method	Observation table for social adaptation of 2- and 3-year-old children	Environmental adaptation, stranger adaptation, companion adaptation, etc.

References

Lander, T. W. (2008). *Transdisciplinary play-based assessment* (C. Xuefeng, Trans). Shanghai: East China Normal University Press.
Pei, D. (2000). *Research methods in education: An introduction.* Hefei: Anhui Education Press.
Wen, Y. (2015). *Psychology and education of infants and toddlers (0–3).* Beijing: Beijing Normal University Press.
Zhang, H. (2014). *Educational measurement and evaluation methods.* Changchun: Jilin University Press.

Chapter 2
Analysis of Motor Development in 2- and 3-Year-Old Children

2.1 Introduction

Motor domain in individual development is mainly divided into two categories, namely, gross motor (such as crawling, independent walking, running, jumping, going upstairs and downstairs, etc.) and fine motor (such as grasping an object, using a spoon, putting on and taking off shoes and socks, drawing or writing with a pen, etc.). Gross motor refers to the motor skills generated by larger muscle groups such as the torso and four limps, including the skills of moving the body in space (displacement skills) and the skills of controlling objects (Ulrich 2000). Fine motor refers to the ability of an individual to complete a specific task mainly by relying on the movements of hands and small muscles or small muscle groups in the hands and other parts with the cooperation of various psychological activities, such as sensory perception and attention (Tang and Li 2011). The infant's motor development is not only an important sign of maturation of the nervous system, but also an important basis for the adaptation to human life and realization of physical and mental development, so it has an important role and value in the healthy growth of individuals (Dong and Tao 2002).

Fine motor skill is not only an important basis for the early children to complete the development tasks, but also an important indicator to evaluate the children's development status. The development of infants and toddlers' hand fine motor is of great significance to the brain development of individuals. Because there are many cells specialized in processing sensory and motor information of fingers, palms, hand backs, and wrists in the brains, the more skillful and finer the fingers' movements are, the more nerve connections can be established in the cerebral cortex, increasing the brain's gyrus and thus promoting the brain development. At the same time, infants and toddlers can strengthen the connection between the sense of touch and vision by playing with or grasping objects and toys, which also promotes the brain development. In addition, the acquisition and development of infants and toddlers' hand movements can expand their ways to acquire environmental information, and thus enrich the forms of infants and toddlers' exploring the environment and make their exploratory behavior more active and effective (Tang and Li 2011). Gross motor development is the earliest motor skills developed by children, laying a foundation for the development of all kinds of sensory perception movements (Guo 1999). The toddlerhood between 1 and 3 years (especially around 2 years old) is a critical period for children's physical and mental development (Cao et al. 2010), and the infant motor development is not only an important sign of the maturation of their neuromuscular system, but also an essential condition for them to gain self-reliance, explore their surroundings, adapt to social life, build confidence and realize their own development, laying an important foundation for the development of other aspects of individuals (Dong and Tao 2002). Therefore, it is very necessary to investigate the status quo of the motor development of 2- and 3-year-old children, which will help researchers to understand the rules of the motor development of 2- and 3-year-old children, which can help researchers to understand the rules of motor development of 2- and 3-year-old children, the practitioners understand the existing problems of infant motor development, and then provide targeted guidance to promote the healthy development of children.

In most of the existing studies on the status quo of infant motor development, the comprehensive scale was employed to evaluate infant motor development level by calculating the score of gross motor and fine motor of infants and toddlers, and then provide the basis for screening, diagnosis, and prediction, and there was no specific descriptive analysis (Jiang et al. 2008; Chen 2004). Moreover, the subjects were mainly infants aged 0–1 year (Yang 2012; Wu et al. 2006; Xu et al. 2007; Hu 2012; Tong et al. 2001) and infants and toddlers aged 1–3 years (Kong et al. 2009; Fan and Zhou 1983; Li et al. 1982; Jia 2013), and there were few studies focusing on the fine motor development of 2- and 3-year-old children (Zhu 2011). Therefore, this study employed the special motor scale to measure the motor development of 130 2- and 3-year-old children in Beijing and analyzed the characteristics of motor development of 2- and 3-year-old children, so as to lay a foundation for follow-up study.

2.2 Methodology

2.2.1 Subjects

In this study, 130 2- and 3-year-old children in Beijing were tested, and their parents were asked to fill out a questionnaire about their children's basic situation. There were 61 boys and 69 girls, 25 children aged 2–2.5 and 105 children aged 2.5–3.

2.2 Methodology

2.2.2 Research Instrument

To effectively measure the motor development of 2- and 3-year-old children, based on the test items reflecting fine motor flexibility and coordination and hand–eye coordination in such scales as Bayley Scales of Infant Development, Peabody Developmental Motor Scale-2, Children Learning Development Assessment Form (Heep Hong Society), Neuropsychological Development Examination Table for Children Aged 0–6, Observation and Assessments of Children Aged 0–3, the *evaluation on motor development of* 2- and 3-year-old children was prepared (see Table 2.1 for the test items for motor development of 2- and 3-year-old children). The scale consists of two parts—basic information and test items. 1. Basic information covers name, gender, age, birth weight, birth status and delivery mode of the infant, mother's childbearing age, parents' occupation and education, only child or not, total family income in 2016, family economic status, scale filler, duration of the infant attending early education, infant education cost in 2016, quantity of books for infants and toddlers at home, feeding situation, time of stopping breastfeeding, allergy, and self-care situation (such as drinking, eating, going to toilet). 2. The test covers fine motor and gross motor. The test items for the former include functional hand skills, object manip-

Table 2.1 Sources of test items for motor development of 2- and 3-year-old children

Item source	Motor domain	Item description
Bayley Scales of Infant Development III (BSID-III) (Bayley 2006)	Fine motor	Grasping, sensory integration, motor planning, and movement speed
	Gross motor	Static posture of four limbs and the torso, movement, and motor planning
Early Childhood Care and Development Checklist (ECCD) (Ledesma 2002)	Fine motor	Grasping, reaching out for objects, functional hand skills, and object manipulation
	Gross motor	Posture, movement
China Developmental Scale for Children (CDSC) (Zhang et al. 2015)	Fine motor	Pinching, grasping
	Gross motor	Crawling, walking, running, and body balance
Development Assessment Form for Children (DAC) (Heep Hong Society 2013)	Fine motor	Reaching out to pick up and place the object, basic manipulation ability, coordination of both hands, hand–eye coordination, holding a pen to write and draw, stationery, and supplies
	Gross motor	Mobility on the floor, basic mobility, advanced mobility, and manipulative movement skills
Peabody developmental motor scale-2 (PDMS-2) (Folio and Fewell 2006)	Fine motor	Grasping and visual-motor integration
	Gross motor	Reflection, posture, movement, and object manipulation

ulation, and object matching; those for the latter include body posture, movement, and object manipulation. All the test items adopt four-point scoring method—0 (Not meet the test requirement at all), 1 (Meet the test requirement a little), 2 (Complete the task fairly but not completely meet the test requirement), and 3 (Completely meet the test requirement), and corresponding scoring standard was set for each point. See Table 2.2 for the specific distribution of test items.

2.2.3 Research Process

In order to measure the real motor development level of 2- and 3-year-old children, the test items, in combination with the infants and toddlers' life situation and game activities, were mainly divided into seven links: dining, reading, art activities, block building activities, physical activities, going upstairs and downstairs, and breaks (see Table 2.3 for the test items and corresponding testing materials included in each link). (Remark: there is no fixed test sequence in all the links except the dining link, which will be arranged according to the current interest and status of the subject and the principle of combining motion and quietness.) The test environment was set up before the test, and then two experimenters carried out the test simultaneously. The items tested in dining, reading, art activities, and block building activities can be tested on 2- and 3-year-old children at the same time. In physical activities, going upstairs and downstairs and breaks, infants and toddlers need to be tested one to one. Before each item began, the tester explained the test requirements to the subjects, demonstrated them, and then allowed the subjects to operate after making sure they understood them. If a subject was unable to complete the test item because of emotional problem or not following instructions, the item was graded and processed as a missing value. After an item was completed, an infant's performance in each item was graded in accordance with the evaluation standards. During the test, the parents were asked to fill in the basic information of their infants and toddlers. Each subject was tested for about 25 min.

2.2 Methodology

Table 2.2 Distribution table of test items for motor development of 2- and 3-year-old children

Domain	Sub-domain	Item indexes	Number of items	Item source
Fine motor	Functional hand skills	Eating with a spoon, page turning, drawing a circle, drawing a horizontal line, drawing a vertical line, drawing a cross, gesture of holding a pen, paper cutting, wearing shoes, and wearing socks	10	Bayley Scales of Infant Development, Peabody Developmental Motor Scale-2, Children Learning Development Assessment Form (Heep Hong Society), Neuropsychological Development Examination Table for Children Aged 0–6, Observation and Assessments of Children Aged 0–3
	Object manipulation	Piling up blocks, building block trains, building block bridges, and threading beads	4	Bayley Scales of Infant Development, Peabody Developmental Motor Scale-2, Children Learning Development Assessment Form (Heep Hong Society), Neuropsychological Development Examination Table for Children Aged 0–6, Observation and Assessments of Children Aged 0–3
	Object matching	Inserting shape blocks	1	Peabody Developmental Motor Scale-2
Gross motor	Body posture	Standing on one leg	1	Bayley Scales of Infant Development, Peabody Developmental Motor Scale-2, Neuropsychological Development Examination Table for Children Aged 0–6
	Movement	Double-leg standing jumping, double-leg continuous jumping, tiptoeing, backward walking, running, going upstairs, and going downstairs	7	Bayley Scales of Infant Development, Peabody Developmental Motor Scale-2, Heep Hong Society's Children Learning Program, Neuropsychological Development Examination Table for Children Aged 0–6
	Object manipulation	Throwing a ball with both hands, receiving a ball with both hands, and kicking a ball	3	Peabody Developmental Motor Scale-2
Total			26	

Table 2.3 Test links and testing materials

Test link	Test item	Testing materials
Dining	Eat with a spoon	Bowls, spoons and food for infants, and toddlers' dining
Reading	Page turning	Picture book
Art activities	Drawing a circle, drawing a horizontal line, drawing a vertical line, drawing a cross, and gesture of holding a pen	Water color pens, A4 paper
	Paper cutting	Safety scissors, A4 paper (half)
	Threading beads	Square beads (with a side length of 1 cm), string for threading bead
Block building activities	Piling up blocks, building block trains, and building block bridges	10 cube blocks (with a side length of 2.5 cm)
	Inserting shape blocks	3D inserting toys (inserting five blocks of different shapes into the corresponding holes)
Physical activities	Standing on one leg, double-leg standing jumping, double-leg continuous jumping, tiptoeing, backward walking, and running	Meter ruler, red ribbon
	Throwing a ball with both hands, receiving a ball with both hands, and kicking a ball	Ball (with a diameter of 15 cm)
Going upstairs and downstairs	Going upstairs, going downstairs	Stairs in the kindergarten
Breaks	Wearing shoes, wearing socks	Shoes, socks (the infants and toddlers' shoes and socks)

2.3 Results and Analysis

2.3.1 Analysis of Status Quo of Motor Development of 2- and 3-Year-Old Children

2.3.1.1 Basic Situation of Fine Motor Development of 2- and 3-Year-Old Children

The basic situation of fine motor development of 2- and 3-year-old children was mainly analyzed from three dimensions: functional hand skills, object manipulation, and object matching.

2.3 Results and Analysis

Overall Development Situation of Fine Motor Items of 2- and 3-Year-Old Children

According to the survey results, in the aspect of functional hand skills, 54% of the surveyed 2- and 3-year-old children could eat with a spoon with a little spilled; 56.3% of them could turn 4 or more pages; more than 50% of them could hold pens with three fingers and reach the highest level when drawing circles, horizontal lines, and vertical lines, but only 32.8% of them could control the inclination of two cross lines with the horizontal line and vertical line within 20° when drawing crosses; 88.3% of them could use scissors to cut papers, but most of them couldn't continue after cutting (49.2%); the majority of them were skilled in wearing shoes and socks (60.9% and 48.8%, respectively). In the aspect of object manipulation, 63.5% of these infants and toddlers could pile up 10 cube blocks with a side length of 2.5 cm; 88.7% of them could line up 5 cube blocks with a side length of 2.5 cm closely and place a block on the block at the end; 70.6% of them could place one block between two blocks and leave a gap between the two blocks below; and 76.6% of them could skillfully thread 5 square beads with a side length of 1 cm. In the aspect of object matching, 83.7% of them could accurately and skillfully place blocks of different shapes into corresponding holes. It is clear that more than 50% of the infants and toddlers participating in the test reached the highest level in each item, which, to some extent, indicates that the fine motor flexibility and coordination and hand–eye coordination of most infants and toddlers are well developed.

According to the survey results, the overall fine motor development level of 2- and 3-year-old children is good. For one thing, it is affected by family economic status because the family economic foundation is the main reason determining the parents' investment in their infants and toddlers. In this study, the families with an annual household income ranging from 100,000 to 300,000 Yuan are in the majority, accounting for 60.3%, and those with an annual household income below 100,000 Yuan account for only 12.7%, which shows that most families enjoy a decent standard of life or better, and can provide children with a better material life. This means the infants and toddlers' diet nutrition, toy categories, and education can be better guaranteed. Rich nutrition lays a good foundation for the infant motor development; various toys for infants and toddlers provide conditions for infants and toddlers to practice their fine motor in many ways, and early learning is a stage when both parents and children grow. Under the guidance of early childhood education teachers, parents can not only improve their values of education, but also can learn a lot of scientific and effective education methods, and then, they can better understand the development needs of the children at all ages, grasp the critical development stages of the children, and thus promote the infants and toddlers' motor development. All of these activities were held with the support of the family financial capability. On the other hand, the parents' education consciousness is also important, because consciousness determines action. Only when parents realize the importance of fine motor development for infants and toddlers of this age group, may they invest time and energy in improving their children's motor development. The survey results showed that 55.3% of the parents spent 5000 Yuan or more on their children's education within 1 year;

57.8% of the parents prepared more than 40 books for their children; 72.8% of the infants and toddlers have received early education, and 29.3% of them have received early education for 1 year or more; and more than 65% of the parents received undergraduate education or higher education (mothers: 72.6%; fathers: 67.7%). It is thus clear that parents participating in this survey have a higher education background, and more scientific parenting concept, pay more attention to children's early education, and can create a growth environment supporting children's motor development and development of other aspects, so that the infants and toddlers can have more opportunities to contact the stimulations of exercises. It is the above reasons that jointly promote the fine motor development of 2- and 3-year-old children.

Comparison of Development Between Fine Motor Items in 2- and 3-Year-Old Children

In this study, the development situations of different aspects of fine motor of 2- and 3-year-old children were compared by comparing the average scores of all the items.

According to the survey results, among the three dimensions of fine motor, the 2- and 3-year-old children got the highest score in object matching, followed by object manipulation and functional hand skills (see Table 2.4 for details). From 6 months to 1 year old, children's hands become increasingly flexible. The most important thing is that the division of labor of five fingers develops, that is, the movements of the thumb and the other four fingers are gradually separated. Moreover, when moving, the five fingers take the opposite direction, instead of grasping by five fingers together; the division of labor of five fingers and the eye–hand coordination develop at the same time, which is a typical action when human beings take things. Around 7 months, when the children take things, the five fingers become more and more flexible in terms of division of labor, which can not only allow the children to take things firmly, but also allow them to change hand gesture according to the shapes, sizes or positions of the objects (Chen 2003). Based on this, the two-hand coordination develops to meet the needs of daily activities. The two-hand coordination can be divided into symmetrical two-hand coordination and asymmetrical two-hand coordination. Symmetrical two-hand coordination requires both hands to participate in an activity in a similar mode, such as clapping hands. And asymmetrical two-hand coordination means that when participating in an activity, two hands play different roles, and when supporting or stabilizing an object, one hand is more passive while

Table 2.4 Distribution table of means of all test dimensions of fine motor about 2- and 3-year-old children

Dimension	Number of people	Mean	Standard deviation	Rank
Object matching	129	2.7442	0.65287	1
Object manipulation	130	2.3846	0.81955	2
Functional hand skills	130	1.9162	0.65684	3

2.3 Results and Analysis

Table 2.5 Distribution table of means of all items about fine motor of 2- and 3-year-old children

Item	Number of people	Mean	Standard deviation	Rank
Inserting shape blocks	129	2.7442	0.65287	1
Building a block train	124	2.6694	0.93463	2
Threading beads	128	2.6094	0.78604	3
Drawing a circle	128	2.4531	0.97899	4
Gesture of holding a pen	127	2.3386	0.90168	5
Wearing shoes	110	2.3182	0.99477	6
Piling up blocks	126	2.2857	1.0944	7
Drawing a horizontal line	128	2.2813	1.20979	8
Building a block bridge	126	2.2778	1.18415	9
Paper cutting	128	1.9844	0.93054	10
Page turning	128	1.8672	1.37108	11
Wearing socks	129	1.845	1.27751	12
Drawing a vertical line	128	1.8359	1.33267	13
Eating with a spoon	126	1.746	0.63165	14
Drawing a cross	128	1.1484	1.38092	15

the other is responsible for operating, such as threading beads. Generally speaking, asymmetrical two-hand coordination doesn't appear until the end of 1 year old, and it is gradually strengthened after 2 years old (Greg et al. 2008). Among the test items for fine motor of 2- and 3-year-old children, the items under object matching and object manipulation are mainly single-hand movements, which mainly reflect hand–eye coordination in fine motor domain; and the items under the functional hand skill mainly test the two-hand coordination and pay attention to the flexibility and coordination of infant fine motor, so the score of the items that require the infants and toddlers to participate with coordination of two hands is lower.

According to the test results of specific items, the score of inserting shape blocks is the highest, followed by building block train and threading beads, and the score of drawing a cross is the lowest (see Table 2.5 for details). The top three items are from three different dimensions. Children start doodling with writing tools when they are 15–20 months. The development of painting ability was divided into four stages: doodling period, combination period, integration period, and painting period. In the aspect of painting, pattern copying is one of the common tasks to measure the development of children's eye–hand coordination. Only after the coordination control ability and purposiveness of infants and toddlers' movements are strengthened, can they more accurately copy and draw basic patterns such as horizontal line, vertical line, circle, normal cross, right angular bisector, square, left angular bisector, cross line, and triangle. Children can reach the level of completing the above nine patterns at about 4 years and 11 months old, and generally can complete the cross at 48 months (Greg et al. 2008), which explains why 2- and 3-year-old children in this study scored lowest when drawing a cross. Spoons are usually the first tools used by infants and toddlers, but the processes of learning to use spoons skillfully are varied and require a lot of practice, and guidance and practice are important factors in cultivating infants and toddlers' proper use of spoons (Greg et al. 2008). 74.8% of the infants and toddlers tested were only children and were often looked after by several adults at home, especially grandparents, who usually over-spoil their children easily and then deprive them of the opportunity to do things by themselves. As a result, the infants and toddlers were accustomed to being dressed and fed, and they needn't use spoons themselves. But using spoons is an important way to cultivate the flexibility and coordination of infant's hand fine motor. Consequently, this affects the fine motor development. The survey results show that the score of infants and toddlers using spoons was only higher than that of drawing a cross, which reflects this phenomenon.

To sum up, the overall level of fine motor development of 2- and 3-year-old children in this study is fair, especially the hand–eye coordination in fine motor domain. The test results show that the scores the infants and toddlers got were higher when they completed the items of object matching and object manipulation that focused on hand–eye coordination than the scores they got when they completed functional hand skill items that focused on finger flexibility and coordination.

2.3.1.2 Basic Situation of Gross Motor Development of 2- and 3-Year-Old Children

The basic situation of gross motor development of 2- and 3-year-old children was mainly analyzed from three dimensions: body posture, movement, and object manipulation.

Overall Development Situation of Gross Motor Items of 2- and 3-Year-Old Children

According to the results of test on gross motor development situation of 2- and 3-year-old children, in the aspect of body posture, 83% of the surveyed 2- and 3-year-old children could stand on one leg for 2 s or more; 54.5% of them could stand on one leg for 3 s or more; and 17% of them couldn't complete it or could only stand for less than 1 s. In the aspect of body movement, more than 90% of the infants and toddlers could complete double-leg standing jumping with two feet jumping and falling to the ground steadily at the same time; about 75% of them could steadily and harmonically complete double-leg continuous jumping for six steps or more; 89.1% of them could tiptoe for six steps or more steadily and harmoniously; nearly 95% of them could backward walk for four steps or more and keep a good direction; and 94% of them could flexibly and harmonically change direction when running. In the dimension of body movement, few infants and toddlers couldn't complete the movements. In the aspect of object control, 12% of the infants and toddlers couldn't throw a ball with both hands; 64% of them could throw a ball with both hands at the same time to a certain direction accurately; 46.8% of them could receive a ball in the arms, and

50% of them failed to receive the ball with the gesture of receiving a ball with both hands; and over 80% of them could keep a good body balance after kicking a ball 2 m away without much deviation from the desired direction. When going upstairs, 72.7% of the infants and toddlers could do it without the help of wall or handrails; 65.6% of them could preliminarily go upstairs with two legs by turn; when going downstairs, 53.1% of the infants and toddlers could complete it without the help of external objects, and 29.7% of them could complete it with two legs by turn.

To sum up, many 2- and 3-year-old children could reach a high level in standing on one leg, double-leg standing jumping, double-leg continuous jumping, tiptoeing, backward walking, running, kicking balls, and develop well in these aspects; the number of infants and toddlers who reach a high level in throwing a ball with both hands, receiving a ball with both hands, going upstairs and downstairs was a little smaller, and their development level was a little lower. It is thus clear that the grass motor of 2- and 3-year-old children develops well in the aspects of body movement, body balance, and body strength, and the flexibility and coordination were a little poorer. But, more importantly, their hand–eye coordination and coordination between upper and lower limbs are not enough, especially the coordination in the control of external moving objects.

Comparison of Development Between Gross Motor Items in 2- and 3-Year-Old Children

In this study, the development of various aspects of gross motor in 2- and 3-year-old children was compared by comparing the average scores of the items.

Among the three dimensions of gross motor, 2- and 3-year-old children scored highest in the dimension of body movement, followed by object control and body posture. In gross motor development, the body movement ability is the most fundamental and important, and the infants and toddlers contact and practice more in daily life, so it develops faster. For infants and toddlers, object control is harder than body movement and it pays more attention to the infants and toddlers' control ability and also requires coordinating several abilities, so it develops a little slowly. For the body posture, only one item was tested this time, namely, standing on one leg. This test item required that the highest level is the infants and toddlers standing on one leg steadily for at least 3 s. For 2- and 3-year-old children, this is really difficult, so it scored lowest (see Table 2.6 for details).

Among all the items, the item scoring highest is running, followed by double-leg standing jumping and tiptoeing. All of the three are under the dimension of body movement. The items are going upstairs and downstairs, receiving a ball, and standing on one leg scored lower (see Table 2.7 for details). Based on the analysis of scoring reasons of the infants and toddlers, the writer thought the following reasons contributed to the results: (1) Difficulty of the test times. Although the researcher has tried his/her best to make the difficulty of the items conform to the development level of 2- and 3-year-old children, there is still a difference in difficulty of the items. (2) Development level of 2- and 3-year-old children. The development of all aspects of

Table 2.6 Distribution table of means of all items about gross motor of 2- and 3-year-old children

Item	Number of people	Mean	Standard deviation	Rank
Running	120	2.94	0.24	1
Double-leg standing jumping	125	2.82	0.70	2
Tiptoe	118	2.81	0.69	3
Backward walking	124	2.70	0.62	4
Kicking a ball	126	2.68	0.78	5
Double-leg continuous jumping	123	2.52	0.98	6
Throwing a ball	125	2.37	1.04	7
Standing on one leg	123	2.35	0.82	8
Receiving a ball	126	2.26	0.82	9
Going upstairs or downstairs	128	1.88	0.83	10

Table 2.7 Distribution table of means of all test dimensions about gross motor in 2- and 3-year-old children

Dimension	Number of people	Mean	Standard deviation	Rank
Body movement	124	2.53	0.45	1
Object control	112	2.46	0.39	2
Body posture	123	2.34	0.81	3

the infants and toddlers' bodily functions is unbalanced, and the development speed varies from infant to infant. An aspect may develop faster while another aspect may develop more slowly. Therefore, the result will also be different. (3) Practice of the items. The test items selected by the researcher are mainly common items in daily life. If the infants and toddlers practice some items more, the score will be higher, and if they practice some items less, the score will be lower.

2.3.2 Difference Analysis of Status Quo of Motor Development of 2- and 3-Year-Old Children

2.3.2.1 Difference Analysis of Motor Development of 2- and 3-Year-Old Children Against External Environmental Factors

The external environmental factors discussed in this study include the parents' occupation and educational background, mother's childbearing age, total family annual income, family economic status, duration of the infant attending early education,

2.3 Results and Analysis

education cost, and quantity of books. Difference analysis of the motor development of functional hand skills, object manipulation, and object matching of 2- and 3-year-old children against the external environmental factors.

Difference Analysis of Motor Development of 2- and 3-Year-Old Children Against Parents' Educational Background

In terms of parents' educational background, there were differences in the fine motor development of 2- and 3-year-old children. There was difference in the infants and toddlers' functional hand skills against the mothers' educational background. The functional hand skills of the infants and toddlers whose mothers obtained bachelor's degree developed significantly better than the functional hand skills of those whose mothers with junior college degree or below ($p < 0.05$). This was specifically shown in wearing shoes and socks. Compared with the infants and toddlers whose mothers with junior college degree or below, the infants and toddlers whose mothers obtained bachelor's degree could more skillfully wear shoes and socks ($p < 0.05$) (see Tables 2.8 and 2.9 for details). Besides, there was difference in the infants and toddlers' object manipulation against the fathers' educational background. The object manipulation of infants and toddlers whose fathers' obtained master's degrees or above developed significantly better than the object manipulation of those whose fathers with junior college degree or below ($p < 0.05$). Although there was no difference in the overall development level of infants and toddlers' functional hand skills against the fathers' educational background ($p > 0.05$), the infants and toddlers whose fathers' obtained master's degrees or above were more skillful in page turning and wearing shoes than those whose fathers with junior college degree or below ($p < 0.05$) (see Tables 2.10 and 2.11 for details). It is thus clear that the fine motor development level of 2- and 3-year-old children, to some extent, is affected by the parents' educational background, and that the infants and toddlers whose parents

Table 2.8 Difference comparison of overall fine motor development level of 2- and 3-year-old children against mothers' educational background

Dimension	Subject	Number of people	Mean	Standard deviation	F-value	p-value
Functional hand skills	Junior college degree or below	35	1.7457	0.59475	2.839[*]	0.028
	Bachelor's degree	62	2.0532	0.64318		
	Master's degree or above	31	1.8290	0.72901		

[*] means $p < 0.05$

Table 2.9 Difference comparison of completion of shoes and socks wearing tasks of 2- and 3-year-old children against mothers' educational background

Dimension	Subject	Number of People	Mean	Standard deviation	F-value	p-value
Wearing shoes	Junior college degree or below	31	2.0000	1.09545	3.341*	0.039
	Bachelor's degree	52	2.5577	0.77746		
	Master's degree or above	26	2.3077	1.08699		
Wearing socks	Junior college degree or below	35	1.4286	1.26690	3.091*	0.049
	Bachelor's degree	62	2.0484	1.17943		
	Master's degree or above	30	2.0333	1.35146		

*means $p < 0.05$

Table 2.10 Difference comparison of overall fine motor development level of 2- and 3-year-old children against fathers' educational background

Dimension	Subject	Number of people	Mean	Standard deviation	F-value	p-value
Object manipulation	Junior college degree or below	41	2.1890	0.96141	3.389*	0.037
	Bachelor's degree	50	2.3700	0.81165		
	Master's degree or above	36	2.6667	0.57941		

*means $p < 0.05$

2.3 Results and Analysis

Table 2.11 Difference comparison of completion of page turning and socks wearing tasks of 2- and 3-year-old children against fathers' educational background

dimension	Subject	Number of people	Mean	Standard deviation	F-value	p-value
Page turning	Junior college degree or below	41	1.5122	1.45124	3.114*	0.048
	Bachelor's degree	49	1.8571	1.39940		
	Master's degree or above	35	2.2857	1.12646		
Wearing shoes	Junior college degree or below	37	1.9730	1.09256	5.444*	0.006
	Bachelor's degree	39	2.3590	0.90284		
	Master's degree or above	32	2.7188	0.77186		

*means $p < 0.05$

have a better educational background can more skillfully turn pages, wear shoes and socks. According to the survey, more than 65% of the parents obtained bachelor's degree or above, accepted good education, have more scientific parenting concepts, know better the development characteristics of infants and toddlers at different age groups and critical development period of various abilities, are more inclined to adopt democratic educational mode, are willing to let the children to do something and pay attention to cultivating the infants and toddlers' self-care ability, so the infants and toddlers with such parents can wear shoes and socks more skillfully. In addition, Kong Ya'nan's survey on fine motor development of children aged 1–3 years also showed that mothers' educational background had an important influence on the children's fine motor development (Kong et al. 2009).

Difference Analysis of Motor Development of 2- and 3-Year-Old Children Against Family Income

In terms of family annual income, although there was no difference in the overall development level of fine motor of 2- and 3-year-old children against family annual income, there was a difference in children's performance in piling up blocks and building block trains against family annual income ($p < 0.05$). In terms of piling up blocks, infants and toddlers living in families with an annual income of 200,000–300,000 Yuan performed significantly better than those with an annual income of 100,000 Yuan or less, and those with an annual income of 100,000–300,000 Yuan performed significantly better than those with an annual income of 400,000–500,000 Yuan; and those with an annual income of over 500,000 Yuan performed significantly better than those with an annual income of 400,000–500,000 Yuan (see Table 2.12 for details). It is thus clear that the infants and toddlers living in families with an annual income of 400,000–500,000 Yuan or over 500,000 Yuan are more skillful in piling up 10 blocks, showing they have a good flexibility and coordination in the fine motor domain. In terms of building block trains, infants and toddlers living in families with an annual income of 100,000–400,000 Yuan performed significantly better than those with an annual income of 100,000 Yuan or less. According to the survey result, the general trend is that the higher the annual income of an infant's family is, the better his/her object manipulation is, and the better his coordination and hand–eye coordination in the fine motor domain. That's because good family economic foundation lays a foundation for the healthy development of infants and toddlers, and also attention is also paid to parents' time investment in children in the process of providing children with material conditions. The survey results show that more than 60% of the parents are middle or senior managers and middle or senior technicians, and the nature of their work is more inclined to management, and their working time is slightly flexible, so they are more likely to devote time to accompanying and educating their children. Jia Yan's study on motor development of infants and toddlers aged 1–3 years also showed that the family economy can affect the infant's motor development level, and that the infant's motor development delay is related to the little family devotion (Jia 2013).

Difference Analysis of Motor Development of 2- and 3-Year-Old Children in Educational Investment

In terms of educational investment, there were differences in object manipulation and object matching of 2- and 3-year-old children against the number of books (see Table 2.13 for details). When the number of books prepared for infants and toddlers in the family is more than 11, the object manipulation and object matching of the infants and toddlers was significantly higher than that of infants and toddlers for whom 5–10 books were prepared in the family ($p < 0.05$), which was specifically shown in the completion of the tasks of inserting shape blocks, wearing shoes and socks. In a family providing more than 11 books for the infant to read, the infant completed the task of inserting shape blocks significantly better than the infant for whom 5–10 books were prepared in the family ($p < 0.05$). In a family providing more than 21 books for the infant to read, the infant could much more skillfully wear shoes than infants and toddlers for whom 5–20 books were prepared in the family ($p < 0.05$). When completing the task of wearing socks, the infants and toddlers for whom more than 31 books were provided were much more skillful than the infants and toddlers for whom more than 11–30 books were provided ($p < 0.05$) (see Table 2.14 for details). Because inserting shape blocks, wearing shoes, and wearing

2.3 Results and Analysis

Table 2.12 Difference comparison of performance in piling up blocks and building block trains of 2- and 3-year-old children against family annual income

Dimension	Subject	Number of people	Mean	Standard deviation	F-value	p-value
Piling up blocks	<100,000 Yuan	15	1.8000	1.37321	2.336*	0.046
	100,000–200,000 Yuan	44	2.3864	1.03914		
	200,000–300,000 Yuan	29	2.5862	0.77998		
	300,000–400,000 Yuan	13	2.0000	1.15470		
	400,000–500,000 Yuan	5	1.2000	1.30384		
	>500,000 Yuan	16	2.3125	1.19548		
Building block trains	<100,000 Yuan	15	1.8667	1.45733	3.425*	0.006
	100,000–200,000 Yuan	43	2.8605	0.63925		
	200,000–300,000 Yuan	28	2.8929	0.56695		
	300,000–400,000 Yuan	13	2.7692	0.83205		
	400,000–500,000 Yuan	5	2.4000	1.34164		
	>500,000 Yuan	16	2.4375	1.20934		

*means $p < 0.05$

Table 2.13 Difference comparison of object manipulation and object matching of 2- and 3-year-old children against quantity of books for infants and toddlers

Dimension	Subject	Number of people	Mean	Standard deviation	F-value	p-value
Object manipulation	<5 books	5	1.8500	1.19373	2.405*	0.041
	5–10 books	9	1.6667	1.21192		
	11–20 books	14	2.4286	0.71675		
	21–30 books	14	2.2500	0.79057		
	31–40 books	12	2.5000	0.84611		
	> 40 books	74	2.5135	0.72491		
Object matching	<5 books	5	2.6000	0.89443	3.244*	0.009
	5–10 books	9	2.0000	1.11803		
	11–20 books	14	2.7857	0.57893		
	21–30 books	14	2.9286	0.26726		
	31–40 books	11	2.9091	0.30151		
	> 40 books	74	2.7973	0.59633		

*means $p < 0.05$

Table 2.14 Difference comparison of performance in specific fine motor items of 2- and 3-year-old children against quantity of books for infants and toddlers

Dimension	Subject	Number of people	Mean	Standard deviation	F-value	p-value
Inserting shape blocks	<5 books	5	2.6000	0.89443	3.244*	0.009
	5–10 books	9	2.0000	1.11803		
	11–20 books	14	2.7857	0.57893		
	21–30 books	14	2.9286	0.26726		
	31–40 books	11	2.9091	0.30151		
	> 40 books	74	2.7973	0.59633		
Wearing shoes	<5 books	5	2.8000	0.44721	4.436*	0.001
	5–10 books	8	1.5000	1.41421		
	11–20 books	13	1.5385	1.05003		
	21–30 books	11	2.6364	0.50452		
	31–40 books	9	2.6667	0.70711		
	> 40 books	63	2.4762	0.89546		
Wearing socks	<5 books	5	2.4000	1.34164	2.979*	0.014
	5-10 books	9	1.5556	1.13039		
	11–20 books	14	1.3571	1.33631		
	21–30 books	14	1.0000	1.24035		
	31–40 books	11	2.3636	0.80904		
	> 40 books	74	2.0676	1.24230		

*means $p < 0.05$

2.3 Results and Analysis

Table 2.15 Difference comparison of gross motor development of 2- and 3-year-old children against participation in early education activities

Dimension	Subject	Number of people	Mean	Standard deviation	F-value	p-value
Overall development	No	18	2.0922	0.57971	−2.261*	0.026
	Yes	69	2.4188	0.53714		
Body posture	No	18	2.2778	0.95828	−0.446*	0.657
	Yes	69	2.3768	0.80625		
Body movement	No	17	2.4706	0.44125	−0.905*	0.368
	Yes	69	2.5797	0.44609		
Object control	No	14	2.1414	0.46360	−3.481*	0.001
	Yes	65	2.5291	0.35808		

*means $p < 0.05$

socks are increasingly difficult, the requirements for the infants and toddlers also become higher and higher. According to the survey result, the performance of the infants and toddlers in completing the three tasks is correlated to the quantity of books provided by the families. The more books a family provides for the infant, the more skillful the infant is when completing the more difficult task. It is thus clear that reading books can promote the finger flexibility and coordination of infants and toddlers, and is positively correlated with the quantity of books. That's because reading books can not only cultivate an interest of the infants and toddlers in books, but also can build up the infants and toddlers' actions of opening and closing the books, build up the infants and toddlers' actions of pinching and twisting under the cooperation of the thumb and index finger, and the actions of rubbing and lifting and turning under the cooperation of the thumb and index finger, which can promote the hand–eye coordination development of the infants and toddlers (Tang and Li 2011). The infants and toddlers' grasping and pinching with fingers and cooperation of fingers are of great significance for them to master the self-care skills in life (Tang and Li 2011).

In terms of educational investment, there was significant difference in gross motor development of 2- and 3-year-old children against participation in early education activities. The overall situation of gross motor development of 2- and 3-year-old children who participated in early education activities was better than that of those who didn't participate in the early education activities. The score of infants and toddlers participating in the early education activities in the dimension of object control was significantly higher than that of the infants and toddlers who didn't participate in the early education activities ($p < 0.01$), which was specifically shown by the result that the infants and toddlers participating in the early education activities scored much higher than those who didn't participate in the early education activities in the items of double-leg continuous jumping, running, and receiving a ball with both hands ($p < 0.01$) (see Tables 2.15 and 2.16 for details). Because the infants and toddlers participating in early education activities have access to richer education

Table 2.16 Difference comparison of performance in specific gross motor development items of 2- and 3-year-old children against participation in early education activities

Dimension	Subject	Number of people	Mean	Standard deviation	F-value	p-value
Double-leg continuous jumping (balance)	No	18	1.8889	1.32349	−2.416*	0.025
	Yes	68	2.6765	0.78114		
Double-leg continuous jumping (coordination)	No	18	1.8333	1.33945	−2.568*	0.018
	Yes	68	2.6765	0.74195		
Running	No	15	2.7333	0.45774	−3.422*	0.001
	Yes	69	2.9710	0.16899		
Receiving a ball with both hands	No	17	1.8824	0.92752	−2.268*	0.026
	Yes	70	2.4000	0.82357		

*means $p < 0.05$

toys, their object control ability can be more trained and naturally develops faster. In the early education activities, infants and toddlers have more opportunities to complete some activities independently and reduce the things completed by parents, which can promote the infant gross motor development. Teachers who design early education activities will take into account the development level and current situation of infants and toddlers, and design more scientific, reasonable and standardized games to promote the development of infants and toddlers (Guo 2011). Participating in early education activities can also promote the psychological development of infants and toddlers, expand their social contact, and help them develop more positive emotions such as optimism, cheerfulness and self-confidence (Wang et al. 2015), foster their interest in exploring, and ability to explore and promote the infant motor development.

Difference Analysis of Motor Development of 2- and 3-Year-Old Children in Kindergarten Environment

In this study, three kindergartens (A, B, D) and an early education center (C) were selected as test points. The test subjects include infants and toddlers receiving early education in these kindergartens/early education institutions and 2- and 3-year-old children in the communities around the kindergartens/early education institutions. The analysis results indicated that there were differences in both the fine motor development and gross motor development of 2- and 3-year-old children against the kindergarten environment.

The test results showed that the fine motor development level of tested infants and toddlers in Kindergarten D was significantly higher than that of the tested infants and

2.3 Results and Analysis

Table 2.17 Difference comparison of fine motor development level of 2- and 3-year-old children against kindergarten environment

Dimension	Subject	Number of people	Mean	Standard deviation	F-value	p-value
Overall level	A	13	1.8821	0.48009	6.282*	0.001
	B	35	1.9410	0.67771		
	C	33	1.9172	0.66249		
	D	49	2.3810	0.47512		
Functional hand skills	A	13	1.5308	0.60330	7.424*	0.000
	B	35	1.8400	0.63718		
	C	33	1.6939	0.72927		
	D	49	2.2224	0.50219		
Object manipulation	A	13	2.4808	0.56330	5.543*	0.001
	B	35	2.0071	1.01367		
	C	33	2.2879	0.83881		
	D	49	2.6939	0.56427		

*means $p < 0.05$

toddlers in A, B, and C, which was mainly reflected by two dimensions—functional hand skills and object manipulation (see Table 2.17 for details). Specifically, the proficiency of tested infants and toddlers in B in eating with a spoon was significantly higher than that in C and D; the proficiency of tested infants and toddlers in B and D in page turning was significantly higher than that in C. The number of tested infants and toddlers in D who could correctly hold a pen was much more than that in C. The proficiency and accuracy of tested infants and toddlers in D in piling up blocks and building block trains were significantly higher than those in B and C, and the completion of tested infants and toddlers in A in the task of building block trains was significantly better than that in B. The proficiency and accuracy of tested infants and toddlers in D in building block bridges were significantly higher than those in A and B. The proficiency of tested infants and toddlers in D in wearing socks was significantly higher than that in A, B, and C (see Table 2.18 for details). It is thus clear that the overall fine motor development level of infants and toddlers in D is significantly higher than that in A, B, and C, and they have some advantages in object manipulation, self-care, and drawing skills.

In terms of gross motor, there was no significant difference in the overall level of gross motor of children aged 2–3 years in the kindergarten environment ($p > 0.05$), but there were significant differences in the two dimensions of body movement and object control ($p < 0.05$) (see Table 2.19 for details). Specifically, in terms of scores of body movement, D > B > C; in terms of scores of object control, D > C. As for the specific test items, the balance of tested 2- and 3-year-old children was significantly better than that in B, D, and C when going downstairs; the balance and coordination of tested infants and toddlers in D in the item of double-leg standing

Table 2.18 Difference comparison of completion of all items in fine motor domain of 2- and 3-year-old children against kindergarten environment

Dimension	Subject	Number of people	Mean	Standard deviation	F-value	p-value
Eating with a spoon	A	13	1.7692	0.72501	3.595*	0.016
	B	35	1.8857	0.40376		
	C	33	1.9091	0.52223		
	D	45	1.5111	0.75745		
Page turning	A	13	1.9231	1.44115	4.692*	0.004
	B	35	1.9143	1.44245		
	C	33	1.1818	1.35680		
	D	47	2.2979	1.14046		
Gesture of holding a pen	A	13	2.3077	1.31559	3.069*	0.030
	B	34	2.2941	0.90552		
	C	32	2.0000	0.91581		
	D	48	2.6042	0.67602		
Piling up blocks	A	13	2.3846	0.86972	6.772*	0.000
	B	33	1.9394	1.27327		
	C	33	1.8788	1.26880		
	D	47	2.7872	0.58741		
Building block trains	A	13	3.0000	0.00000	6.290*	0.001
	B	32	2.1875	1.33047		
	C	32	2.5313	1.10671		
	D	47	3.0000	0.00000		
Building block bridges	A	13	1.9231	1.32045	4.041*	0.009
	B	32	1.8125	1.37811		
	C	33	2.3030	1.18545		
	D	48	2.6667	0.85883		
Wearing shoes	B	33	2.0606	1.08799	17.175*	0.000
	C	29	1.7241	1.03152		
	D	48	2.8542	0.54537		
Wearing socks	A	13	1.1538	1.40512	10.774*	0.000
	B	35	1.5143	1.19734		
	C	33	1.3939	1.32144		
	D	48	2.5833	0.89522		

*means $p < 0.05$

2.3 Results and Analysis

Table 2.19 Difference comparison of gross motor development of 2- and 3-year-old children against kindergarten environment

Dimension	Subject	Number of people	Mean	Standard deviation	F-value	p-value
Overall level	A	11	2.4436	0.53262	1.025*	0.384
	B	33	2.2918	0.58478		
	C	31	2.2655	0.46185		
	D	47	2.4485	0.54031		
Body posture	A	12	2.4167	0.79296	2.338*	0.77
	B	33	2.2121	0.96039		
	C	31	2.1290	0.88476		
	D	47	2.5745	0.61661		
Body movement	A	12	2.4167	0.64079	3.173*	0.027
	B	34	2.4824	0.39117		
	C	32	2.4000	0.55183		
	D	46	2.6870	0.33374		
Object control	A	11	2.5518	0.34005	3.459*	0.019
	B	30	2.4087	0.40147		
	C	30	2.3113	0.52598		
	D	41	2.5927	0.24131		

*means $p < 0.05$

jumping were significantly better than that in B and C; the score of backward walking of the infants and toddlers in D was significantly higher than that in A, B, and C; the development level of throwing a ball of tested infants and toddlers in C and B was significantly higher than that in D, and the development level of receiving a ball of tested infants and toddlers in D was significantly higher than that in B and C, presenting a phenomenon that the level of throwing a ball and that of receiving ball are not consistent; the development level of balance of tested infants and toddlers in D when kicking a ball was significantly higher than that in B and C, and the tested infants and toddlers in D performed significantly better than those in A, B, and C in mastering the kick direction and the running distance of the ball, showing that the infants and toddlers in D had a stronger strength in legs and control ability (see Table 2.20 for details).

It is thus clear that the overall motor development level of tested infants and toddlers in D is better than that in A, B, and C. For one thing, the test subjects of D are all 2- and 3-year-old children accepting full-time nursery-class education and the teachers organize some activities to promote infants and toddlers' motor development every day. After having breakfast every day, the infants and toddlers can freely play with various materials for fine motor development (such as table splicing toys, jigsaws, drawing, and handwork). Besides, the teachers organize various activities and games to promote infants and toddlers' gross motor development (for exam-

Table 2.20 Difference comparison of completion of all items in gross motor domain of 2- and 3-year-old children against kindergarten environment

Dimension	Subject	Number of people	Mean	Standard deviation	F-value	p-value
Going downstairs (balance)	A	13	2.3846	0.76795	2.835*	0.041
	B	35	1.6571	0.76477		
	C	33	1.8182	0.68258		
	D	47	1.7021	0.93052		
Double-leg continuous jumping (balance)	A	12	2.6667	0.88763	7.122*	0.000
	B	35	2.4571	0.95001		
	C	31	1.9355	1.43609		
	D	45	2.9333	0.25226		
Double-leg continuous jumping (coordination)	A	12	2.5000	0.90453	6.057*	0.001
	B	34	2.6765	0.76755		
	C	31	1.9355	1.41269		
	D	45	2.8222	0.53466		
Backward walking	A	12	2.5000	0.90453	4.049*	0.009
	B	33	2.5152	0.79535		
	C	32	2.6250	0.60907		
	D	47	2.9362	0.24709		
Throwing a ball with both hands	A	12	2.5833	0.90034	2.903*	0.038
	B	35	2.5143	0.70174		
	C	32	2.6250	0.60907		
	D	46	2.0217	1.39027		
Receiving a ball with both hands	A	12	2.0833	0.90034	3.595*	0.016
	B	35	2.1714	0.74698		
	C	32	2.0000	0.87988		
	D	47	2.5532	0.74625		
Kicking a ball (balance)	A	12	2.8333	0.38925	7.206*	0.000
	B	34	2.5882	0.55692		
	C	32	2.7500	0.50800		
	D	48	3.0000	0.00000		
Kicking a ball (distance and direction)	A	12	2.3333	0.98473	9.413*	0.000
	B	34	2.1765	0.79661		
	C	32	2.1563	0.84660		
	D	48	2.8750	0.39275		

*means $p < 0.05$

ple, exercising the infants and toddlers' walking, running, jumping and crawling by imitating the movements of different animals). For another, D attaches great importance to the quality of health care and education. It can not only put diversified game materials, but also creates a good physical environment for children to promote the motor development. For example, the teachers will also put some small clothes in the doll's home, so that the infants and toddlers can cultivate the flexibility of fine motor by buttoning up and unbuttoning. At the same time, education is integrated into life. D pays attention to incorporating education element in the daily activities, so that the infants and toddlers can progress their fine motor in activities of daily life. For example, when eating, the infants and toddlers will be taught to hold a spoon in the posture of small pistol with the index finger and thumb; and the infants and toddlers can also hold a pen to draw pictures in the same way. The tested infants and toddlers in A, B, and C are live scattered. Some ever accepted early education for 1–2 h every time. And the early education instruction is parent-dominant and pays more attention to guiding the parents to scientifically parent children at home. Some infants and toddlers from the communities have never accepted early education and thus have fewer opportunities to promote the motor development. Therefore, the motor development of these infants and toddlers is weaker.

To sum up, in terms of external environmental factors, parents' educational background, family annual income, number of books, and standardized early education have positive effects on improving the flexibility, coordination, and hand–eye coordination ability of 2- and 3-year-old children in fine motor domain well as the coordination, balance, and stability in the gross motor domain. However, there is no significant difference in the motor development level of 2- and 3-year-old children in terms of mothers' childbearing age, parents' occupation, delivery mode, feeding situation, time of stopping breastfeeding, and number of children in the family.

2.3.2.2 Difference Analysis of Motor Development of 2- and 3-Year-Old Children Against Their Personal Factors

The infants and toddlers' personal factors discussed in this study include the sex, age, birth weight, birth status, and allergy of the infants and toddlers. Difference analysis of the motor development of functional hand skills, object manipulation, and object matching of 2- and 3-year-old children against the infants and toddlers' personal factors.

Difference Analysis of Motor Development of 2- and 3-Year-Old Children Against Sex

In terms of sex, there was difference in fine motor development level of 2- and 3-year-old children. Girls' overall fine motor development level was significantly higher than boys', which is mainly reflected by functional hand skills. Specifically, girls were more proficient than boys when completing the tasks of page turning, drawing a cross,

Table 2.21 Difference comparison of completion of all dimensions in fine motor domain of 2- and 3-year-old children against sex

Dimension	Subject	Number of people	Mean	Standard deviation	T-value	p-value
Functional hand skills	Boy	61	1.7115	0.67382	−3.482*	0.001
	Girl	69	2.0971	0.58911		
Object manipulation	Boy	61	2.3443	0.84306	−0.526*	0.600
	Girl	69	2.4203	0.80268		
Object matching	Boy	61	2.7049	0.78197	−0.646*	0.520
	Girl	68	2.7794	0.51386		
Overall level	Boy	61	1.9464	0.63337	−2.620*	0.010
	Girl	69	2.2261	0.58323		

*means $p < 0.05$

Table 2.22 Difference comparison of completion of all items in fine motor domain of 2- and 3-year-old children against sex

Dimension	Subject	Number of people	Mean	Standard deviation	T-value	p-value
Page turning	Boy	61	1.5738	1.41961	−2.339*	0.021
	Girl	67	2.1343	1.27797		
Drawing a cross	Boy	60	0.7833	1.24997	−2.913*	0.004
	Girl	68	1.4706	1.41917		
Gesture of holding a pen	Boy	59	2.0508	0.89873	−3.496*	0.001
	Girl	68	2.5882	0.83282		
Wearing shoes	Boy	53	2.0943	1.11397	−2.296*	0.024
	Girl	57	2.5263	0.82603		
Wearing socks	Boy	61	1.4918	1.29901	−3.054*	0.003
	Girl	68	2.1618	1.17956		

*means $p < 0.05$

gesture of holding a pen, and wearing shoes and socks ($p < 0.05$) (see Tables 2.21 and 2.22 for details). This means that girls' flexibility, coordination, and hand–eye coordination in the fine motor domain are better than boys'. The surveys of Peng et al. (2007), Hao et al. (2005) and Wu et al. (2006) on the fine motor development of infants aged 0–1 year also showed that girls' fine motor development was better than boys. It is thus concluded that girls' fine motor development being better than boys' is a common characteristic of infants and toddlers aged 0–3 years.

In terms of sex, there was difference in infant gross motor development level. Although there was no difference in the dimensions of body posture, body movement, and object control, girls scored much higher than boys in the items of double-leg standing jumping and backward walking ($p < 0.05$) (see Table 2.23 for details).

2.3 Results and Analysis

Table 2.23 Difference comparison of gross motor development of 2- and 3-year-old children against sex

Dimension	Subject	Number of people	Mean	Standard deviation	T-value	p-value
Double-leg standing jumping (jumping and landing)	Boy	58	2.63	0.91	−2.580*	0.012
	Girl	67	2.97	0.38	−3.135*	0.002
Double-leg standing jumping (landing steadily)	Boy	58	2.41	0.87	−3.033*	0.003
	Girl	67	2.83	0.56	−2.580*	0.012
Backward walking	Boy	59	2.52	0.72	−3.135*	0.002
	Girl	65	2.86	0.46	−3.033*	0.003

*means $p < 0.05$

Double-leg standing jumping reflects the development of strength in leg, body balance and coordination of infants and toddlers, and backward walking mainly reflects the development of vestibular function of the infants and toddlers. The average score of the girls for task completion was higher than that of the boys, showing that the girls' development is better than the boys' in these items and abilities. It can indicate that among 2- and 3-year-old children, girls' development of physical function and control of nervous system are a little faster than boys' in some ways. Studies have shown that in the period from 0 to 12 years old, the development level of girls' physical indexes and abilities is higher than that of the boys on the whole (Guo 2011), which explains why the overall gross motor development level of girls aged 2–3 years is higher than that of boys aged 2–3 years.

Difference Analysis of Motor Development of 2- and 3-Year-Old Children Against Age

In terms of age, there was difference in fine motor development level of 2- and 3-year-old children. The overall fine motor development level of children aged 2.5–3 years was significantly higher than that of children aged 2–2.5 years, which is mainly reflected by functional hand skills, object manipulation, and object matching. Specifically, the proficiency, flexibility, and accuracy of children aged 2.5–3 years were significantly higher than those of children aged 2–2.5 years when completing the tasks of drawing a circle, drawing a horizontal line, drawing a vertical line, drawing a cross, paper cutting, piling up blocks, building block trains, building block bridges, inserting shape blocks, threading beads, and wearing shoes and socks ($p < 0.05$) (see Tables 2.24 and 2.25 for details). 2- and 3-year-old children are more flexible

Table 2.24 Difference comparison of completion of fine motor dimensions of 2- and 3-year-old children against age

Dimension	Subject	Number of people	Mean	Standard deviation	T-value	p-value
Functional hand skills	2–2.5 years old	25	1.4840	0.68110	−3.852*	0.000
	2.5–3 years old	105	2.0190	0.61034		
Object manipulation	2–2.5 years old	25	1.4300	0.92003	−6.116*	0.000
	2.5–3 years old	105	2.6119	0.60544		
Object matching	2–2.5 years old	25	2.3600	1.03602	−2.242*	0.034
	2.5–3 years old	105	2.8365	0.48493		
Overall level	2–2.5 years old	25	1.5280	0.70024	−4.713*	0.000
	2.5–3 years old	105	2.2298	0.51904		

*means $p < 0.05$

in hand movements, and they can relatively accurately and skillfully use the objects, hold a pen with fingertips to draw randomly on the paper. Some infants and toddlers even can draw a straight line or vertical line. Holding a pen with three fingers is an important index to evaluate the finger differentiation ability of children aged 25–30 months (Zhou 2012), so as the infants and toddlers grow, their motor flexibility will be improved gradually. In addition, the thumb control ability of the infants and toddlers will be further improved when they are around 35 months. They can not only open the scissors to a large degree, but also can close the scissors smoothly. And in this period, their forearms can gradually rise to the midline location, so they can cut a short line (Zhou 2012).

The period from 2 to 6 years old is a stage when the children's motor skill of holding a pen develops rapidly. The earliest gesture of holding a pen of the infants and toddlers requires the movement of the whole hand and arm, and the infants and toddlers perform "grasping with palm up", which means that the infants and toddlers hold a pen with the help of palm and fingers with palm up. In this clumsy gesture of holding a pen, it is difficult for the infants and toddlers to draw or write purposely. As they make accidental attempts in drawing and writing activities and learning to adjust the action of holding a pen under the guidance of teachers and parents, the children's pen-holding action of "grasping with palm up" is gradually replaced by the action of "grasping with palm down", and thumb and the other four fingers begin to play a more and more important role in drawing and writing skills. Children who just learn to hold a pen usually adjust the position of the pen through the movement

2.3 Results and Analysis

Table 2.25 Difference comparison of completion of fine motor items of 2- and 3-year-old children against age

Dimension	Subject	Number of people	Mean	Standard deviation	T-value	p-value
Drawing a circle	2–2.5 years old	25	2.0400	1.13578	−2.396*	0.018
	2.5–3 years old	103	2.5534	0.91532		
Drawing a horizontal line	2–2.5 years old	25	1.8000	1.38444	−2.253*	0.026
	2.5–3 years old	103	2.3981	1.14052		
Drawing a vertical line	2–2.5 years old	25	1.0800	1.35154	−3.281*	0.001
	2.5–3 years old	103	2.0194	1.26786		
Drawing a cross	2–2.5 years old	25	0.5600	1.15758	−2.420*	0.017
	2.5–3 years old	103	1.2913	1.39769		
Paper cutting	2–2.5 years old	25	1.5600	1.00333	−2.599*	0.010
	2.5–3 years old	103	2.0874	0.88680		
Piling up blocks	2–2.5 years old	24	1.1667	1.37261	−6.394*	0.000
	2.5–3 years old	102	2.5490	0.82807		
Building block trains	2–2.5 years old	23	1.6957	1.52061	−6.363*	0.000
	2.5–3 years old	101	2.8911	0.54591		
Building block bridges	2–2.5 years old	23	1.0870	1.23998	−6.045*	0.000
	2.5–3 years old	103	2.5437	0.99781		
Inserting shape blocks	2–2.5 years old	25	2.3600	1.03602	−3.410*	0.001
	2.5–3 years old	104	2.8365	0.48493		
Threading beads	2–2.5 years old	25	2.0400	1.01980	−4.307*	0.000
	2.5–3 years old	103	2.7476	0.65257		

(continued)

Table 2.25 (continued)

Dimension	Subject	Number of people	Mean	Standard deviation	T-value	p-value
Wearing shoes	2–2.5 years old	21	1.6667	1.11056	−3.505*	0.001
	2.5–3 years old	89	2.4719	0.90566		
Wearing socks	2–2.5 years old	25	1.0800	1.18743	−3.476*	0.001
	2.5–3 years old	104	2.0288	1.23427		

*means $p < 0.05$

of the arm and elbow, but after the development of the coordinated movement of the fingers, children gradually become more accustomed to using the fingers to adjust the gesture of holding a pen and the position of the pen, and the movement frequency of the arm and elbow drops rapidly. In addition, the point at which children hold the pen gradually moves close to the tip. Children aged 2–3 years hold a pen at the point close to the tip, mainly rely on the movements of the shoulder joint for only drawing and writing, and then gradually they develop to control the movement of the pen with the elbow. It is thus clear that with the growth of age, the development of motor patterns and skill characteristics adopted by children follows the "economic principle", that is, children gradually move the point at which they hold a pen closer to the tip. On the other hand, the posture of sitting and standing tends to be vertical while the movement of using pen is more mature. This posture reduces the supporting role of the arms and makes the movement of the hands freer. In other words, when holding a pen to draw or write, the children moves the parts closer to the midline of the torso less, but moves the limbs far from the torso more. Flexible use of pens is the precondition for children to carry out drawing and writing activities (Dong and Tao 2004). Therefore, with the growth of children's age and the improvement in their pen-holding skills, their level of drawing various patterns also becomes higher.

In terms of age, there was significant difference in gross motor development level of 2- and 3-year-old children. The overall gross motor development of children aged 2.5–3 years was significantly higher than that of children aged 2–2.5 years ($p < 0.05$), which is mainly reflected in the dimensions of body posture, body movement, and object control. Specifically, children aged 2.5–3 years performed significantly better than children aged 2–2.5 years in the aspects of the balance in double-leg standing jumping, balance and coordination in double-leg continuous jumping and tiptoeing, and balance and strength in receiving a ball with both hands and kicking a ball (see Tables 2.26 and 2.27 for details). In her study, Guo Xiaoyan (2011) pointed out that age has a significant influence on the infants and toddlers' standing on one leg, throwing and receiving a ball and long jump, and that age is positively correlated with the test result.

2.3 Results and Analysis

Table 2.26 Difference comparison of completion of gross motor dimensions of 2- and 3-year-old children against age

Dimension	Subject	Number of people	Mean	Standard deviation	T-value	p-value
Body posture	2–2.5 years old	24	1.66	0.91	24.724*	0.000
	2.5–3 years old	99	2.51	0.70		
Body movement	2–2.5 years old	123	2.34	0.81	13.030*	0.000
	2.5–3 years old	25	2.24	0.49		
Object control	2–2.5 years old	99	2.60	0.42	18.262*	0.000
	2.5–3 years old	124	2.53	0.45		
Overall level	2–2.5 years old	21	2.15	0.58	21.409*	0.000
	2.5–3 years old	91	2.53	0.30		

*means $p < 0.05$

Difference Analysis of Motor Development of 2- and 3-Year-Old Children in Birth Weight

In terms of birth weight, there was a significant difference in gross motor development of 2- and 3-year-old children, which is mainly reflected in double-leg continuous jumping and kicking a ball, as well as coordination of double-leg continuous jumping ($p < 0.01$). The body coordination of normal birth weight infants is better than that of the low birth weight infants or high birth weight infants (see Table 2.28 for details). Because it is more difficult for high birth weight infants to move, it may be slower for them to develop the exercise and motor functions; the less exercises they have, the more easily they gain weight, forming a vicious circle, which will affect the infant's gross motor development. As a result, their motor abilities, especially sense of balance, coordination, and agility, are weaker than normal birth weight children (Sun and Jiang 2012). In addition, in the test item of strength in legs, the ball kicked by the normal birth weight infants ran the furthest, indicating that the development of strength in legs of normal birth weight infants is better than the high or low birth weight infants. Zhang et al. (2004), according to the diagnostic criteria of malnutrition determined by WHO, made a diagnosis on underweight, growth retardation and emaciation, and employed Neuropsychological Development Checklist for Children Aged 0–6 years to analyze the neuropsychological development of 68 children aged 6.5–28 months, with the results expressed with development quotients. At the same time, they investigated the relevant social environmental factors. The results showed

Table 2.27 Difference comparison of completion of gross motor items of 2- and 3-year-old children against age

Dimension	Subject	Number of people	Mean	Standard deviation	T-value	p-value
Standing on one leg	2–2.5 years old	24	1.66	0.91	24.724*	0.000
	2.5–3 years old	99	2.51	0.70		
Double-leg standing jumping (balance)	2–2.5 years old	24	2.29	1.12	6.597*	0.011
	2.5–3 years old	101	2.72	0.61		
Double-leg continuous jumping (balance)	2–2.5 years old	25	1.80	1.38	18.512*	0.000
	2.5–3 years old	98	2.70	0.78		
Double-leg continuous jumping (coordination)	2–2.5 years old	24	2.00	1.35	9.118*	0.003
	2.5–3 years old	98	2.65	0.82		
Tiptoeing (balance)	2–2.5 years old	22	2.50	1.22	5.793*	0.018
	2.5–3 years old	96	2.88	0.47		
Tiptoeing (coordination)	2–2.5 years old	22	2.40	1.09	10.010*	0.002
	2.5–3 years old	96	2.88	0.47		
Receiving a ball with both hands	2–2.5 years old	25	1.72	0.79	15.102*	0.000
	2.5–3 years old	101	2.39	0.77		
Kicking a ball (balance)	2–2.5 years old	25	2.52	0.65	15.575*	0.000
	2.5–3 years old	101	2.88	0.32		
Kicking a ball (directional deviation)	2–2.5 years old	25	2.16	0.94	4.557*	0.035
	2.5–3 years old	101	2.52	0.71		
Kicking a ball (distance)	2–2.5 years old	25	2.44	0.91	8.138*	0.005
	2.5–3 years old	101	2.86	0.58		

*means $p < 0.05$

2.3 Results and Analysis

Table 2.28 Difference comparison of completion of gross motor items of 2- and 3-year-old children against birth weight

Dimension	Subject	Number of people	Mean	Standard deviation	F-value	p-value
Double-leg continuous jumping (coordination)	Low birth weight infants (birth weight < 1500 g)	5	2.40	0.54	3.407*	0.037
	Normal birth weight infants: 2500–4000 g	96	2.63	0.93		
	Giant infants: weight ≥ 4000 g	9	1.77	1.30		
Kicking a ball (distance)	Low birth weight infants (birth weight < 1500 g)	5	1.80	1.30	5.836*	0.004
	Normal birth weight infants: 2500–4000 g	100	2.83	0.62		
	Giant infants: weight ≥ 4000 g	10	2.80	0.63		

*means $p < 0.05$

that the average development quotient of malnourished children is 87.84, falling in the normal range but lower than norm, which is significantly lower than that of the control group. The low birth weight infants may become malnourished easily, so it affects the infant gross motor development.

To sum up, in terms of sex, girls' flexibility, coordination, and hand–eye coordination in fine motor domain are significantly better than the boys', which is specifically reflected by the proficiency in completing the tasks of page turning, drawing a cross, gesture of holding a pen, and wearing shoes and socks. In the aspect of gross motor development, girls perform significantly better than boys when completing the tasks of double-leg standing jumping and backward walking, which indicates that girls' strength in their legs, body balance, and coordination are significantly better than the boys'. In terms of age, children aged 2.5–3 years perform significantly better than children aged 2–2.5 years when completing the tasks under functional hand skills, object manipulation and object matching, which is specifically reflected by the proficiency, flexibility, and accuracy in completing the tasks of drawing a circle, drawing a horizontal line, drawing a vertical line, drawing a cross, paper cutting, piling up blocks, building block trains, building block bridges, inserting shape blocks, threading beads, and wearing shoes and socks. In terms of birth weight, the gross motor development level of normal birth weight infants is the highest.

2.4 Conclusion

According to the survey results, because the living condition of the current 2- and 3-year-old children is superior, the parents accepted good education and have more scientific parenting concepts, most 2- and 3-year-old children have received early education to varying degrees, contacted with more materials and stimulations for promoting fine and gross motor development. Because of the above reasons, the flexibility, coordination, and hand–eye coordination in fine motor domain and coordination, balance, and stability in gross motor domain of 2- and 3-year-old children develop well.

Family environment and kindergarten environment have important effects on infant motor development. Parents' educational background, family annual income, number of books, and standardized early education have positive effects on improving the flexibility, coordination, and hand–eye coordination ability of 2- and 3-year-old children in fine motor domain well as the coordination, balance, and stability in the gross motor domain. However, there is no significant difference in the motor development level of 2- and 3-year-old children in terms of mothers' childbearing age, parents' occupation, delivery mode, feeding situation, time of stopping breastfeeding, and number of children in the family.

There are significant differences in the development fine motor and gross motor of 2- and 3-year-old children against both sex and age. Girls' flexibility, coordination, and hand–eye coordination in fine motor domain are significantly better than the boys', which is specifically reflected by the proficiency in completing the tasks of page turning, drawing a cross, gesture of holding a pen, and wearing shoes and socks. Children aged 2.5–3 years perform significantly better than children aged 2–2.5 years when completing the tasks under functional hand skills, object manipulation, and object matching, which is specifically reflected by the proficiency, flexibility, and accuracy in completing the tasks of drawing a circle, drawing a horizontal line, drawing a vertical line, drawing a cross, paper cutting, piling up blocks, building block trains, building block bridges, inserting shape blocks, threading beads, and wearing shoes and socks. In terms of gross motor, girls' strength in their legs, body balance, and coordination are significantly better than the boys'. Children aged 2.5–3 years perform significantly better than children aged 2–2.5 years when completing the tasks under the dimensions of body posture, body movement, and object control, which is specifically reflected by standing on one leg, two-leg jumping, tiptoeing, receiving a ball, and kicking a ball. In addition, the gross motor development of normal birth weight infants is significantly higher than that of high or low birth weight infants.

References

Bayley, N. (2006). *Bayley scales of infant and toddler development, third edition: administration manual*. San Antonio, TX: Harcourt.
Cao, R. X. et al., (2010). Noncompliant behavior in toddlerhood predicted social adaptation at 4 to 11 years of age. *Acta Psychologica Sinica, 42*(5), 581–586.
Chen, G. M. (2003). *Preschool psychology*. Beijing: People's Education Press.
Chen, S. X. (2004). Analysis of clinical test results of Bailey Infant Development Scale. *China Journal of Health Psychology, 12*(1), 19–21.
Dong, Q., & Tao, S. (2002). *Motor and psychological development*. Beijing: Beijing Normal University Press.
Dong, Q., & Tao, S. (2004). *Motor and psychological development*. Beijing: Beijing Normal University Press.
Fan, C. R., & Zhou, Z. F. (1983). Discussion on the law of intelligent development of children from birth to six years old. *Acta Psychologica Sinica, 04,* 429–444.
Folio, M. R., & Fewell, R. R. (2006). *Peabody developmental motor scale* (I) (M. Li, Z. Huang, Trans.). Beijing: Peking University Medical Press.
Greg, P., et al. (2008). *Introduction to human motor development*. Beijing: People's Education Press.
Guo, H. J. (1999). *Childhood development psychology*. Nanjing: Nanjing University Press.
Guo, X. Y. (2011). *The effectiveness of infant classes education experience in kindergartens for children aged 3–6 on motor development*. Unpublished doctorial dissertation, Sichuan Normal University, Chengdu.
Hao, Y., et al. (2005). Analysis of fine motor development and influencing factors of infants aged 8–12 months in Luohu community. *Journal of Community Medicine, 3*(8), 8–9.
Heep Hong Society. (2013). *Development assessment form for children (revised)*. Hong Kong: The Green Pagoda Press Ltd.
Hu, X. Q. (2012). *A study on differences and influencing factors about the fine motor development between preterm and term infants*. Unpublished doctorial dissertation, Chongqing Medical University, Chongqing.
Jia, Y. (2013). *A study on motor development of infants and toddlers aged 1–3*. Unpublished doctorial dissertation, Shanxi University, Shanxi.
Jiang, W., et al. (2008). The influence of early development guidance of 0~1 years old on the intelligent development of normal infants. *Maternal and Child Health Care of China, 23*(2), 198.
Kong, Y. N., et al. (2009). Study on infants and toddlers aged 1-3 years old fine motor development situations and influencing factors. *Chinese Journal of Child Health Care, 02,* 145–146.
Ledesma, L. (2002). *The early childhood care and development (ECCD) checklist: Technical and administration manual*. Quezon City: University of the Philippines, Diliman.
Li, H. T., et al. (1982). An investigation on the intelligent development of children less than three years old. *Journal of Psychological Science, 01*(29–41), 66.
Peng, X. S., et al. (2007). Analysis of the influence factor of infant motor development. *Chinese Journal of Child Health Care, 22*(25), 3548–3549.
Sun, W. Q., & Jiang, Fan. (2012). Research progress of main factors influencing gross motor development of infants and toddlers. *Chinese Journal of Child Health Care, 2*(7), 145–146.
Tang, M., & Li, G. X. (2011). *Motor development and education of infants and toddlers aged 0–3*. Shanghai: Fudan University Press.
Tong, M. L., et al. (2001). A study on the effect of early education on infant motor development. *Chinese Journal of Child Health Care, 05,* 298–299.
Ulrich, D. A. (2000). *Test of gross motor development (Second Edition) Examiner's Manual*. Austin, TX: pro-ed Publishers.
Wang, X. Q., et al. (2015). Study on gross motor development situation and influencing factors of preschool children. *Chinese Journal of Child Health Care, 23*(2), 188–191.
Wu, J. H., et al. (2006). Analysis of motor development and influencing factors in 458 infants aged 8–12 months. *International Medicine and Health Guidance News, 09,* 106–107.

Xu, X., et al. (2007). A study on infant fostering environment and their motor development. *Chinese Journal of Child Health Care, 15*(5), 455–457.

Yang, Y. (2012). *A study on motor development for infant in age 0–1*. Unpublished doctorial dissertation, Shanxi University, Shanxi.

Zhang, F. R., et al. (2004). The effects of malnutrition on neuropsychological development of children. *Maternal and Child Health Care of China, 19*(4), 51–52.

Zhang, L. L., et al. (2015). China Developmental Scale for children norm in Beijing (0–4 years old) revision and reliability analysis. *Chinese Journal of Child Health Care, 23*(06), 573–576.

Zhou, N. L. (2012). *Observations and assessments of children aged 0–3 years old*. Shanghai: East China Normal University Press.

Zhu, H. Y. (2011). A *study on strategies of promoting the fine motor development for infant in age 0–3*. Unpublished doctorial dissertation, Northeast Normal University, Changchun.

Chapter 3
Analysis on Cognitive Development of 2–3 Years Old Children

3.1 Introduction

Cognition involves the individual's psychological processes of perception, attention, memory, thinking, problem-solving, language, and reasoning. Cognition is the main way for babies and infants to understand the world, and it is also the basis for learning ability of infants and young children (Chen et al. 2013; Carlson et al. 2004; Linder and Linas 2009; Jiang and Ma 2013). People rely on cognitive activities for the characteristics and nature of objective things, and for the relationships and connections between things. It occupies a very important position in the person's entire mental activity. Cognitive development refers to the change of cognitive activities in a person's life, specifically the formation of cognitive structures and cognitive abilities and the regular changes that occur with age (Kelly-Vance et al. 1999; Kelly-Vance and Ryalls 2005; Lobo et al. 2014; Nilsen et al. 2016; Pellegrini and Hou 2011). Cognitive development of infants and young children has an important influence on their mental development such as intelligence level, academic achievement, and social adaptation in their school age, adolescence and even the entire adult period (Paro and Pianta 2001). Only by fully understanding the physical and psychological development characteristics of infants and children can they be provided with appropriate conservation and education. In that case, It is necessary to monitor and evaluate children's cognitive development. This study used a questionnaire method, a random interview method, and play-based evaluation method to perform cognitive development tests on 142 infants and toddlers aged 2–3 years in Beijing. The characteristics of cognitive development in 2–3 years old children were analyzed to provide ideas for follow-up studies.

3.2 Research Methods

3.2.1 Research Object

This study explored the cognitive development and characteristics of 2–3 years old children. A total of 142 2–3 years old children were investigated in 3 kindergartens and 3 early education institutions in Beijing. The above kindergartens include both urban kindergartens and rural kindergartens; the 3 early education institutions are located in Haidian District, Chaoyang District, and Daxing District respectively. The 142 children are between 23 months and 37 months old, with an average age of 33.04 months and a standard deviation of 3.46. Among them, 68 were boys, accounting for 47.9%, with an average age of 32.91 months, with a standard deviation of 3.28; there were 74 girls, accounting for 52.1%, with an average age of 33.16 months and a standard deviation of 3.63. The age distribution of young children is shown in Table 3.1.

Table 3.1 Month age * gender crosstabulation count

Month age	Gender Male	Gender Female	Total
23	2	0	2
24	1	3	4
25	0	2	2
26	1	2	3
27	1	2	3
28	1	2	3
29	2	3	5
30	4	1	5
31	8	1	9
32	6	4	10
33	5	6	11
34	10	11	21
35	14	17	31
36	7	13	20
37	6	7	13
Total	68	74	142

3.2 Research Methods

3.2.2 Specific Research Methods

3.2.2.1 Questionnaire Method

In order to fully understand the profile, family background and parenting of 2–3 years old children, investigations on the caregivers of 2–3 years old children were made. The questionnaire includes age, gender, preterm birth, only child, participation in early childhood education courses, parents' age, occupation, and family economy.

3.2.2.2 Play-Based Evaluation Method

In the play-based evaluation method, the evaluator allows the children to be close to nature, thereby observing the play initiated by the children and quantifying the children's performance in the play so as to obtain indicators of development dimensions (Sha 2016; Tory 2008). The game guider (the experimenter) shall organize a room with corresponding toys and equipment. The children were provided with tools. In a suitable case, children shall understand the activity and the rule so as to be more involved in play. Children's cognitive development was evaluated during play. This study designed the corresponding play situations and materials according to different evaluation dimensions. Specific methods are described in the Research Tools and Research Process.

3.2.2.3 Random Interview

The parents of the children aged 2–3 were randomly interviewed during play, with an aim to have a deeper understanding of the play level and play performance of them at home and to provide some references for scoring.

3.2.3 Research Tools

Cognitive Development Assessment Scale for Children Aged 2–3 was adopted in the study. The subject of the Scale was formulated based on play-based TPBA, with reference to Children Development Scale by Heep Hong Society, Bailey Scale, and some cognitive tests. Cognitive Development Assessment Scale for Children Aged 2–3 includes six aspects, that is, symbolization and representation, problem-solving, correspondence, attention, and participation, graph recognition, exploration construction, as shown in Table 3.2. According to statistics, all dimensions are commonly used evaluation dimensions of cognitive development tools at home and abroad. In addition to the independent scoring, other items use the five-point scoring method.

Table 3.2 Measurement dimensions selection and source

Survey dimension selection and source	
Symbolization and representation	It is generally believed that games can promote early childhood cognitive development. In this study, symbolization and representational dimension rating grades mainly use TPBA symbolization and representational game dimension observation guidelines
Problem-solving	With reference to TPBA problem-solving observation guideline in method dimension, including strategies to fulfill objectives, ways to fulfill challenging tasks, interests in objects with causal relationship and events. For grades, see appendixes
Graphical recognition	The specific rating refers to P93, Graphic Recognition Scoring Standard, under the Learning Program of Heep Hong Society
Exploration and construction	With reference to TPBA observation guideline to problem-solving construction games and goods application in early childhood. During construction games, children are asked to have an ultimate goal to remold an object
Attention and participation	With reference to TPBA attention scope guideline and flexible conversion in REEF
One-to-one correspondence	With reference to TPBA observation guideline in correspondence dimension. In addition, in the third edition of the Bailey Scale, counting is used for capacity measurement in the cognitive dimension. Children aged 2.5 could recognize objects and know orders of numbers

3.2.4 Research Process

All survey tasks are based on certain play situations. Common toys that correspond to the dimensions of cognitive development were selected. Play-based evaluation can effectively stimulate the enthusiasm of young children to participate in the evaluation, and can show their cognitive development ability to the maximum in the test. The paper below introduces play situations and materials, as shown in Table 3.3: first of all, the play situation was arranged. Placement of the toys and occlusion between areas were arranged, so that children would not be attracted by colorful toys and abstracted. Then, the children entered the game area in the sequence of situation 1 and situation 2. The experimenter observed children's game activities, filled in the score sheet and filmed. Before the observation, the researchers carried out pre-observation in the room with the camera to eliminate the children's curiosity with the observer and the camera. Sometimes, children had to play games alone as instructed by the experimenter. Parents could not give any tip; during parent–child play, parents could get involved. However, such play was dominated by children who were accompanied by their parents. Parents could not control their children nor the play. If necessary, the experimenter could intervene. In this part, the experimenter could also interview

Table 3.3 Play situations and materials

Play situation and materials		
Case 1	**Play-based evaluation:** ① Problem-solving ② Three-dimensional pattern matching **Material:** Toy locks (10 locks with different shapes) Toys for three-dimensional pattern matching (5 graphs of round, triangle, square, pentagram, cross)	Children were tested to play independently
Case 2	**Play-based evaluation:** ① Symbolization and representation ② Exploration and construction **Material:** Toy tableware: Oven, gas stove, pot, shovel, bowl, spoon, vegetables, fruit Magnetic sheets	Parents are involved in parent–child games

parents so as to add information. Two children were allowed to play games together. As they were not disturbed, they were tracked by two experimenters. The children were given 30 min to play.

3.2.5 Data Analysis

During the data collection process, the researchers entered the results of the infant test and the questionnaire interview into SPSS 19.0, and verified all the data. In this study, statistics methods including descriptive statistics, independent sample test, one-way analysis of variance, correlation, and regression analysis were used to analyze data.

3.3 Research Results and Analysis

3.3.1 Cognitive Development of Children Aged 2–3 Years Old

The survey measured a total of 142 children aged 2–3 years. In the cognitive field, there were 115 valid data for total scores, the lowest score was 10 points, the highest score was 47 points, the average score was 28.72 points, and the standard deviation was 9.49 points. Among them, there are 53 valid data for boys, the lowest score is 10 points, the highest score is 47 points, the average score is 28.77 points, the standard deviation is 8.93; the valid data for girls is 62, the lowest score is 11 points, the highest score is 47 points, the average score is 28.68 points, standard deviation 10.00. According to age, children aged 23–30 months are classified into the low-age group, and 31–37 months of age are classified into the high-age group. In the low-age group, there are 21 valid data, the lowest 10 points, the highest 35 points, the average 19.29 points, and the standard deviation 7.58; the high-age group has 94 valid data, the lowest score 12 points, the highest score 47 points, the average score 30.83 points. The standard deviation is 8.56. An independent sample T-test was used to analyze the difference in gender and age for the total score. The results showed that there was no significant difference in scores of children with different genders (t = 0.054, $p = 0.957 > 0.05$); the scores of children in different age groups had extremely significant differences (t = $-5.695, p = 0.000 < 0.05$). There is no gender difference in the cognitive level of children aged 2–3 years. However, children's cognitive level significantly increases with age. This also shows that children's cognition develops rapidly when they are 2–3 years old, and parents and teachers should pay attention to guiding children during this period.

Next, a more detailed analysis on the cognitive development of children aged 2–3 years will be made in different dimensions.

3.3.2 Number–Concept Recognition of 2–3 Years Old Children

There were 123 valid data in the number–concept cognition survey task, the lowest score was 0 points, the highest score was 10 points, the average score was 4.17 points, and the standard deviation was 3.73. Among them, there are 59 valid data for boys, the lowest score is 0 points, the highest score is 10 points, the average score is 4.08 points, and the standard deviation is 3.81; There are 64 valid data for girls, the lowest score is 0 points, the highest score is 10 points, the average score is 4.25 points, and the standard deviation is 3.69 points. The low-age group had 24 valid data, the lowest score was 0, the highest score was 10, the average score was 1.04, and the standard deviation was 2.29; the high-age group had 99 valid data, the lowest score was 0, the highest score was 10, the average score was 4.93, and the standard deviation was 3.62.

An independent sample T-test was adopted to analyze the difference in sex and age for logarithmic conceptual cognitive scores. The results showed that there was no significant difference in the number of conceptual cognitive scores among children of different genders (t = −0.244, $p = 0.807 > 0.05$); there was an extremely significant difference in the number of conceptual cognitive scores among children of different age groups (t = −6.555, $p = 0.000 < 0.05$).

The results show that there is no gender difference in the concept of the logarithmic concept of infants and young children aged 2–3 years. Before two and a half years old, young children hardly understand the meaning of numbers; after two and a half years old, children gradually understand the meaning of quantity, with limited degree. Degree and speed of development of number cognition differ with children aged 2–3. Some children can count from 1 to 10 before two and a half years old, and some children cannot count a figure after two and a half years. Of course, this is also related to the children's emotions, willingness, self-control, and understanding of language during the test. Some young children cannot follow the tester's instructions to complete the task. Instead, they played with the toy bricks.

3.3.3 Three-Dimensional Pattern Matching of 2–3 Years Old Children

There are 123 valid data for graphic cognitive tasks, the lowest score is 0 points, the highest score is 5 points, the average score is 3.79 points, and the standard deviation is 1.39. Among them, there are 58 valid data for boys, the lowest score is 0 points, the highest score is 5 points, the average score is 3.86 points, and the standard deviation is 1.38; there are 65 valid data for girls, the lowest score is 1 point, the highest score is 5 points, the average score is 3.72 points, and the standard deviation is 1.41. The low-age group has 24 valid data, the lowest score is 0, the highest score is 5, the average score is 2.54, and the standard deviation is 1.50; the high-age group had 99 valid data, the lowest score was 1 point, the highest score was 5 points, the average score was 4.09 points, and the standard deviation was 1.19.

An independent sample T-test was used to analyze the difference in gender and age for the graphical cognitive scores. The results showed that there was no significant difference in the cognitive scores of children of different genders ($t = 0.551$, $p = 0.583 > 0.05$); the cognitive scores of children in different age groups had extremely significant differences ($t = -4.706$, $p = 0.000 < 0.05$).

The results show that children between the ages of 2 and 3 have some knowledge of graphics. In many studies, infants can distinguish between round squares and triangles, and can match objects by color, shape, and size (Learning Guideline by Heep Hong Society, TPBA Review Guideline). In this survey, cross-shapes and pentagonal shapes were added. The results of the survey showed that children aged 2–2.5 can basically understand (identify and match the features of graphics) two or three simple graphs, while children aged 2.5–3 can understand four simple graphs on average. At least one can recognize a graphic. There is no gender difference in the perception of graphics between 2- and 3-year olds, and the cognitive level increases with age. Among the five types of graphics, crosses are the most difficult to be understood, and triangles are the easiest to be understood. However, there are differences in the other three graphs among these children. For younger children who can only recognize two or three figures, it seems that circles are rarely identified, and stars are easier to identify than squares; however, older children who can identify three or four figures can easily recognize triangles, squares, and circles, but some children will be confused when recognizing stars and crosses.

From the photos below, we can see that many young children put cruciform blocks into star-shaped holes, and a few children put common star block blocks into cross-shaped holes. This shows that young children can not distinguish these two shapes.

3.3.4 Symbolization and Representation of 2–3 Years Old Children

In the play of symbolization and representation, there are 126 valid data, the lowest score is 3 points, the highest score is 15 points, the average score is 8.05 points, and the standard deviation is 3.56 points. Among them, there are 60 valid data for boys, the lowest score is 3 points, the highest score is 15 points, the average score is 8.07 points, and the standard deviation is 3.35; there were 66 valid data for girls, the lowest score was 3 points, the highest score was 15 points, the average score was 8.03 points, and the standard deviation was 3.77. The low-age group had 24 valid data, the lowest score was 3 points, the highest score was 15 points, the average score was 6.17 points, and the standard deviation was 3.24; there are 102 valid data in the high-age group, the lowest score is 3 points, the highest score is 15 points, the average score is 8.49 points, and the standard deviation is 3.51.

3.3 Research Results and Analysis

The three dimensions of the play of symbolization and characterization were analyzed. Among them, there were 126 valid data for object substitution, with an average of 2.58 points and a standard deviation of 1.49. Among them, there are 60 valid data for boys, with an average score of 2.53, a standard deviation of 1.49, and 66 valid data for girls with an average score of 2.62 and a standard deviation of 1.51. There were 24 valid data in the low-age group with an average score of 1.88 and a standard deviation of 1.30. The high-age group had 102 valid data with an average score of 2.75 and a standard deviation of 1.49. There were 127 valid data for role recognition, with an average of 2.59 points and a standard deviation of 1.22. Among them, there were 61 valid data for boys, with an average of 2.62 points and a standard deviation of 1.66; for girls, there were 66 valid data with an average score of 2.56 and a standard deviation of 1.29. There were 24 valid data in the low-age group with an average score of 2.04 and a standard deviation of 1.08. The high-age group had 103 valid data with an average score of 2.72 and a standard deviation of 1.22. There are 127 valid data of game plots with an average of 2.88 points and a standard deviation of 1.23. Among them, there are 61 valid data for boys, with an average score of 2.92, a standard deviation of 1.16, and 66 valid data for girls with an average score of 2.85 and a standard deviation of 1.29. There were 24 valid data in the low-age group with an average score of 2.25 and a standard deviation of 1.19. The high-age group had 103 valid data with an average score of 3.03 and a standard deviation of 1.19. The symbol and representation data are detailed in Table 3.4.

An independent sample T-test was used to analyze the difference in gender and age for the total score and the three dimensions. The results showed that there was

Table 3.4 Symbolization and characterization of descriptive statistics

Grouping/Dimensions			Characterization score	Object substitution	Role recognition	Game plot
Gender	Male	N	60	60	61	61
		M	8.07	2.53	2.62	2.92
		SD	3.35	1.49	1.16	1.16
	Female	N	66	66	66	66
		M	8.03	2.62	2.56	2.85
		SD	3.77	1.51	1.29	1.29
Age	Lower age group	N	24	24	24	24
		M	6.17	1.88	2.04	2.25
		SD	3.24	1.30	1.08	1.19
	Higher age group	N	102	102	103	103
		M	8.49	2.75	2.72	3.03
		SD	3.51	1.49	1.22	1.19
Total		N	126	126	127	127
		M	8.05	2.58	2.59	2.88
		SD	3.56	1.49	1.22	1.23

no significant difference in the total scores of the children of different genders and the three dimensions (t-score $= 0.057$, $p = 0.955 > 0.05$; t-object substitution $= -0.329$, $p = 0.743 > 0.05$; t-role perception $= 0.286$, $p = 0.776 > 0.05$; t-game plot $= 0.318$, $p = 0.751 > 0.05$); There was a significant difference between the total scores of the children of different age groups and the three-dimensional scores (t-total score $= -2.962$, $p = 0.004 < 0.05$; t-object substitution $= -2.628$, $p = 0.010 < 0.05$; t-role perception $= -2.490$, $p = 0.014 < 0.05$; t-Game Plot $= -2.885$, $p = 0.005 < 0.05$).

The results show that there is no gender difference in the Symbolization and representational capabilities of infants between the ages of 2 and 3 years. The level of representation play for children aged 2.5–3 is significantly higher than that for children aged 2–2.5 years. In the token game, the average score for each young child in the young age group is about 2 points. They can simply use items similar to real items to play, and they are not unimpressive about play characters and game plots. However, their play are still not systematic. They still do not understand the play of symbolic characters, and occasionally show behaviors that embody higher levels of symbolism and representation. To the contrary, the play for children over two and a half years old is simple but obviously systematic. They know the responsibilities of the roles they play, the richness of the play plots, and the connections between the plots. Besides, they can use more abundant materials to substitute for their own play purpose in the play.

Parents can participate in role-play. From the picture below, we can see that some parents have significant differences in parent–child play. For example, some parents attach great importance to children's "cognitive" ability, they will teach children to identify simulated fruits; some parents can play with young children, and some parents are more often accompanied. In terms of the selection of play materials, young children aged 2–3 prefer the fruits of the image and even peel off the skin of toy bananas. However, most young children prefer the toys in the kitchen. They will explore how the tap is turned on, how the fire is turned on, and how the condiment bottle is used. They also like small spoons, knives, and forks. Many children were pretending to cut fruit with a knife. However, their understanding of the knife is not the same. Some children between the ages of 2 and 3 cannot distinguish between the blade and the blade. They do not know that the knife in their hand is reversed.

Many children 2–3 years old know how to use the kitchen faucet to boil water, wash hands, and wash fruits. They also like to put food in the pot, and then cook on the stove. Some children can show very specific characteristics of the play characters, for example, they can imitate the chefs cooking and toss the wok. The play for children aged 2–3 years old have plots. They will not only use the toy as a tool to play, but also pretend to have dinner with their parents. Sometimes children will invite teachers alongside to play together.

Their play objects are not only parents, but some young children will notice dolls on the side. They take care of the dolls and play with the dolls. They fed dolls, cooked, wore hats for dolls or pulled blankets off them, and coaxed the dolls to sleep. Young children have limited knowledge of the tools in the kitchen. Some children did not recognize the colander, and saw the colander as a toothbrush. They would take care of the doll and brushed teeth for the doll. Their play plot is more abundant. In addition, using a colander as a toothbrush is also a manifestation of characterization. Children can replace objects with similar shapes but different functions to complete their own play. However, the use of alternatives not only satisfies the child's emotional needs, but also reflects the child's image thinking development. According to Piaget's cognitive development theory, preschool children are in the pre-operational stage. As the experience grows and language develops, children begin to think symbolically. The children in the pre-computation stage began to be able to think about and imagine things that are not in sight, and there have been a large number of symbolic play and pretend play. In the game, the child pretends to be a character, such as a teacher, a mother, or a character in a cartoon, and uses some nearby objects instead of other objects, such as a pillow representing a baby and a glasses box representing a phone. In role-playing games, children can increase their experience and understanding of the outside world, which helps individuals construct the external world. Role games can promote the development of children's symbolic representation and can promote the generalization and abstract development of young children's thinking.

3.3.5 Exploration and Construction of 2–3 Years Old Children

There were 126 valid data for the exploration and construction game, the lowest score was 1 point, the highest score was 5 points, the average score was 2.98 points, and the standard deviation was 1.46. Among them, there are 59 valid data for boys, the lowest score is 1 point, the highest score is 5 points, the average score is 3.17 points, and the standard deviation is 1.44; there are 67 valid data for girls, the lowest score is 1 point, the highest score is 5 points, the average score is 2.81 points, and the standard deviation is 1.46. There were 24 valid data in the low-age group, the lowest score was 1 point, the highest score was 5 points, the average score was 1.83 points, and the standard deviation was 1.31; there were 102 valid data in the high-age group, the lowest score was 1 point, the highest score was 5 points, the average score was 3.25 points, and the standard deviation was 1.36.

An independent sample T-test was used to analyze differences in gender of construction and exploration of gender–age dimensions. The results showed that there was no significant difference in the exploration–construction scores of children of different genders (t = 1.404, $p = 0.163 > 0.05$); the exploration–construction scores of children in different age groups had extremely significant differences (t = −4.607, $p = 0.000 < 0.05$).

The results show that there is no gender difference in the exploration and construction of children between the ages of 2 and 3. The ability to explore and construct of children aged 2–3 years grows with age, but most children aged 2–3 still do not have the ability to build awareness. Many young children between the ages of 2–2.5 and even 2.5–3 do not realize that the materials provided can be constructed, or have no desire to be constructed, but simply explore the characteristics of the materials themselves. The children who could build blocks in a simple way had no clear building objectives. They told the experimenter what they built after the completion of the game. This shows that most children aged 2–3 are still in the stage of intuitive action thinking.

In addition, in terms of constructive complexity, repeated overlaps, horizontal extensions and extensions are the salient features of early childhood construction activities. This simple construction activity has attracted young children for a long time (Ungerer et al. 1981; Zelazo and Frye 1997). Two–threee-year-old children are interested in the concept of length and height. Most of the children stacked magnetic sheets with same shapes, or put the magnetic sheet with same shape in a row. When materials are not enough, they will continue to create their own with other shapes of magnets. The children who knew their building objectives stacked them or put them in a row after the objectives were fulfilled.

Those who are not strong in construction awareness or construction purposes will combine role-playing games and construction games during tests. For example, some children say that they want to put a bed for their favorite doll, as shown below.

3.3.6 Problem-Solving Capability for 2–3 Years Old Children

Problem-solving ability is a more comprehensive cognitive ability. Children aged 2–3 years can use the thinking process to create ways to reach their goals; manipulate toys with mechanical devices, recognize the operation methods of many mechanical devices; have a certain ability to anticipate actions, can anticipate results, or point out causes; link an experience with another experience; plan actions in mind. Based on this, this study selected the play situation of unlocking a box. In this test, the problem-solving play had 124 valid data, the lowest score was 1 point, the highest score was 5 points, the average score was 3.00 points, and the standard deviation was 1.07. Among them, there are 59 valid data for boys, the lowest score is 1 point, the highest score is 5 points, the average score is 3.14 points, and the standard deviation is 1.03; there are 65 valid data for girls, the lowest score is 1 point, the highest score is 5 points, the average score is 2.88 points, and the standard deviation is 1.10. The low-age group has 25 valid data, the lowest score is 1, the highest score is 4 points, the average score is 2.44 points, the standard deviation is 0.87; the high-age group has 99 valid data, the lowest score is 1 point, the highest score is 5 points, and the average score is 3.14 points. The standard deviation is 1.07.

An independent sample T-test was used to analyze the difference in gender and age for problem-solving scores. The results showed that there was no significant difference in problem-solving scores among children of different genders (t $= 1.353$, $p = 0.179 > 0.05$); the problem-solving scores of children in different age groups had extremely significant differences (t $= -3.034$, $p = 0.003 < 0.05$).

The results show that there is no gender difference in the problem-solving ability of children aged 2–3 years. The problem-solving strategy and persistence increase

3.3 Research Results and Analysis

with age. The problem-solving ability of children aged 2.5–3 is higher than that of 2–2.5 year olds.

Although the tests were based on unlocking, during tests, children's problem-solving capacity would not only reflected in the task. For example, they had to refine their motions. Sometimes, they unlocked but failed to open the door, and they would find other solutions. Sometimes, the children would pull the door with their hands from other holes.

When unlocking was difficult, some children would change the direction to unlock. Some of them put the lock on their laps, some of them looked down, and even lied on the blanket. They changed gestures. Some of them even shook the box, trying to unlock it with methods.

Although the muscles are not yet fully developed, and it's difficult to unlock with keys, according to the observation, the children are interested in keys, and they keep unlocking with the help of the key. Some of them even refused to unlock doors without keyholes, instead, they were thinking the correspondence of the key in their hands and the door. During the period, positive learning quality and insistence were reflected.

3.3.7 Attention and Participation Development of Children Aged 2–3

There are 122 valid data for attention and participation development assessment, with a minimum score of 2 points, a maximum score of 10 points, an average score of 6.57 points, and a standard deviation of 2.15. Among them, there are 58 valid data for boys, the lowest score is 2 points, the highest score is 10 points, the average score is 6.31 points, the standard deviation is 2.24; the valid data for girls is 64, the lowest score is 2 points, the highest score is 10 points, the average score is 6.81 points. The difference is 2.05. The low-age group had 24 valid data, the lowest score was 2 points, the highest score was 9 points, the average score was 5.04 points, the standard deviation was 1.85; the high-age group had 98 valid data, the lowest score was 2 points, the highest score was 10 points, and the average score was 6.95 points. The standard deviation is 2.06.

Two different dimensions of attention are analyzed. Among them, there are 125 valid data for attention maintenance, with an average score of 3.03 and a standard deviation of 1.16. Among them, there were 59 valid data for boys, with an average score of 2.80, a standard deviation of 1.20, and 66 valid data for girls with an average score of 3.24 and a standard deviation of 1.08. There were 26 valid data in the low-age group with an average score of 2.35 and a standard deviation of 0.89. The high-age group had 99 valid data with an average score of 3.21 and a standard deviation of 1.15. There are 122 valid data for flexible conversions with an average of 3.52 and a standard deviation of 1.25. Among them, there were 58 valid data for boys, with an average score of 3.48, a standard deviation of 1.22, and 64 valid data for girls with an average score of 3.56 and a standard deviation of 1.28. In the low-age group, there were 24 valid data with an average score of 2.58 and a standard deviation of 1.18. The high-age group had 98 valid data with an average score of 3.76 and a standard deviation of 1.16. The attention data is shown in Table 3.5.

An independent sample T-test was used to analyze the difference in gender and age in the two dimensions of attention total score, attention maintenance, and flexible transition. The results showed that there was no significant difference in the total score of attention between children of different genders (t = −1.291, p = 0.199 > 0.05); There was no significant difference in the flexible transition (t = −0.351, p = 0.726 > 0.05); however, there was a significant difference in attention maintenance (t = −2.184, p = 0.031 < 0.05). There were significant differences in the total scores of attention and attention maintenance and flexible conversion in children of different age groups (t-score = −4.146, p = 0.000 < 0.05; t-attention retention = −3.553, p = 0.001 < 0.05; t-Flexible Conversion = −4.429, p = 0.000 < 0.05).

The results indicate that there is no gender difference in the flexible transition of attention between infants and children aged 2–3 years, but the performance of girls in attention maintenance is significantly better than that of boys. This may be related to the gender difference in brain structure. The prevalence of boys in adolescents with ADHD is 2–9 times higher than in girls; in the general population, the prevalence of boys is three times higher than in girls. This is partly due to that education of children differs with genders. Girls are encouraged to be obedient and quiet, boys are allowed to be naughty. As we age, the attention-maintaining and flexible switching abilities of children aged 2–3 years are significantly enhanced, and the brain is constantly

Table 3.5 Statistics of attention

Grouping				The total score of attention	Maintenance of attention	Flexible conversion
Gender	Male		N	58	59	58
			M	6.31	2.80	3.48
			SD	2.24	1.20	1.22
	Female		N	64	66	64
			M	6.81	3.24	3.56
			SD	2.05	1.08	1.28
Age	Lower age group		N	24	26	24
			M	5.04	2.35	2.58
			SD	1.85	0.89	1.18
	Higher age group		N	98	99	98
			M	6.95	3.21	3.76
			SD	2.06	1.15	1.16
Total			N	122	125	122
			M	6.57	3.03	3.52
			SD	2.15	1.16	1.25

3.3 Research Results and Analysis

Table 3.6 Differential tests on total scores, genders, and aged with different tasks and in different dimensions

		Gender		Age	
		t	Sig. (two-tailed)	t	Sig. (two-tailed)
Total score		0.054	0.957	−5.695	0.000
Points		−0.244	0.807	−6.555	0.000
Characterization	Total scores of characterization	0.057	0.955	−2.962	0.004
	Object substitution	−0.329	0.743	−2.628	0.010
	Role recognition	0.286	0.776	−2.490	0.014
	Game plots	0.318	0.751	−2.885	0.005
Construction games		1.404	0.163	−4.607	0.000
Problem-solving		1.353	0.179	−3.034	0.003
Graphic matching		0.551	0.583	−4.706	0.000
Attention	Total scores of attention	−1.291	0.199	−4.146	0.000
	Maintenance of attention	−2.184	0.031	−3.553	0.001
	Flexible conversion	−0.351	0.726	−4.429	0.000

maturing. Most of the children aged 2–3, especially those who are aged over 2, could finish tasks as instructed by the experimenter and their parents.

Table 3.6 is about differential tests on total scores, genders, and aged with different tasks and in different dimensions.

In summary, in addition to maintaining attention in attention assessment, female children are significantly better than boys, and there are no gender differences in other dimensions. Regardless of the total score or tasks and the subitems in each task, the performance of young children aged 2–3 (2.5–3 years old) is significantly better than that of young children aged 2–3 years old (i.e., 2–2.5 years old). During the period of 24–36 months, the children's cognitive development ability increased significantly.

3.4 Case Studies

Two–three years old is an important stage of development for young children. Therefore, in this not-too-short time frame, it is inevitable that children perform differently. Besides, some of the testees come from rural areas, while some were born into well-off families in urban areas, even in middle-class families in Beijing. Many differences are expected. However, even if children are similar in age and growth environment, their performance may be very different. To this very note, the paper below introduces two girls with not so obvious differences in the family environment.

3.4.1 Sensible Geng Geng

At the time of the survey, Geng Geng was almost 3 years old in a few days and was almost the oldest child in the survey. Therefore, he is also expected to perform better. However, Geng Geng is very logical. This kind of reasoning cannot be seen in children of the bottom and middle classes. For example, although the graphic matching task is relatively simple, because the infant's hand–eye coordination is limited. They may not be able to accurately put the figure in the right place. The children with inaccurate knowledge of graphics would immediately try the other holes, while the other children who knew their judgments kept smashing the correct hole. However, they didn't know the direction to adjust the graphics. With only five graphic matching plays, to ensure that they could recognize the graphic features through strategies other than trial-and-error strategy, the experimenter would put it in the correct place during the game. During the test, Geng Geng didn't need tips. She could do simple graphics once. For the difficult cross, though she got the correct hole, she failed to put inside once. This time, she didn't try anxiously, instead, she removed the blocks, and carefully observed the holes and graphics in her hands. Then, she made the correct direction, and put the cross in the hole correctly.

Geng Geng is a child with mild personality and is not easily excited. In the box unlocking play, he may not have shown a strong interest at first. However, when the teacher told her to open more door locks as much as possible, she would be able to focus on exploring how to open each door lock of different shapes and colors. When she opens the lock, she may look at the teacher and see the children around. This shows that she was not very interested in this play and did not actively open other locks. However, when she knew she had to unlock another door, she explored in the task, rather than crying to play others. In the end, Geng Geng unlocked many doors.

Character and symbol play are parent–child games that require parents to be on site. The father of Geng Geng played with Geng Geng. His father is also gentle and refined. As many parents were tested, given limited space, some of them had to wait aside together with their children. The parents and their children felt anxious. Although Geng Geng and her dad were the last to be tested, her dad was not anxious, instead, he was really patient and polite. When the father and daughter played together, the dad was asked to sit on a mat or a small chair and play with his daughter. However, in order not to affect the video recording, the daddy kindly rejected it, and kept squatting when playing with his daughter. The two play are more autonomous and Geng Geng knows what she wants to do. She wanted to make a bridge. She knew she could complete the task and did not turn to her father for help. Finally, although she built a long bridge without much technical content, she did achieve her goal.

3.4 Case Studies

In the kitchen play, at first, Geng Geng found materials and their corresponding purposes in the kitchen, then she "juiced" for the baby. The fruity material in the kitchen is also very attractive. Some parents eagerly asked children to identify fruits but ignored this was a role game. Geng Geng's father also wanted her to recognize fruit, but the father did not interrupt her daughter's game. To the contrary, he told his daughter, "Let's feed the dolls to eat starfruit," and later said, "Let's make a mango for the baby."

3.4.2 Negative Luo Luo

During the test, Luo Luo was 33 months old. As a girl in the higher age group, she outdid other children in development level. However, she was found that her language skills are particularly strong compared to the other children, as she said in a clear way. She did as the experimenter instructed, and she could concentrate on the task. She could fulfill all the tasks, with the score at the intermediate level. She, so to speak, is not an incompetent or troublesome child. But she always touched the material and said she would not do it, and then refused to try and explore. She is impressive.

At first, she said she would not count in the counting activity. I asked her several times to "try again", and she started to count. However, she actually could count one after another. Afterward, we did the unlocking game. Luo Luo had the box turned around, so as to find what it was on each face, and she stood up and said, "I can't!" She didn't lack confidence. Children like her would turn to teachers or parents. To the contrary, she didn't want to try, nor had the intention to fulfill the task. I encouraged her to try again. However, she refuted loudly, "it's boring!" So, I had to ask her to play graphic matching games. She said again, "I did it in the classroom!" I asked her to play again in a more careful way, so as to do it correctly once. She did not reject me and soon put a few plastic figures into the correct hole.

In the process of matching the graphics, she found a key to the box on the blanket and asked me what it was. I told her that the key could unlock the box. She seemed to have a little interest in it and started to try. She failed after several times (of course, she also didn't insert the key into the hole, instead, she just explored at random). She found another keyhole, and told me that there was another lock. I encouraged her to unlock it. However, she said immediately, "I can't!" Luckily, she didn't stop what she was doing. However, she gave up soon. This time, she didn't leave or refuse the activity, instead, she invited me to unlock for her. I encouraged her that she could open some doors without the help of keys, and asked her to try. I also gave her tips of the easiest door. She said in an inpatient way, "I don't know!" Then, she gave the key to me. With the key, I still asked her to try the doors without the help of keys. On hearing this, she tried at random. I found that she had some interest in the game, and started to record some typical behaviors without observing her. Luo Luo's mom was filling out the parental questionnaire, and let her alone. This time, Luo Luo could concentrated on the game, and explored the methods to unlock the doors.

After a while, I made a simple note. The mother completed the questionnaire and started observing her daughter's game and guided her to unlock it. Many parents immediately go to help their children when they see that their children cannot unlock. To the contrary, instead of helping her daughter immediately, she told her daughter what to do next. She told her daughter to "observe and be patient". Luo Luo was still exploring. She was lying on the blanket, trying to unlock the door. This time, Luo Luo's mom told her to turn the box over. However, Luo Luo said afterward, "I don't do it." Then, she ran to toys aside.

Her mother was not happy and said: "Hey, the teacher hasn't said you can play this, you haven't unlocked yet!" Luo Luo was unhappy. She pouted and stood akimbo, "no!" Luo Luo successfully unlocked the door. Then, I asked her to play role games aside. Luo Luo and her mother's role game went smoothly, during which she cut apples, peeled bananas, made coffee for her mom. However, the mom still directed what her daughter should do. She told her child to pour water and boil water before making coffee. Luo Luo pretended to have made the coffee, and poured it into the small cup. At this time, she found the small bottle next to her very interesting. Sometimes she used it as a condiment bottle and sometimes she put it in the cup as a stirring stick. However, the mother felt anxious, and asked her daughter, "have you made the coffee? Can I drink?" Luo Luo pretended she didn't hear it, and put the spoon and fork in the cup. Her mother was all the more inpatient, and asked again, "Can I?" Luo Luo looked at her mom at a loss. Her mom said again, "Let me drink!" The mom changed her moods, and discussed with her daughter, "You could play others after giving the coffee to me." Luo Luo offered it to her mom, and the mom became gentle, "this is for me? Thank you!" However, the mom said, "Could you put the spoon outside the cup, my sweetie?" However, she did not seem to listen to her mother, playing with fruit.

3.4.3 Analysis

The different performances of parents in two different cases are impressive. Typical excellent behaviors or bad behaviors of young children are influenced by parents. Geng Geng performed well, so did Luo Luo. These two parents guided their children with strategies, rather than playing games aside, or ignoring what the experimenter instructed and doing all things for their children. However, their parents had different performance. Geng Geng's dad respected children's games. Even if he had some requirements, he would be in line with the games, rather than asking children to do what he wanted. Luo Luo's mom is more patient and regular than the other mothers, however, she kept interfering with her child. Of course, her interventions were not doing for her child. Instead, she always told the "shortcuts to the games", that is, how to play games in an efficient way and in accordance with the rules of the adult world. Luo Luo's mother did not attach importance to the child's attempts and experience. By emphasizing the correctness, she inadvertently denied her child. Therefore, Luo Luo always said that she could not and would not try. She actually avoided the frustration of errors in an adult way and was, therefore, more willing to do simple tasks. Luo Luo's mom did value her child's education. Other good performances of Luo Luo could not go without her mother. However, because of her mother's strong intervention and lack of attention to her child's initiative, the child "cleverly" refused to try and even formed a habit of refusing to try. This is very dangerous for children. The courage to explore and try is an important learning quality. To the contrary, by analyzing Geng Geng's father, we could know the reasons of Geng Geng's patience and reasonability. There is of course inheritance. However, Geng Geng does like her father. This means, teaching by personal example as well as verbal instruction make a difference. Sometimes, setting examples is more important than educating children. Of course, in comparison to two parents, we find that respecting children is really essential.

References

Carlson, S. M., Mandell, D. J., & Williams, L. (2004). Executive function and theory of mind: Stability and prediction from ages 2 to 3. *Developmental Psychology, 40*(6), 1105–1122.

Chen, G., Feng, X., & Pang, L. (2013). *Preschool children's developmental psychology* (3rd ed.) Beijing: Normal University Press.

Jiang, X., & Ma, Y. (2013). Investigation on influencing factors of cognitive development in 480 normal infants. *China Children's Health Magazine, 12*(12), 1321–1323.

Kelly-Vance, L., Needelman, H., Troia, K., & Ryalls, B. O. (1999). Early childhood assessment: A comparison of the bayley scales of infant development and play-based assessment in two-year old at-risk children.

Kelly-Vance, L., & Ryalls, B. O. (2005). A systematic, reliable approach to play assessment in preschoolers. *School Psychology International, 92*(4), 398–412.

Linder, T., & Linas, K. (2009). A functional, holistic approach to developmental assessment through play: The transdisciplinary play-based assessment, second edition. *Zero to Three, 30*(9), 28–32.

Lobo, M. A., Kokkoni, E., Campos, A. C. D., & Galloway, J. C. (2014). Not just playing around: Infants' behaviors with objects reflect ability, constraints, and object properties. *Infant Behavior & Development, 37*(3), 334–351.

Nilsen, E. S., Huyder, V., Mcauley, T., & Liebermann, D. (2016). Ratings of everyday executive functioning (reef): A parent-report measure of preschoolers' executive functioning skills. *Psychological Assessment, 29*(1).

Pellegrini, A. D., & Hou, Y. (2011). The development of preschool children's (Homo sapiens) uses of objects and their role in peer group centrality. *Journal of Comparative Psychology, 125*(2), 239.

Paro, K. M. L., & Pianta, R. C. (2001). Predicting children's competence in the early school year: A meta-analytic review. *Review of Educational Research, 70,* 443–484.

Sha, F. (2016). Research on the construction strategies of building blocks. *The Road to Success, 02,* 69.

Tory, W. L. (2008). *Evaluating children in games* (p. 37). (X. Chen, Trans.). Shanghai: East China Normal University Press.

Ungerer, J. A., Zelazo, P. R., Kearsley, R. B., & O'Leary, K. (1981). Developmental changes in the representation of objects in symbolic play from 18 to 34 months of age. *Child Development, 52*(1), 186–195.

Zelazo, P. D., & Frye, D. (1997). Cognitive complexity and control: A theory of the development.

Chapter 4
Status and Analysis of Language Development in 2- and 3-Year-Old Children

4.1 Introduction

Language is a tool of communication and thinking, and also has a significant impact on learning and development in other fields. Therefore, language learning and development of children is crucial for individual development. The period from birth to 3 years old is the stage when children's language develops most rapidly, and also the sensitive period of children's language development. Therefore, it is of great significance to study the rules of language development of infants and toddlers aged 0–3 years and the ways and methods to improve their language ability. Infants and toddlers' language develops in several stages, and the period from 2 to 3 years old is the stage when the infants and toddlers basically learn spoken language. Compared to the previous stage, the infants and toddlers make remarkable progress in mastering pronunciation, vocabulary, grammar, and oral expression ability, and they are able to use language for general daily communication at this stage (Zhang 2001). To clarify the normal level of language development and understand the characteristics of language development of infants and toddlers at this stage are the preconditions is the premise to identify whether the infants and toddlers' language ability is lagged or not and to develop a reasonable language education program.

However, compared with studies on children with language development disorder and exceptional children, studies on language development with normal children as the subjects are not abundant. In addition, compared with empirical studies on the characteristics of language development of children aged 3–6 years, the studies on the characteristics of language development of 2- and 3-year-old children at home are very limited. Only a few studies employed the longitudinal method to record the language development of children during the first 3 years (Wu and Xu 1979). Therefore, this study aims to measure the language development level of 2- and 3-year-old children, and explore the overall characteristics and individual differences of language development of 2- and 3-year-old children by evaluation test.

Table 4.1 Basic information of subjects

	N (people)	Total
Boys	69	145
Girls	76	
2–2.5 years old	27	145
2.5–3 years old	118	

Language development usually contains two aspects—understanding and expression. Language understanding refers to the ability to associate language symbols to objects or activities based on experience, memory, and impressions of things. Language expression is the ability to express a particular meaning consistently with the same sign (Heep Hong Society 2013). In this study, the test of language development level of 2- and 3-year-old children covers language understanding and language expression.

4.2 Methodology

4.2.1 Subjects

In this study, the purposive sampling method was employed to select 150 2- and 3-year-old children and their parents in Beijing as the subjects, and 145 of them were effective subjects in the end, including 69 boys and 76 girls. The mean age of these 145 infants and toddlers was 33.15 months (SD = 3.505), of which 27 were 2–2.5 years old and 118 were 2.5–3 years old. The mothers were aged between 20 and 45 years, with an average age of 32.64 (SD = 4.087); and the fathers were aged between 25 and 46 years, with an average age of 34.58 (SD = 4.899) (Table 4.1).

4.2.2 Research Instrument

In this study, the test items for language in the revised Children Development Assessment Form (revised) developed by Heep Hong Society in Hong Kong were used to test the language competence of 2- and 3-year-old children. The Children Development Assessment Form (revised) contains assessment forms for six age groups and six subdomains. 17 test items (7 for language expression, 10 for language understanding) for 2–3-year-old children in the language competence assessment form were extracted and retained in this study. Among the original test items, there was not the item testing the children's use of multiple-word phrases, in order to improve the dimensions of language expression assessment, a test item, namely, "the chil-

4.2 Methodology

dren can use at least two multiple-word phrases," was added to this study to assess the application level of children using multiple-word phrases. In addition, this study included the understanding of the nouns of locality "up, down" of 2.5–4-year-old children in Children's Learning Program.

The content of the final scale mainly evaluated two aspects of language competence (as shown in Table 4.2): language expression and language understanding. In the part of language expression, there were 8 test items for children's use of vocabulary (nouns: be able to tell the names of clothes and be able to tell the names of body parts; verbs: be able to tell the names of actions; adjectives: be able to say the adjectives "clean and dirty" and be able to say the adjectives "big and small"), two-word phrases (be able to say two-word phrases consisting of the name of an action and the name of an object and be able to say two-word phrases consisting of a negative adverb and a verb) and multi-word phrases, excluding the children's pronunciation. The part of the language understanding specifically covers 11 items for vocabulary understanding (nouns: know the names of animals; verbs: know the names of common actions; adjective: be able to understand the adjectives "clean and dirty", and be able to understand the adjectives "big and small"; be able to understand the nouns of locality "up, down"), two-word phrase understanding (be able to understand the instructions consisting the name of an object and the name of its location; be able to understand the instructions consisting of names of two actions, and be able to understand the instructions consisting of an adjective and the name of an object) and question understanding (be able to understand the questions starting with "Is there…", alternative questions and questions starting with "Is it/this/that…").

4.2.3 Research Process

4.2.3.1 Test Tools and Materials

1 desk, 3 chairs, pictures for the test, objects for the test, recording pen, record form (see Table 4.3 for specific materials).

4.2.3.2 Test Process

The test was conducted for individuals one by one in a separate and quiet room. Under the guidance of the usher, a child entered the room together with the guardian. The child sat opposite the experimenter while the guardian sat next to the child. The host first asked the name and age of the child, made simple communication with the child to create a good communication atmosphere, and then asked the child the test questions one by one. After the test was completed, the experimenter said goodbye to the child. During the examination, the experimenter was required to make a complete recording of the child's answers to supplement the information that was not recorded in time during the test.

Table 4.2 Distribution table of test items for language development of 2- and 3-year-old children

Domain	Subdomain	Item indexes	Number of items
Language Expression	Vocabulary use	Be able to tell the names of clothes, be able to tell the names of body parts; be able to tell the names of actions; be able to say the adjectives "clean and dirty" and be able to say the adjectives "big and small"	5
	Two-word phrase use	Be able to say two-word phrases consisting of the name of an action and the name of an object and be able to say two-word phrases consisting of a negative adverb and a verb	2
	Multi-word phrase use	Be able to use multi-word phrases	1
Language Understanding	Vocabulary understanding	Know the names of animals; know the names of common actions; be able to understand the adjectives "clean and dirty"; be able to understand the adjectives "big and small"; and be able to understand the nouns of locality "up, down"	5
	Two-word phrase understanding	Be able to understand the instructions consisting the name of an object and the name of its location; be able to understand the instructions consisting of names of two actions, and be able to understand the instructions consisting of an adjective and the name of an object	3
	Question understanding	Be able to understand the questions starting with "Is there…"; be able to understand alternative questions, and be able to understand questions starting with "Is it/this/that…"	3
Total			19

4.2 Methodology

Table 4.3 Materials for test items for language development of 2- and 3-year-old children

Test items	Materials
Be able to tell the names of clothes	6 photos: shoes, socks, coat, trousers, hat, skirt
Be able to tell the names of body parts	6 photos: eyes, ears, mouth, nose, hands, feet
Be able to tell the names of actions	6 photos: washing hands, sleeping, writing, combing one's hair, brushing one's teeth, and taking a bath;
Be able to say the adjectives "clean and dirty"; be able to understand the adjectives "clean and dirty"	Two objects: a clean paper towel, a dirty paper towel
Be able to say the adjectives "big and small"; be able to understand the adjectives "big and small"; be able to understand the instructions consisting of an adjective and the name of an object	4 objects: a big cube, a small cube, a big triangle, a small triangle
Be able to say two-word phrases consisting of the name of an action and the name of an object	2 photos for demonstration: eating bread, putting on a coat; 3 photos for test: cutting fruit, drinking orange juice, pouring milk
Know the names of animals	6 photos: dog, rabbit, pig, cattle, cow, elephant, giraffe
Know the names of common actions;	6 photos: crying, sweeping the floor, swimming, taking photos, queuing, laughing
Be able to understand the nouns of locality "up, down", and be able to say two-word phrases consisting of a negative adverb and a verb; be able to understand alternative questions, and be able to understand questions starting with "Is it/this/that…"	2 objects: a big cube, a small cube
Be able to understand the questions starting with "Is there…"	2 objects: a small cube, a dish

4.2.3.3 Scoring Method

After each item was completed, the child's performance was scored by 2 points—0 and 1. 0 means that the child has never demonstrated the language competence indicated by this item, and 1 means that the child has demonstrated the language competence indicated by this item. At the same time, the child's answers to each item should be recorded on the record form (if the child's answers were not recorded in time, the experimenter should transcribe the recording).

Table 4.4 Distribution table of average scores of test items for vocabulary use of 2- and 3-year-old children

Item	Accuracy rate (%)	Order
Name of clothes	97.0	1
Body parts	97.0	1
Adjectives "big and small"	94.8	3
Name of actions	94.1	4
Adjectives "clean and dirty"	23.6	5

4.3 Results and Analysis

4.3.1 Analysis of Basic Situation of Language Development of 2- and 3-Year-Old Children

The basic status of language development of 2- and 3-year-old children mainly contains two dimensions: language expression and language understanding. According to the data processing results, 2–3-year-old children could basically complete the language test and have a high accuracy rate, with an average accuracy rate of over 90%. The average accuracy rate of the language expression part was 81.6% and that of the language understanding part was 93.5%. The following is a detailed analysis of the development characteristics of language expression and language understanding.

4.3.1.1 Basic Situation of Language Expression Development of 2- and 3-Year-Old Children

In this study, the language expression development of 2- and 3-year-old children mainly covers three dimensions: vocabulary use, two-word phrase use, and multi-word phrase use. Among the three dimensions, the children performed best in the dimension of vocabulary use, and the average accuracy rate of 4 items under it was above 90%. The score of multi-word phrase use was the lowest among all the items, with an average accuracy rate of 76.3%.

Vocabulary Use

The part of vocabulary use mainly focuses on testing children's use of names of clothes (noun), body parts (noun), actions (verb), "big and small" (adjective), "clean and dirty" (adjective). According to the data (see Table 4.4), 97.0% of the children could tell the names of clothes and body parts, and the average score of nouns was the highest in the vocabulary use dimension. According to the "noun dominance" theory (Gentner 1982), most of the words first mastered by children are nouns, and clothes

4.3 Results and Analysis

Table 4.5 Distribution table of average scores of test items for use of two-word phrases and multi-word phrases of 2- and 3-year-old children

Item	Accuracy rate (%)	Rank
Phrases consisting of negative adverbs and verbs	90.3	1
Verb–object phrases	79.3	2
Multi-word phrases	76.3	3

and body parts are related to children's direct experience, so only a few children did not name clothes and body parts. 94.1% of the children could name the actions (such as washing their hands, sleeping, writing, combing one's hair, brushing one's teeth and taking a bath). However, due to the lack of relevant life experience, some children had trouble identifying the name of the action "writing", which was usually expressed as "drawing". 94.8% of children were able to say "big and small". However, in terms of use of the adjectives "clean and dirty", only 23.6% of the children could use "clean and dirty" to describe the characteristics of the objects for the test. For example, "The paper is very clean; the paper is very dirty." Children aged about 2 years experience the stage of "vocabulary explosion" and have a high mastery degree of nouns, verbs, and adjectives. Zhang (2001) pointed out that infants aged 1–1.5 years can understand many nouns and verbs. The nouns are mainly names of the familiar household objects around the infants and toddlers, names of the characters, animals and the body parts with obvious features. Verbs that they can understand are mainly verbs indicating body actions, followed by modal verbs and judgment verbs indicating events and activities. Therefore, the study results conform to the rules of children's language development.

Use of Two-Word Phrases and Multi-Word Phrases

The use of two-word phrases and multi-word phrases mainly studies the children's use of such verb–object phrases as "cut fruit, drink orange juice, pour milk," and such two-word phrases and multi-word phrases as "do not eat, do not comb hair, do not drink." According to the data (see Table 4.5), 90.3% of the children were able to say a phrase consisting of a negative adverb and a verb, and this item scored highest on average in the dimension of the use of two-word phrases and multi-word phrases. 79.3% of the children were able to say verb–object phrases (including the accurate expression of "cut fruit, drink orange juice, pour milk," but because of differences in life experience and picture recognition, some children said similar phrases like "make salad, cook dishes, cut watermelon, drink beverage, pour water"). During the test, 76.3% of the children were able to use multi-word phrases (such as "can I eat this one on the floor" or "he brushed his hair with a toothbrush") to talk to the experimenter or guardian. Children aged 2–3 years can use a variety of simple sentence patterns and initially develop compound sentences (Zhang 2001). Therefore, children can better master two-word phrases consisting of the name of an action and name of an

Table 4.6 Distribution table of average scores of test items for an understanding of vocabulary and two-word phrases of 2- and 3-year-old children

Item	Accuracy rate (%)	Rank
Names of animals	99.3	1
Names of actions	99.3	1
Instructions about actions	99.3	1
Instructions about objects	98.5	4
Adjectives "big and small"	97.8	5
Instructions about adjectives	96.3	6
Adjectives "clean and dirty"	89.1	7
Locality words "up and down"	61.0	8

object, two-word phrases consisting of negative adverbs and verbs and multi-word phrases. The research result is consistent with the existing studies. According to paired-samples T-test, there is no significant difference in expression of vocabulary, two-word phrases and multi-word phrases among children aged 2–3 years.

4.3.1.2 Basic Situation of Language Understanding Development of 2- and 3-Year-Old Children

In this study, the development of language understanding in 2- and 3-year-old children mainly covers three dimensions: vocabulary understanding, two-word phrase understanding, and question understanding. Except the understanding of the adjectives "clean and dirty", the average accuracy rate of all the other items was above 90%.

Understanding of Vocabulary and Two-Word Phrases

The part of vocabulary understanding mainly tests whether the children understand the names of animals, names of common actions, adjectives "big and small", and adjectives "clean and dirty". The part of two-word phrase understanding mainly tests whether the children can understand the instructions consisting the name of an object and the name of its location, the instructions consisting of names of two actions, and the instructions consisting of an adjective and the name of an object. According to the data (see Table 4.6), the children understood nouns and verbs best. 99.3% of the children knew the names of animals (such as dog, rabbit, pig, cow, elephant, giraffe) and the name of common actions (such as crying, sweeping the floor, swimming, taking photos, queuing, smiling), but because of the limitation of life experience, some children couldn't accurately point out the picture of "taking photos". 97.8% of the children could understand the adjectives "big and small", and 89.1% could

4.3 Results and Analysis

Table 4.7 Distribution table of average scores of test items for question understanding of 2- and 3-year-old children

Item	Accuracy rate (%)	Rank
Alternative questions	100	1
Questions starting with "Is there…"	97.0	2
Questions starting with "Is it/this/that…"	91.0	3

understand the adjectives "clean and dirty". The children's ability to understand the adjectives "clean and dirty" is much higher than their ability to use them.

In terms of two-word phrase understanding, most children could act according to the instruction and point out the appropriate items. 99.3% of the children could understand the instructions consisting of names of two actions, such as "clap"; 98.5% children could understand the instruction consisting of the name of an object and the name of its location such as "put the apple in the basket," 96.3% of the children could understand the instructions consisting of an adjective and the name of an object, such as "big box". Thus, it is clear that children aged 2–3 years basically can understand simple words and two-word phrases.

In addition to the above test items for language understanding, the test of nouns of locality "up and down" was also carried out, in which the experimenter asked children to place objects above or below the table. The result showed that 61.0% of the children could understand "up" and "down". As the understanding of "up and down" involved spatial orientation perception, it was difficult for 2- and 3-year-old children. In particular, some children could understand "up" but could not understand "down". In this study, it was found that children could less accurately understand locality words "up" and "down" than other words. The mastery level of locality words of children aged 2–6 years can be divided into two stages with the development of age: the first stage is the period from 2 to 3, and the second stage is the period from 4 to 6, and in the period from 3 to 4, the level improves most quickly. Children begin to understand "up and down" at the age of 2 and basically master them at the age of 3. It is thus clear the results of this study conform to the development law of children's spatial term understanding (Zhu 1986).

Question Understanding

The part of question understanding mainly tests whether children could understand questions starting with "Is there…", questions starting with "Is it/this/that…"and alternative questions. According to the data (see Table 4.7), among the three types of questions, children have the best command of the alternative questions. 100% of the children could understand the alternative questions. When the experimenter asked the children they like large squares or small squares, the children could choose the appropriate items according to their preferences. 97.0% of the children could understand questions starting with "Is there…" and 91.0% could understand questions starting with "Is it/this/that…". Most children could respond to questions starting with "Is there…" and questions starting with "Is it/this/that…" in a nonverbal way, such as nodding or shaking their heads, or in a verbal way, such as " Yes, it is; No, it isn't; Yes, there is; No, there isn't". It is thus clear that the children aged 2–3 years have been able to understand simple questions. During this period, children's vocabulary increases greatly, and they can basically understand the sentences used by adults. According to the paired sample T-test, there is no significant difference in the understanding of vocabulary, two-word phrases and questions among children aged 2–3 years.

4.3.2 Analysis of Difference Between Language Understanding and Language Expression

Language understanding and language expression are two aspects of children's language learning. Language understanding is the foundation of language expression, and children can also promote language understanding in the process of language expression. It can be seen from Table 4.8 that there is no significant difference between the score of language expression and that language understanding of children aged 2–3 years.

4.3.3 Analysis of Difference in Language Development Between Children Aged 2–2.5 Years and Children Aged 2.5–3 Years

According to the independent-samples T-test, there was a significant difference between the scores of children aged 2–2.5 years and children aged 2.5–3 years. The average score of children aged 2–2.5 years was 13.2308, and that of children aged 2.5–3 years was 15.5253. It is thus clear that the language development level of children aged 2.5–3 years is significantly higher than that of children aged 2–2.5 years. According to the analysis, the proportion of children aged 2.5–3 years getting high scores is much higher than that of children aged 2–2.5 years (Table 4.9).

Specifically, according to the independent-samples T-test in all aspects of language expression and understanding in Table 4.10, it can be seen that there are significant differences in vocabulary use, two-word phrase use, two-word phrase understanding and question understanding between children aged 2–2.5 years and children aged 2.5–3 years, but there is no difference in vocabulary understanding. According to the analysis, the difference between children aged 2–2.5 years and children 2.5–3 years is mainly reflected in the number of children with low scores; and the number of children aged 2–2.5 years with low scores is significantly larger than that of children aged 2.5–3 years.

4.3 Results and Analysis

Table 4.8 Paired-samples T-test of language understanding and language expression

Paired differences

		Mean	Std. deviation	Std. error mean	95% confidence interval of the difference Lower	95% confidence interval of the difference Upper	t	df	Sig (2-tailed)
Pair 1	Language understanding–Language expression	0.00000000	0.89666166	0.07745977	−0.15321242	0.15321242	−0.000	133	1.000

Table 4.9 Independent-samples T-test of total scores of language development of children aged 2–2.5 years and children aged 2.5–3 years

		F	Significance	t	df	Sig (2-tailed)	Mean difference	Std. error difference	95% confidence interval of the difference Upper	Lower
Total score of language development	Assumed equal variance	37.226	0.000	−5.626	123	0.000	−2.29448	0.40784	−3.10179	−1.48718
	Not assumed equal variance			−3.480	26.851	0.002	−2.29448	0.65934	−3.64769	−0.94127

4.3 Results and Analysis

Table 4.10 Independent-samples T-test among all aspects of language expression and language understanding

		F	Significance	t	df	Sig (2-tailed)	Mean difference	Std. error difference	95% confidence interval of the difference Upper	95% confidence interval of the difference Lower
Vocabulary use	Assumed equal variance	41.880	0.000	−3.401	124	0.001	−0.50692	0.14907	−0.80197	−0.21188
	Not assumed equal variance			−2.105	26.877	**0.045**	−0.50692	0.24081	−1.00113	−0.01272
Two-word phrase use	Assumed equal variance	15.163	0.000	−3.238	123	0.002	−0.43162	0.13329	−0.69545	−0.16779
	Not assumed equal variance			−2.606	31.395	**0.014**	−0.43162	0.16565	−0.76929	−0.09396
Vocabulary understanding	Assumed equal variance	80.900	0.000	−3.928	123	0.000	−0.30769	0.07833	−0.46273	−0.15265
	Not assumed equal variance			−1.990	25.000	**0.058**	−0.30769	0.15461	−0.62612	−0.01074
Two-word phrase understanding	Assumed equal variance	87.944	0.000	−4.209	123	0.000	−0.30769	0.07311	−0.45241	−0.16297
	Not assumed equal variance			−2.132	25.000	**0.043**	−0.30769	0.14432	−0.60493	−0.01046

(continued)

Table 4.10 (continued)

		F	Significance	t	df	Sig (2-tailed)	Mean difference	Std. error difference	95% confidence interval of the difference Upper	Lower
Question understanding	Assumed equal variance	98.817	0.000	−5.536	123	0.000	−0.43124	0.07790	−0.58544	−0.27703
	Not assumed equal variance			−3.347	26.590	**0.002**	−0.431242	0.12884	−0.69579	−0.16668

4.3 Results and Analysis

4.3.4 Relationship Between Other Factors and Children's Language Development Level

Through one-way analysis of variance, it was found that there was no significant difference in the language development level of children aged 2–3 years from parents with different educational backgrounds and professions, and there was no significant difference in the language development level of children in families with different economic levels. According to the results of independent-samples T-test, there was no significant difference in language development between children of different sexes or with different birth conditions (premature delivery spontaneous delivery).

4.4 Conclusion

The period from 2 to 3 years old is the critical period for children to learn spoken language. In this period, children's vocabulary and sentences develop rapidly, from simple sentences to compound sentences. In this study, children aged 2–3 years have good language development and can basically complete the test. The following two conclusions are drawn, discussed, and analyzed.

4.4.1 Children Aged 2–3 Years Have a Good Language Development, with no Significant Difference in Language Understanding and Language Expression

There are studies showing that children aged 2 years not only have more than 60% complete simple sentences, but also have compound sentences. Children's speech development starts with simple sentences, followed by compound sentences, which appear when simple sentences are not quite perfect (Zhu 1986). This is consistent with the finding of this study that most children aged 2–3 years are able to use multi-word phrases.

4.4.2 There Are Significant Differences in Language Development Level Between Children Aged 2–2.5 Years and Children Aged 2.5–3 Years

There are significant differences between children aged 2–2.5 years and children aged 2.5–3 years in vocabulary use, two-word phrase use, two-word phrase understanding, and question understanding, and there is no significant difference in vocabulary understanding. Zhang (2001) pointed out that infant language development can be divided into four stages: simple sentence stage (25–27 months) interrogative sentence generation stage (28–30 months), interrogative sentence peak stage (31–33 months), multi-word phrase, and compound sentence stage (34–36 months). It is thus clear that the period from 2 to 3 years old is the germination and development stage of compound sentences for children, which can explain the significant difference between children groups at different ages in two-word phrase understanding and question understanding. In addition, the age difference in vocabulary use may be caused by the life experience of children. With the growth of age, after most children enter nursery classes and join a group from their families, the changes in their life experience and peer relationship, to some extent, will also affect their language development level.

References

Gentner, D. (1982). Why nouns are learned before verbs: Linguistic relativity versus natural partitioning. Technical report no. 257. *Child Language, 2,* 86.
Heep Hong Society. (2013). *Children's learning program.* Hong Kong: The Green Pagoda Printing Co., Ltd.
Wu, T. M., & Xu, Z. Y. (1979). A preliminary analysis of language development of children during the first three years. *Acta Psychologica Sinica, 02,* 153–165.
Zhang, M. H. (2001). *Pre-school children language education.* Shanghai: East China Normal University Press.
Zhu, M. S. (1986). *Studies on children language development.* Shanghai: East China Normal University Press.

Chapter 5
Study on the Developmental Characteristics of Social Adaptation of 2–3-Year-Old Children

5.1 Introduction

Social adaptation is a process in which individuals interact with the surrounding environment and achieve a harmonious relationship with the social environment (Chen 2010). The relationship between individuals and social environment changes with age. Therefore, the content and focus of social adaptation in an individual's life will change with age (Mahoney and Bergman 2002). Chen Huichang divides social adaptation into stranger adaptation, unfamiliar environmental adaptation and peer interaction (Chen 1994). The World Health Organization (WHO) believes that "health is not only free from diseases, but also includes physical health, mental health, good social adaptation, and ethical health.". It can be seen that social adaptation is important for individual development. Guide to Learning and Development for Children Aged 3–6 puts social adaptation as one of the two major subfields in the social field. "Social adaptation is a major part of early childhood social learning, and it is also a major way for its social development." Social adaptation plays an important role in the process of socialization.

Toddlerhood (1–3 years old), especially the age of 2, is an important period for children's physical and psychological development (Cao et al. 2010). Children between the ages of 2 and 3 will soon face a change in their living environment, that is, the transition from family life to kindergarten group life. This is an important step in the socialization of children. In this process, young children's mind and body will be greatly affected (Li 2016). Due to abrupt changes in the living environment, the transformation of interpersonal relationships from parent–child interactions to strange peer interactions and teacher–student interactions, and the new code of conduct, most of the young children lost their sense of security at the beginning of admission, resulting in separation anxiety (Zhang 2000) and other unadaptable performance. Due to differences in social adaptability, the time for children to adapt to the kindergarten is also different. Some young children, because of their low social adaptability, will not adapt to the kindergarten for a long time, which will have a negative impact on their physical and mental development. Before children enter kindergarten, an in-depth understanding of the characteristics of children's social adaptation can help educators adopt appropriate education and caring methods. Now, there have been more studies on the social adaptation of young children aged over 3, but fewer studies on that of children aged less than 3. It is difficult to understand the adaptive development of 2–3 years old children through existing studies, nor give advice on the improvement of their social adaptation capacity. Thus, this study focuses on children under the age of 3, especially young children aged 2–3 who are about to adapt to admission. This study aims to fully understand the abovementioned children's social adaptation and provide a scientific basis for follow-up education.

Children's social adaptation has a clear age trend, and social adaptability increases with age (Shi et al. 2006). Unlike preschool and elementary and middle school children among whom girls' social adaptability is better than that of boys (Wang et al. 2005), Cao (2014) pointed out that the developmental level of social adaptation behavior of boys aged from 30 to 33 months was significantly higher than that of girls, and there was no significant difference among children of other months (Shi et al. 2006). The developmental features of social adaptation of 2–3-year-old infants are yet to be verified by further studies.

This study explores the developmental characteristics of social adaptation of 2–3-year olds, studies their gender and age characteristics, and explores in depth the development characteristics of 2–3-year olds in various dimensions of social adaptation.

5.2 Research Design

5.2.1 Research Objects

With purpose sampling method, this study selected 150 children aged 2–3 years old in Beijing. The final target groups consist of 124 children, 61 of whom are boys, 63 of whom are girls, 28 of whom are aged 24–30 months (2–2.5 years old), 96 of whom are aged 30–36 months (2.5–3 years old), together with 124 parents (Table 5.1).

Table 5.1 Information of the target groups

	N	Total number
Boys	61	124
Girls	63	
24–30 months	28	124
30–36 months	96	

5.2.2 Research Methods

(1) Purposes of observation
To understand the developmental characteristics of social adaptation for children aged 2–3 years old, social adaptation of young children was observed with structured observation method in stranger situation, unfamiliar environment situation, and peer interaction situation.

(2) Observation tools
According to The Third Edition of the Bayley Infant Development Scale (BSID-III), the Early Childhood Care and Development Scale (ECCD), and the Development Assessment Chart. Common items in the three scales were selected and 2–3 years old social adaptation observation table was formulated. The observation table consists of 12 items. In the three contexts, the children were observed in terms of the developmental characteristics of stranger adaptation, unfamiliar environment adaptation, peer interaction adaptation, and behavioral adaptation. With the rating method, children's social adaptation performance was scored. The children would score 0, 1, 2, and 3. Each item's score has a corresponding standard description.

According to Chen Huichang's definition of social adaptation structure, this study, based on the characteristics of the development of children aged 2–3 years old and social environment, the social adaptation structure is divided into stranger adaptation, unfamiliar environment adaptation, peer interaction adaptation, and behavioral norms adaptation. Stranger adaptation refers to 2–3-year-old children, accompanied by their parents, communicate with strangers; unfamiliar environment adaptation refers to, adaptation of 2–3-year-old children to a strange environment when they are accompanied by parents, when their parents are away and when their parents are not present; peer interaction adaptation refers to, adaptation of two 2–3-year-old children to peer communication, game and peer conflict resolution; behavioral norms adaptation refers to adaptation of 2–3-year-old children to social norms, social etiquette and rules (Table 5.2)

(3) Observations and procedures
In the coherent three situations, the children interacted with the strange experimenter under the guidance of their parents and entered a strange environment. They explored the new environment accompanied by their parents or when their parents left. Then they then saw peers of the same age and interacted with them.

In the context of interaction with strangers, the experimenter met with children for the first time. As a stranger, the experimenter interacted with children and observed how young children adapt to interacting with strangers, including attitudes to strangers, communicating with strangers, friendliness to strangers, greeting strangers, and answering stranger questions.

In the context of an unfamiliar environment, the researchers created an unfamiliar environment and provided young children with attractive toys. They observed young children's adaptation to strange environments accompanied by their par-

Table 5.2 Observation indicators and source of social adaptation for young children

No.	Items	Source
1	Very friendly to strangers	ECCD
2	When others say hello, they will respond appropriately (e.g.,: say "hello")	BSID-III
3	Answer simple personal questions (e.g., gender, age and name)	Development Assessment Chart
4	In the new environment, within the reach of parents, they can explore the new environment alone	BSID-III; ECCD
5	In the absence of parents, they can continue their original activities.	BSID-III; Development Assessment Chart
6	Say hello to other children (e.g., say "hello")	BSID-III
7	Invite people to join their game/actively request to join someone else's game.	BSID-III; Development Assessment Chart
8	Play simple games with their companions	BSID-III
9	Do not fight for toys, willing to discuss solutions	BSID-III
10	Participate in an activity in order	BSID-III; Development Assessment Chart
11	Obey the rules of a game	BSID-III
12	When receive a gift or praise from someone else, they would say "thank you"	BSID-III; Development Assessment Chart

ents, the separation anxieties and attachment patterns of young children when parents left, and the children's adaptation when parents were absent.

In the context of peer interaction, the experimenter created interactive contexts for two children, in ways to observe the interactions between children, including peer interaction, game types, and conflict resolution. The experimenter observed whether the two children would greet each other. The experimenter provided the children with some toys, and asked them to play with the toys, in order to observe the types of the play, whether they would invite others to play with them or join in other games, and conflicts solution during the games. Finally, the experimenter presented an attractive toy, and observed whether the children discussed to solve the problem of lack of toys, and whether the children could follow rules and wait for their own order after the game rules were formulated. In the three contexts, the experimenter observed the behavioral adaptations of young children including social norms and social etiquette and rules in public places.

(4) Materials

A toy car, two sets of kitchen toys, 2 toy tables, 2 jigsaws, 4 picture books, 2 chairs, 2 carpets, some stickers, test charts, pens, timers.

5.2 Research Design

Table 5.3 Average scores in social adaptation of children aged 2–3 in all dimensions

	M	SD
Stranger adaptation	1.727	0.3741
Strange environment adaptation	2.565	0.6407
Peer interaction adaptation	1.205	0.8886
Behavioral norm adaptation	1.560	0.5852
Total scores	1.651	0.4227

5.2.3 Data Analysis

The researchers used SPSS 22.0 to analyze the data to understand the characteristics of social adaptation of 2–3 years old.

5.3 Research Results

5.3.1 Overall Analysis on Social Adaptation of Children Aged 2–3

The mean total score of toddlers on 12 items is 1.651 (SD = 0.4227). The testees scored above average, with average social adaptability. In the four dimensions, the testees scored highest in strange environment adaptation (M = 2.565, SD = 0.6407), and scored lowest in peer interaction adaptation (M = 1.205, SD = 0.886), the score of stranger adaptation (M = 1.727, SD = 0.3741) is higher than that of behavioral code adaptation (M = 1.56, SD = 0.5852) (Table 5.3).

5.3.2 Analysis of Development Features of Children Aged 2–3 in All Dimensions

In the stranger's adaptation dimension, the mean value of the infant's score was 1.727 (SD = 0.3741), and the stranger adaptation was at a medium level. 84.3% of young children are friendly when meeting strangers. When interacting with strangers, most of the children were not active. When the experimenter was active in interacting with them, 34.7% of the children would respond the experimenter through eye expressions or languages, while 60.5% of them would answer simple questions of the experimenter. 27.4% of the children did not respond to the experimenter's greetings (Table 5.4).

In the dimension of unfamiliar environment adaptation, children generally have higher scores and better adaptability to strange environments. Most young children

Table 5.4 Scoring percentage of stranger adaptation (100%)

	0	1 point	2 points	3 points
Attitude to strangers	2.6	13.1	34.1	50.2
Greeting with a stranger	35.5	29.8	22.6	12.1
Answering simple personal questions	27.4	12.1	21.0	39.5

have better adaptability to strange environments. 79.1% of children can explore the strange environment in the presence of parents. 71% of children can continue their original activities in a strange environment while their parents leave for a short time. They are very happy to see parents returning and separation anxiety is not obvious (Table 5.5).

In terms of peer interaction, children generally have lower scores. When meeting with their peers, more than half of the children (56.5%) ignored their peers, and only 2.4% of children took the initiative to greet other children. 85.5% of the children did not join or invite other children to join the play while playing with their peers. The child playing ignored other children, and the children who wanted to play only looked at the side and did not ask. 66.9% of children played along, without communications with each other. In the event of a contradiction, only 4% of the children would discuss solutions with each other and 60.5% of the children would remain silent. They would neither continue playing games nor discuss countermeasures with each other. 11.3% of young children directly grabbed toys or cried (Table 5.6).

In terms of behavioral norm adaptation, rule awareness and social etiquette are measured. When it comes to norm awareness, 64.9% of young children will abide by the rules of games, and 80.6% of children would wait in order. 14.6% of children are unwilling to wait in a queue, but fight for toys. In terms of social etiquette, children score low. Only 4% of young children would say thank you after receiving gifts from

Table 5.5 Scoring percentage of strange environment adaptation (100%)

	0 (%)	1 point (%)	2 points (%)	3 points (%)
Explore in the environment when parents are present	4.8	4.8	11.3	79.1
Explore in the environment when parents are present	9.7	3.2	16.1	71.0

Table 5.6 Percentage of peer interaction scores (100%)

	0 (%)	1 point (%)	2 points (%)	3 points (%)
Greeting with partners	7.3	56.5	33.8	2.4
Playing games together	6.5	85.4	7.3	0.8
Type of play	3.2	66.9	28.2	1.7
Conflict resolution	11.3	60.5	24.2	4.0

5.3 Research Results

Table 5.7 Percentage of behavioral adaptation scores (100%)

	0 (%)	1 point (%)	2 points (%)	3 points
Willing to wait in queue	4.8	14.6	39.5	41.1%
Abide by game rules	9.7	25.8	51.6	12.9%
Say "thank you" when receiving gifts	21.0	75.0	4.0	0

others. 75% of children would say thank you after being reminded, and 21% would not say thank you (Table 5.7).

5.3.3 Age and Gender Differences in Social Adaptive Development of 2–3 Year Old Children

The study divided children aged 2–3 into two groups, that is, a group of children aged 2–2.5, and the other group of children aged 2.5–3. The results show that the adaptive development of young children's society increases with age. The total score of social adaptation for children aged 2–3 years old was higher than that of children aged 2–2.5 old, and there are significant differences in terms of the total score ($p = 0.000$), stranger adaptation ($p = 0.003$), unfamiliar environment adaptation ($p = 0.045$), and behavioral adaptation ($p = 0.001$). It can be seen that the development of a social adaptation of children aged 2.5–3 years is significantly higher than that of children aged 2–2.5 years old, especially in terms of stranger adaptation, adaptation to unfamiliar environments and adaptation to behavioral norms. and adaptation to peer interaction, 2–3 years old children develop slowly. In terms of gender, there was no significant difference between boys and girls in total scores and in all dimensions (Table 5.8).

Table 5.8 Analysis of differences in social adaptation of young children aged 2–3 years at different age groups

Dimension	2 years–2 years and a half M (SD)	2 years old–3 years old M (SD)	p
Stranger adaptation	1.1250 (0.76164)	1.2318 (0.89175)	0.003
Unfamiliar environment adaptation	2.3214 (0.73553)	2.6354 (0.59595)	0.045
Peer interaction adaptation	1.1250 (0.33679)	1.2318 (0.38259)	0.185
Behavioral norm adaptation	1.1905 (0.60470)	1.6667 (0.53639)	0.001
Total scores	1.3899 (0.40891)	1.7274 (0.39726)	0.000

5.4 Analysis and Discussion

5.4.1 The Characteristics of Social Adaptation of 2–3 Years Old

Children aged 2–3 years old are at a moderate level of social adaptation. In terms of age, 2.5 years old can be used as the zero point of social adaptation and development of young children in this age group. The social adaptation development of children aged 2.5–3 years is significantly higher than that of children aged 2–2.5 years old. The social adaptive development of young children increases with age. This is consistent with most of the existing research results (Cao 2014; Zou et al. 2013).

The physical and mental development of children increases with age, and children's social experience also becomes richer. The development of both will contribute to the improvement of children's social adaptation. In terms of gender characteristics, the results of this study show that there is no significant gender difference in the social adaptation development of children aged 2–3 years old. Studies have shown that overall, at other ages, girls' social development is better than that of boys (Shi et al. 2006). The reason for the results of this study may be that gender is not a sensitive variable that affects the development of social adaptation in this age group. Children between 2 and 3 years old do not show obvious gender preference and characteristics.

6 months–2 years old is a period to develop a strong parent–child attachment, during which, children are emotionally connected with their main caregivers, showing a strong separation anxiety and stranger anxiety. In this period, children like to stay with their caregivers. 2–3 years old is a period to develop peer relations. In this period, children could consider needs of their mothers, and adjust their behaviors (Fu et al. 2016), so that the strong parent–child attachment was replaced by peer interaction and other social relations. Therefore, in this study, children aged 2–3 performed better in stranger adaptation and strange environment adaptation. The developmental level of children aged 2.5–3 years old is significantly higher than that of children aged 2–2.5 years old. Children between 2–2.5 years old are in the early stages of transition. Strangers and separation anxiety are more severe than children between 2.5 and 3 years of age. They show more obvious problems of inadaptation. The research results are consistent with the development stage of infant and child attachment of Bowlby and Ainsworth.

There is a common development trend in the social adaptation of young children aged 2–3 years, that is, social adaptability increases with age. However, there are also obvious individual differences. Children of the same age are different in social adaptation and development.

5.4 Analysis and Discussion

5.4.2 Developmental Characteristics of Social Adaptation of 2–3 Years Old in All Dimensions

In all directions, children had the highest scores in terms of strange environment adaptation, followed by stranger adaptation, behavioral norm adaptation and peer interaction adaptation. Children's behavioral norms and peer interactions have lower scores. In terms of behavioral adaptation, most children can answer other people's questions, but very few children can actively express gratitude to others when they are praised by others or receive gifts. Most children will thank the experimenter when they are prompted by others. Children of this age do not fully know social etiquette. Children between 2 and 3 years old are transitioning from intense parent–child attachment to peer interaction. The ability to communicate with peers is still in its infancy, which leads to the lowest score of peer interaction adaptation. As age increases, the experience of intercourse with young children increases, and the adaptability of peer interaction increases.

5.5 Suggestion

5.5.1 Parents Should Encourage Young Children to Come into Contact with the New Environment and Increase Opportunities for Young Children to Interact with Their Peers

Social adaptation focuses on the interaction between individuals and the social environment. Only by exposing to a new environment and increasing social experience can young children improve their social adaptability in their life. Therefore, parents need to encourage children to have more exposure to, experience and feel a new environment. They need to bring children to different places, to get exposure to different people, so as to overcome timidity, strangeness, fear and develop social adaptability. Good peer-communicative competence is of great significance to the child's future development. As 2–3 years old have already had a sense of interaction with their peers, Parents should help create an environment for playing games with their peers and increase opportunities for peer interaction. For example, they can bring young children to parks, amusement parks, neighbors' relatives, find playmates for young children, and in the process guide children to learn to establish and maintain friendships with their peers. At the same time, parents should also give their children enough sense of security in the process of children's exposure to strange environments and strangers. Children shall not be alone for a long time in a strange environment, which exacerbates young children's fear of strange environments and strangers.

On the one hand, parents should help young children to dispel inadaptation to unfamiliar circumstances and strangers. On the other hand, parents must also help young children to establish their own safe awareness in the face of strange environments and strangers.

5.5.2 Parents Should Be Good at Guiding Young Children to Establish Good Behavior Standards and Foster Pro-social Behaviors

A good code of conduct is an important prerequisite for young children to adapt to society. Spoiled children who are 2–3 years old are often difficult to establish good rule awareness and ritual awareness. After attending kindergarten, they do not observe the day-to-day routines and class rules of the kindergarten. There are also no social etiquette in dealing with teachers and peers, resulting in serious inadaptation. Therefore, parents should help their children establish a good standard of behavior before they enter the kindergarten and infuse basic social norms into their children in daily life. Parents should also set an example for young children so that young children can learn social etiquette and rules in family life and social life, such as waiting in line and obeying traffic rules. Parents should promptly correct their children's improper behaviors. For example, for aggressive behaviors, parents should help children to reduce the frequency of aggressive behaviors through appropriate education in a timely manner. Parents should pay attention to fostering the pro-social behaviors of young children, such as sharing toys with others, comforting and helping others, and allowing children to follow the elder's teachings to gradually understand the meaning of pro-social behaviors.

References

Cao, R., Xia, M., & Chen, H. (2010). Noncompliance of children aged 2 and forecast of social adaptation of children aged 4 to 11. *Journal of Psychiatry, 42*(5), 581–586.

Cao, X. (2014). *Development of a Questionnaire for Evaluating the Development of Social Adaptation Behaviors in Children Aged 0–3 Years*. M.A. Thesis, Shanxi University, Shanxi.

Chen, H. (1994). Development and normative formulation of children's social development scale. *Psychological Development and Education, 10*(4), 52–63.

Chen, J. (2010). On social adaptation. *Journal of Southwest University (Social Science Edition), 36*(1), 11–15.

Fu, C., Wang, Y., Jin, J., & Liu, J. (2016). *Social education of preschool children* (Vol. 06, p. 31). Zhejiang Gongshang University Press.

Li, Y. (2016). *Study on Problems of Kindergarten Admission Adaptation and Countermeasures*. M.A. Thesis, Shandong Normal University, Shandong.

Mahoney, J. L., & Bergman, L. R. (2002). Conceptual and methodological considerations in a developmental approach to the study of positive adaptation. *Applied Developmental Psychology, 23*(2), 195–217.

References

Shi, S., Wu, J., & Zhang, J. (2006). Investigation on social adaptation behavior of preschool children in Wuhan. *Chinese Public Health, 22*(8), 924–925.

Wang, Y., Lin, C., & Yu, G. (2005). Compilation and application of children's social life adaptation scale. *Psychological Development and Education, 01,* 109–114.

Zhang, B. (2000). Study on problems of Kindergarten admission adaptation and countermeasures (part I). *Early Childhood Education, 9,* 7–8.

Zou, W., Liu, Y., & Li, X. (2013). Comprehensive assessment of adolescents' social adaptation in seven cities in China. *Journal of Beijing Normal University (Social Science Edition), 1,* 51–60.

Chapter 6
Analysis of Infants' Emotional Development

6.1 Introduction

Emotion is subjective experience of human brain that whether the objective reality meets our needs and is essential to children's development. With the concept of emotional quotient, emotional intelligence, and other concepts deeply rooted in people's minds, people are increasingly concerned about the development of young children's social–emotional ability. Studies have shown that emotional competence is a major development task in the early childhood period and a focus on the social field (Wang 2010); the emotional ability of young children is of great significance for the development of their physical and mental health, cognitive ability, social adaptability, and interpersonal skills (Tang and Xue 2015). Emotional ability in childhood, instead of IQ, is the best predictor of their success in later life (Ji 2013). Emotional ability determines the harmony of interpersonal relationships and the cultivation of innovative abilities. Therefore, understanding the development of children's emotions and their characteristics helps to better care for and educate children. The formation of emotional ability in young children is influenced by both genetics and education. Genetic is not controllable, while education makes a difference. Improving children's emotional ability is an important issue in early childhood education. In addition, since the 1980s, China has implemented the one-child policy. Compared with multiple children, there has been a new change in the growing environment for one child, and accordingly, the child's social–emotional ability has also shown new features. The opening of the two-child policy has brought new challenges to children's emotional ability (Hua 2015). According to reports, a brother who believes that his sister had stripped his own love brutally killed his sister who was a year and a half (Qian 2014). For this reason, it is imperative to cultivate children's social–emotional ability at the younger age.

Foreign countries have already studied the social emotions of young children (Branson and Demchak 2011). Many early educators, researchers, and policy-makers realize that emotional education is part of basic education. Wei Wei, a Chinese scholar, who was inspired by a foreign social–emotional learning project, promotes educating children from young age under the idea of "learning by doing" (Wei 2015) and "scientific education" (Ministry of Education 2001). He has achieved positive results in a small range of social–emotional education. However, there is little attention and research on young children in the early stage.

According to Dr. Camers, a well-known American child psychological development expert, emotional ability is the ability to achieve a specific purpose in a proper way in a specific cultural context (Tian et al. 2009). Saarni (1999) classifies children's emotional abilities into eight aspects, that is, perceptions of their own emotions, recognition of other people's emotions, use of emotional language, sympathy and empathy, differentiation of internal emotions and external expressions, coping with stressful emotions and situations, use of appropriate emotions for communication, and emotional self-efficacy. Denham et al. (2003) believe that children's emotional ability includes emotional expression ability, emotional knowledge ability, and emotional regulation ability. Domestic scholar Yao believes that children's emotional abilities include emotional understanding and emotional regulation (Yao et al. 2004). This article focused on the child's emotional recognition, emotional understanding, and emotional regulation. Denham and his colleagues' research (2003) found that the acquisition of children's emotional ability and the development of social capabilities are crucial. At the age of 3–4, children's emotional expression could positively predict their emotional knowledge and emotional self-regulation. However, only emotional self-regulation could positively predict children's social ability. At the kindergarten stage, the situation had changed. Emotional expression ability enhanced the predictability of emotional knowledge and social ability, and the influence of emotional self-regulation on social interaction was no longer that important.

Emotion recognition refers to the ability to recognize the emotional expression of others. Emotion understanding is the identification and interpretation of children's emotional behaviors and emotional situations. It involves understanding emotional information, interpreting emotional expression, and understanding the relationship between emotions and other psychological activities, behaviors, and situations. The recognition of facial expressions reflects the ability of infants to express themselves through external emotions and infer their intrinsic emotional and psychological states. This is a key indicator of emotional recognition. It examines young children's emotion recognition ability by recognizing pictures of facial expressions such as happiness, sadness, anger, and fear through line drawings and photos. For example, Izard (1980) compiled the "Facial Expression Recognition System" (Affex) test for facial expression recognition, which included interested, happiness, surprise, sadness, anger, disgust, scorn, and fear, and Denham (1986) further developed a research program for measuring the emotional recognition ability of infants and toddlers aged 2–4.

Emotional regulation ability refers to the adjustment of one's own emotional experience and expression to an appropriate level for achieving personal goals. Most emotion regulation measurements refer to laboratory setting up experiments. The common ones are disappointing experimental paradigms, such as Saarni's (1984)

6.1 Introduction

Mie's disappointed gift paradigm, the experimental paradigm separating from parents, and Kogan's (1997) "mother–baby separation experiment", as well as a delay-satisfying paradigm, such as the gift delay experimental paradigm designed by Funder et al. (1983). Wang and Chen (1998) used five stress scenarios, including gift delay experiments, to measure the emotional regulation strategies and characteristics of 140 2 years old in stress situations, and coded emotional expression and emotional regulation strategies. The emotional regulation strategies adopted by the 2-year-old children in China under stressful situations were classified into the following six types, active activities, distractions, seeking comfort from others, passive behaviors, self-consolation, and avoidance. In this study, the ratings of emotional performance and emotional regulation strategies were high, scoring 0.82 and 0.89. This study referred to six strategies for emotion regulation.

Looking at the research results of children's emotional development, there are still several issues: (1) in terms of the target groups, the study focused more on preschool (4–6 years old) children but less on young children aged 2–3; (2) in terms of research methods, the interview method facilitates an in-depth understanding of the respondent's attitude and thinking. This method is not suitable for young children and is interfered by young children's language ability. However, it is practically feasible to examine the emotional development of young children with experimental methods and implicit social cognition and preference measurement; (3) in terms of research materials, most of studies are from western countries, and there is a problem of cross-cultural validity. According to China's actual conditions, it is necessary to adapt the materials and make them more suitable for local researches; (4) in terms of research results, there are contradictions and inconsistencies. For example, Liang et al. (2011) found that girl's emotional recognition ability was significantly better than that of boys, but Zhan (2005) discovered there was no significant gender difference in emotional cognitive ability of 3–5-year-old children through facial expression recognition and story situation methods.

Therefore, this study focused on the emotional development of 2–3 years old. With parent report surveys and situational tests, the development of children's social emotions, emotion recognition, emotional understanding and emotion regulation strategies, their characteristics, and their relationships were invested to understand the emotional development of 2–3 years old, so as to provide reference for early childhood care and education in this age.

6.2 Methods

6.2.1 Participants

145 2–3 years old and their parents were selected as participants. Among them, 125 parents (fathers or mothers) filled out the questionnaire on social emotions of the Bayley Childhood Development Scale (Third Edition); 59 children (boys 25, girls

34) were tested to have more emotional recognition and emotional understanding data. 134 children (63 boys and 71 girls) participated in the emotional regulation experiment.

6.2.2 Measures

6.2.2.1 Social–Emotional Scale (The Third Edition)

Social–Emotional Scale in Bayley Scales of Infant and Toddler Development Third Edition was used to assess the emotional development of infants and young children aged 2–3. The questionnaire, including 38 aspects, assesses the shortcomings of early social–emotional development, social and emotional health, early interpersonal communication, and social–emotional development. The questionnaire was filled in by the target fathers or mothers, and a 6-point scale was used. 0–5 indicates the frequency of behavior from low to high. For each skill in each item and social adaptation scale, frequency of behaviors was summarized to obtain the raw scores. The column for the age of the month was determined to find the standard score for the original score and converted into a composite score, percentile, and confidence interval. The paper uses items 1–8 to assess a child's sensory processing capabilities (e.g., sensitivity to color, sound, touch, or movement), so as to check whether children's development in this area is imperfect. The paper used the adjusted age of preterm delivery to determine the appropriate age range and converts all sensory processing scores into full mastery, just mastery, or potentially challenging by age suitability.

6.2.2.2 Emotion Recognition Test

According to Denham's (1986) research on the emotion recognition ability of infants and toddlers aged 2–4 years, children's emotion recognition ability was measured. This research method has been widely used in children's emotion recognition tests (Zhao et al. 2006; Liang et al. 2011). Four pictures of basic expressions expressing happiness, sadness, anger, and fear were compiled into a picture book. All face pictures were confirmed by 30 male and female college students. The typical characteristics of the above four kinds of expressions can be reflected. In order to reduce the possibility of difficult recognition caused by the gender of the face, the boys and girls version pictures were designed. First, the experimenters randomly presented the subjects with facial expressions of happiness, sadness, anger, and fear. The experimenter asked the child, "When a child looks like this, how does she/he feel?" The child responded to the mood of the person in the picture to measure the infant's expressive naming ability; second, the experimenter randomly put four kinds of facial expressions in front of the children, and asked the subjects to identify "What is the appearance of happiness (sadness, anger, and fear)?" to measure infants' sen-

6.2 Methods

sitive naming ability. Scores: 2 points for identifying or answering correctly; only 1 point for correctly saying the category (positive or negative emotions such as "He doesn't feel good" instead of he feels sad, angry, and fearful); 0 point for completely wrongness. The sum of expressive naming and sensitivity naming scores is the score of emotion recognition, and the total score is 0–16 points (Figs. 6.1, 6.2, 6.3, 6.4, 6.5, and 6.6).

Fig. 6.1 Emoticons—boys edition

Fig. 6.2 Emoticons—girls edition

Figs. 6.3–6.4 Emotional cognitive expression naming test—male/female edition

Figs. 6.5–6.6 Emotional cognitive receptive naming test—male/female edition

6.2.2.3 Emotional Understanding Test

The understanding of the emotional externality of Test of Emotion Comprehension (TEC) compiled by Pons and Harris (2000) which was used mainly for measuring the level of emotional understanding of 3–11 years old was selected to measure the emotional understanding of young children. According to previous studies, the internal consistency coefficient of TEC is 0.68 (Pons et al. 2003), and the replica reliability coefficient is 0.90 (Pons et al. 2004). Zhuo (2008) used TEC to measure the level of emotional understanding of 2–9 years old in China. The factor analysis results showed that TEC has a good structural validity and is applicable to young children in China. The subjects were asked to respond to the emotions of the heroes in five-story situations: (1) The little turtle that the child loved is dying; (2) The child receives gifts from Grandma; (3) The child is waiting for the bus; (4) The child wants to paint but her little sister has been disturbing her; (5) The child is being chased by the monster. Story scenes, alternative facial expressions were made into a picture book (in both male and female editions). The experimenter told the child about the story and presented the picture book. Child was asked to select the most appropriate one from the four facial expressions based on the emotional characteristics of the leading character. Child's answers were nonverbal, closed, and spontaneous. Each question is answered correctly with 1 point, otherwise 0 point (Figs. 6.7, 6.8, 6.9, 6.10, 6.11, and 6.12).

Fig. 6.7 Emoticons—boys edition

6.2 Methods 103

Figs. 6.8–6.12 Emotion understanding quiz comics book—boys edition

6.2.2.4 Frustration Situation Experiment

The frustration context experiment adapted from the experimental program designed by Day and Smith (2013) was used to measure the emotional regulation ability of infants and young children. Concretely, there were a floor mat, a table, a chair, andthree transparent boxes, three kinds of food, a chronograph stopwatch, an adult chair, and a video recorder in a quiet room. In an experimental case, the parents accompanying their children were told the objectives of the experiment and were asked not to give their children help. It was timed from the moment when the child understood the task and was given the bottle. The child would be tested in a frustration case in which the child had to open a sealed bottle with snacks for 3 min during which his/her emotional responses would be recorded, scores would be given on the spot, and time samples would be obtained. The experimenter recorded the emotional regulation behavior of the child every 10 s and coded according to Table 6.1. The average score for each emotional regulation strategy is calculated and represents the frequency with which the child showed this strategy. 0 indicates that the child never

Table 6.1 Emotional regulation experiment code

Coding	Definition	Example
Active activity	Young children work hard to achieve goals	Try to screw or bit the bottle
Seeking help	Go to the mother or the experimenter or ask someone for help, or put the bottle in front of the mother or the experimenter, or say, "how can I open it?"	
Self-comfort	Including symbolic self-comfort and physical self-comfort	Symbolic self-comfort: statements or activities indicate that frustration is handled through cognition/symbols, such as self-directed statements, "I can open" or "the bottle is too tight"; physical self-comfort: including body-directed behaviors (moving, catching clothes or goods, such as, grabbing hands, hair and face, sucking fingers, rubbing face or clothes) and getting comfort and sense of safety with soft or familiar goods (such as holding his/her own water bottle)
Seeking comfort	Including symbolic seeking comfort and body comfort	Symbolic seeking comfort: words like "I can't open it", "I have no enough strength"; body comfort: want to be held, touching hair and clothes of the parents or the experimenter, lying on the parent or the experimenter's lap
Distraction	Attention was not paid to the bottle for over 2 s	Including singing, glancing around, focusing on or holding a task-independent object, talking with the mother or the experimenter about non-task-related topics (not seeking help); or holding the bottle in one hand, but looking away (not trying to open the bottle)
Venting	Negative emotional or motion expression	Such as stomping, bending backwards, kicking a leg, throwing a bottle, shaking a bottle, flapping a bottle

6.2 Methods

showed this emotional regulation strategy. 1 indicates that the child demonstrated this emotional regulation strategy.

6.3 Analysis of Results

6.3.1 Emotional Development of Young Children

6.3.1.1 Social Mood Development

The standard scores and comprehensive scores of the Social–Emotional Development Scale were calculated, and frequency statistics were made, as shown in Table 6.2. In summary, the score of social mood development of 2–3 years old concentrates between 80 and 105, with less distribution on both ends.

Table 6.3 shows classification of sensory processing capability of the tested children according to age suitability, fully mastered, just mastered or may be challenging, with proportions of 49.6%, 42.7%, and 7.7%, respectively. It can be seen that about half of the children aged 2–3 years have completely mastered the sensory processing capability. The vast majority of others were just mastered, and few 2–3 years old felt difficult in sensory processing ability.

In the column with the highest mastering, the highest stage would be recorded (in Social–Emotional Scale). It means items 4 and 5 would be circled among all the items

Table 6.2 Social–emotional development scale score frequency statistics

Standard score	Comprehensive score	Frequency	Percentage	Cumulative percentage
3	65	5	5.1	5.1
4	70	5	5.1	10.1
5	75	4	4	14.1
6	80	15	15.2	29.3
7	85	14	14.1	43.4
8	90	12	12.1	55.6
9	95	12	12.1	67.7
10	100	9	9.1	76.8
11	105	10	10.1	86.9
12	110	8	8.1	94.9
13	115	1	1	96
15	125	2	2	98
17	135	1	1	99
18	140	1	1	100
In total		99	100	

Table 6.3 Classification of sensory processing capability according to age suitability

	Frequency	Percentage	Cumulative percentage
May be challenging	9	7.7	7.7
Just mastered	50	42.7	50.4
Fully mastered	58	49.6	100.0
In total	117	100.0	

answered. This information is used to explain the scores of the Social–Emotional Scale, and it can also be used to help chart children's social–emotional development. Table 6.4 shows the statistics of the highest stage frequency of social emotions for 2–3 years old. Apart from 8 children who were not in the six phases circled, reasons might be differences in parental understanding of the item statement or the influence of self-modesty in the context of Chinese culture; 2–3 years old were mostly in phase 5a and phase 6 in terms of mastering of social emotions (21.1, 17.1, and 20.3%), a few of them were in phase 3–4b (8.1, 13, 9.8%), and few of them were in phase 2 (4.1%). It can be seen that the individual differences in the control of social emotions of 2–3 years old are very large.

Table 6.4 The highest stage frequency table for mastering social emotions

The highest stage of emotional development	Frequency	Percentage	Cumulative percentage
Not at the above phases	8	6.5	6.5
Phase 1: Show self-discipline and interest in the world	0	0	0
Phase 2: Develop relationships	5	4.1	10.6
Phase 3: Use of emotional emotions in an interactive, purposeful way	10	8.1	18.7
Phase 4a: Use interactive emotional signals or gestures to communicate	16	13	31.7
Phase 4b: Use interactive emotional signals or gestures to solve problems	12	9.8	41.5
Phase 5a: Use symbols or concepts to convey intentions or feelings	26	21.1	62.6
Phase 5b: Use symbols or ideas to express the need beyond basic needs	21	17.1	79.7
Phase 6: Build a logical bridge between emotions and concepts	25	20.3	100
In total	123	100	

6.3 Analysis of Results

Table 6.5 Descriptive statistical analysis of emotion recognition and emotion understanding

		Minimum value	Maximum value	Mean	Standard deviation
Emotion recognition ability	Expressive naming	0.00	2.00	0.76	0.57
	Sensitive naming	0.00	2.00	1.38	0.53
Emotional understanding		0.00	1.00	0.49	0.22

6.3.1.2 Emotion Recognition and Emotional Understanding

A descriptive statistical analysis was performed on the scores of young children's emotion recognition and emotional understanding tests, as shown in Table 6.5. It can be seen that the expressive naming capacity of 2–3 years old was still relatively low, and the dispersion degree of distribution was also relatively large ($\bar{X} = 0.76$, SD = 0.57); sensitive naming capability was relatively higher relative to the total score and the dispersion degree of the distribution was also relatively large ($\bar{X} = 1.38$, SD = 0.53); the expressive naming score was lower than the susceptibility naming score (0.76 < 1.38). Significant difference still need to be further examined; children's emotional understanding ability was not high and their distribution was relatively concentrated ($\bar{X} = 0.49$, SD = 0.22).

6.3.1.3 Emotion Regulation Strategy

A descriptive statistical analysis of the six strategies for emotion regulation is shown in Table 6.6. It can be seen that in the frustration situation experiment, the frequency of emotional regulation strategies adopted by children aged 2–3 years was decreasing in accordance with active activities, distraction, seeking help, self-comfort, seeking comfort, and venting.

Six strategies for emotion regulation were used as clustering centers for rapid cluster analysis, as shown in Table 6.7. It can be seen that infants and young children's emotional regulation strategies can be divided into three categories, and the inter-

Table 6.6 Descriptive statistical analysis of emotion regulation strategies

	Minimum value	Maximum value	Mean	Standard deviation
Active activities	0.00	1.00	0.45	0.27
Seeking help	0.00	1.00	0.31	0.27
Self-comfort	0.00	0.78	0.27	0.20
Seeking comfort	0.00	0.72	0.17	0.18
Distraction	0.00	1.00	0.37	0.28
Venting	0.00	0.83	0.16	0.17

Table 6.7 Cluster analysis of infant mood regulation strategies

Type	Number (%)	Active activities	Seeking help	Self-comfort	Seeking comfort	Distraction	Venting
1	46 (34.3%)	0.74	0.20	0.23	0.16	0.22	0.14
2	39 (29.1%)	0.39	0.66	0.22	0.24	0.16	0.23
3	49 (36.6%)	0.24	0.14	0.35	0.12	0.67	0.11
F		106.43***	136.49***	5.60**	5.44**	127.29***	6.41**

Note +$P < 0.1$, *$P < 0.05$, **$P < 0.01$, ***$P < 0.001$

type *F*-tests of the dimensional mean of infants and toddlers of all types reached a significant level.

As can be seen from Fig. 6.13, the characteristics of the three types of emotion regulation strategies are as follows: type 1—active: Children in this type scored below the average in terms of seeking help, comforting themselves, seeking comfort, distractions, and venting. They had the highest scores in active activities; type 2—seeking help: Children in this type scored below average in positive activity, self-comfort, and distraction. Their scores for seeking comfort and venting were at an intermediate level. They had the highest scores in seeking help; type 3—abstracted: Children in this type were below average in terms of active activities, seeking help, seeking comfort, and venting. They had the highest scores in abstraction. According to Table 6.7, the proportions of the three types were 34.3%, 29.1%, and 36.6%, respectively. The following is three-case descriptions of the three strategies (Fig. 6.13).

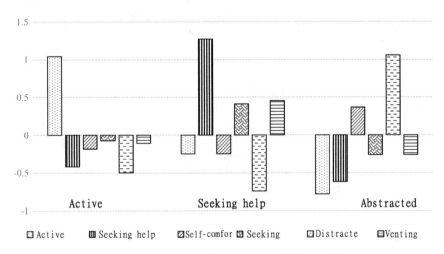

Fig. 6.13 Clustering analysis of infant mood regulation strategies boys edition

6.3 Analysis of Results

Positive Explorer, Xiao Yi: Female of 29 Months

She just put the box on her leg when she got it. With the box in one hand, she tried to open the lid, and kept staring at the camera from time to time. She tried to open the box in different postures, and her eyes were not staring at the box. Later, she put the box on one side and observed it. Then she put the bottom of the box on her lap. She held the box with one hand and tried to open the lid with the other hand. During this process, the box dropped once from her hand, but she immediately picked up the box.

The above method did not work. Then she took the box from her thigh and placed her hands on the lid and the bottom of the box. She shook the box and tried to pull out the lid. Later, she fixed the bottom of the box with her elbow joint. She held the box with one hand and tried to open the box with the other hand on the side of the lid. It didn't work. So she changed her strategy. She grasped the lid with one hand and supported the bottom of the box with the other hand, trying to pull the lid out.

"Mom, mom, mom", she looked at the camera and her movements did not stop.

There was no response. She tried the previous method again and repeatedly changed the positions of her little hand on the bottle. She screwed the lid with her facial muscles pulled tight. She then shook the box with her hands to her chest and put the box on her lap. She held the box in one hand, and placed her other hand on the lid, trying to open the box. However, the method didn't work. She held the lid with her left hand and shook it above her head. She said,

"Mom, I can't open it!" She stared at the camera.

"Try!" With her mother's response, she quickly sat back. She looked at the ceiling and said something. At the same time, she picked up the box, placed it on the box, placed one hand on the bottom of the box, placed the thumb of the other hand at the junction of the box and the lid, and pressed the other four fingers on the lid, trying to open the box.

"Mom, I can't." Her body was facing her mother, with her tummy on the bottom of the box and two hands on the lid.

Without any response, she sat back to her original position. She continued to try to open the box with one hand at the bottom of the box, the thumb of the other hand at the junction of the box and the lid, and the other four fingers pressed on the lid. Still, she failed. So she asked again for the help.

"I can't open it." She said while holding the lid with her left hand and shaking the box on her right side.

"Come on!" With a response, she once again sat back. She lifted it from the bottom of the box with her right hand, and she wobbled it on her right eye. Then she took it down. She held the box with one hand and tried to open the lid with the other hand. With her facial muscles tight, she said, "I can't open it".

Help Seeker, Hao Hao: Male of 29 Months

(It was not smooth before the experiment began. The child was reluctant. Two minutes after the experimenter talked with him, he was willing to sit on the mat and asked his grandma to sit beside him.)

When the experimenter handed the box to him, he walked to his grandmother and sat down under the grandmother's gesture.

The box was placed on its side. He had one hand on the bottom of the box, the other hand's thumb at the junction of the box and the lid, and the other four fingers pressed against the lid, trying to open the box. However, it didn't work. Then he handed the box to his grandmother.

"Come on!" With the response, he tried to open the lid with his mouth, but he gave up quickly.

"I can't open it." He said as he looked at the experimenter and pushed the box in the direction of her grandmother.

"How?" He rubbed the wall on his back. While speaking, he raised the box with one hand over his head and sent it to his grandmother.

"Do it by yourself". He still insisted on giving the box to his grandma, and cried.

"The auntie asked you to do it by yourself". He seemed to understand what his grandma said. He scratched his head with one hand and looked in the direction of the experimenter.

He tried to open the box again, but he quickly sent the box to the grandma. The grandmother pretended to watch the mobile phone message under the experimenter's reminder but still failed to stop him from seeking help. He got up and his body leaned forward to her grandmother. He also brought the box to her side and said, "You opened it", with a little crying. His grandma ignored himself. Then he stood up, holding the box in one hand, and shaking his grandmother's arm with the other: "Grandma opens", trying to make his grandmother stop doing anything else.

"If you want to eat, just do it yourself." The grandma's words did not work. When she spoke, he sent the box to her grandmother and said something. Finally, he put the box directly on the grandmother's lap.

When the grandmother saw it, she used the thigh to hold the box and motioned him to unscrew it. He put his right hand on the lid for a second and said, "I can't open it". While he was talking, he took a step back, holding his hand against the wall, touching his head with one hand and looking at the experimenter.

With grandma's encouragement, he picked up the box and walked in the direction of the experimenter, trying to seek help from the experimenter. The experimenter rejected him on the ground that he was busy. Then he walked in the direction of his grandmother.

His grandma encouraged him again. He took another second to try to open the box, but he handed the box to the grandma's hand and said, "I can't." His grandmother pretended to be unable to open by herself, hoping he would open it. He left and turned away from his grandmother. Then he hummed a few times. After that, he took back the bottle. However, he did not want to open the box and returned the box to his grandmother. Grandmother then encouraged him to ask the experimenter how to

6.3 Analysis of Results

open. He hesitated, holding both hands above the head with his hands, then walked in the direction of the experimenter and said "hmm".

The experimenter told him to think of a solution. So he went straight to hand over the box to his grandmother and made a crying voice. Then he walked around in front of his grandma. His grandma put the box on the table beside him and encouraged him to open it. He picked up the box, tried to open the box with the previous method, and gave the box to his grandma, "give you". Refused by his grandma, he did not give up. He walked around his grandmother and made a crying voice.

Grandma encouraged him again. This time, instead of taking the box, he jumped on the floor and said, "I can't open it, give you." He stayed away from the box, leaning back against the wall, pointing to the box, and wanting her grandmother to open.

Distractor Who Is Not in the State, Meng Yang: Female of 34 Months

After she got the box, she placed the box on the table and looked at the box for 2 s. Then she looked to her left, turned her head to the left, and stuck her tongue out. After 13 s, she turned her head, looked at the box for 1 s, turned her head to the right, and watched for 7 s. She also stuck her tongue in the same way as before. During this process, she put her hands on her chest.

She raised the box to nose height, and stood up, looking forward for 3 s. After sitting down again, she held the box 1 cm from the desk. She kept her hands constantly rubbing at the bottom of the box and the lid. She looked at the left side for a while, stared at the experimenter in a daze, and took a look at the right side. This state lasted for 20 s during which she occasionally turned her head or tongue out.

She stared at the box for 3 s and turned her head to the left for 15 s. She lifted the box as she did before, the hands kept rubbing against the bottom of the box and the lid. After that, she looked at the camera for 2 s and looked at the left for 10 s; she looked at the camera for 3 s and looked at the left side for 18 s.

She looked at the camera again, but her eyes kept rolling for 8 s. Then she stared at the box for 3 s and tried to open it.

She left the small chair from the right side of the table, holding the box in her hand, and licked lip with her tongue. After standing still, she leaned against the table and her arm rested on the table. She glanced at the box and looked at the right side for 18 s. The box was in her hand. She holds the bottom of the box with one hand. The other hand holding the cover of the box kept moving, without any strength.

Finally, she looked back at the camera for 2 s.

Table 6.8 Cross-tabulation analysis of children's sensory processing ability at different ages

Classification of sensory processing capability according to age suitability	≤30 months old (%)	>30 months old (%)	Df	X^2	P
May be challenging	1 (4.2%)	8 (8.6%)	2	1.15	0.56
Just mastered	9 (37.5%)	41 (44.1%)			
Fully mastered	14 (58.3%)	44 (47.3%)			
In total	24 (100%)	93 (100%)			

6.3.2 Characteristics of Young Children's Emotional Development at Different Ages

6.3.2.1 Characteristics of Children's Social–Emotional Development at Different Ages

The children were divided into two groups according to less than 30 months of age and more than 30 months of age. The sensory processing capabilities of young children in different age groups were cross-tabulated according to their age suitability, as shown in Table 6.8. In the three levels of sensory processing ability classified by age suitability, the proportion of young children in the 30-month-old group was similar to the proportion of young children in the 30-month-old group. The difference test also showed that the age difference was not significant ($P = 0.56 > 0.05$).

Cross-tabulation analysis of the emotional development of young children divided into different age groups is shown in Table 6.9. Young children less than or equal to 30 months old did not reach the level of stage 6; however, 26.0% of children younger than 30 months had reached stage 6; there were also differences in the proportion of children in other stages. The difference test also showed that the emotional development of children older than 30 months was significantly higher than that of children younger than 30 months ($P = 0.05$).

6.3.2.2 Characteristics of Children's Emotion Regulation Strategies in Different Age Stages

An F-test was performed on the emotional regulation strategies of young children in different age groups, as shown in Table 6.10. It can be seen that the frequency of using active activity strategies for children older than 30 months was extremely significantly higher than that of children younger than 30 months ($0.50 > 0.28$, $F = 14.454^{***}$); the frequency of using help-seeking strategies for children older than 30 months of age was significantly less than that of young children with 30 months of age ($0.29 < 0.41$, $F = 4.677^*$); and other strategies in the frequency of use of the two groups of children had no significant difference.

6.3 Analysis of Results

Table 6.9 Cross-tabulation analysis of emotional development of young children with different age stages

The highest stage of emotional development	≤30 months old (%)	>30 months old (%)	Df	X^2	P
Phase 1: Show self-discipline and interest in the world	0 (0)	0 (0)	7	14.00	0.05+
Phase 2: Develop relationships	1 (3.7%)	4 (4.2%)			
Phase 3: Use of emotional emotions in an interactive, purposeful way	2 (7.4%)	8 (8.3%)			
Phase 4a: Use interactive emotional signals or gestures to communicate	9 (33.3%)	17 (17.7%)			
Phase 4b: Use interactive emotional signals or gestures to solve problems	6 (22.2%)	15 (15.6%)			
Phase 5a: Use symbols or concepts to convey intentions or feelings	5 (18.5%)	11 (11.5%)			
Phase 5b: Use symbols or ideas to express the need beyond basic needs	4 (14.8%)	8 (8.3%)			
Phase 6: Build a logical bridge between emotions and concepts	0 (0)	25 (26.0%)			
Not at the above phases	0 (0)	8 (8.3%)			
In total	27 (100%)	96 (100%)			

Table 6.10 Differences in emotion regulation strategies among young children at different ages

	Age group	Average	Standard deviation	Minimum	Maximum	F value
Active activities	≤30 months old	0.29	0.26	0	0.94	14.45***
	>30 months old	0.47	0.26	0	1	
Seeking help	≤30 months old	0.41	0.28	0	1	4.68*

(continued)

Table 6.10 (continued)

	Age group	Average	Standard deviation	Minimum	Maximum	F value
	>30 months old	0.29	0.27	0	1	
Self-comfort	≤30 months old	0.27	0.17	0	0.61	0.01
	>30 months old	0.27	0.21	0	0.78	
Seeking comfort	≤30 months old	0.16	0.15	0	0.5	0.23
	>30 months old	0.17	0.18	0	0.72	
Distraction	≤30 months old	0.44	0.27	0	1	2.33
	>30 months old	0.35	0.28	0	1	
Venting	≤30 months old	0.19	0.18	0	0.83	0.98
	>30 months old	0.15	0.16	0	0.72	

Note $+P < 0.1$, $*P < 0.05$, $**P < 0.01$, $***P < 0.001$

6.3.3 Characteristics of Emotional Development of Children in Different Gender

Cross-tabulation analysis of sensory processing abilities of young children of different genders classified by age suitability is shown in Table 6.11. In three levels of classification of sensory processing capability according to age suitability, there were differences between boys and girls, but the difference test showed no significant difference between genders ($P = 0.58 > 0.05$).

Cross-tabulation analysis of emotional development of young children with different genders is shown in Table 6.12. Difference tests showed no significant difference in emotional development between boys and girls aged 2–3 years ($P = 0.19 > 0.05$).

Table 6.11 Cross-tabulation analysis of children's sensory processing ability in different genders

Classification of sensory processing capability according to age suitability	Boys (%)	Girls (%)	Df	X^2	P
May be challenging	5 (8.9%)	4 (6.6%)	2	1.08	0.58
Just mastered	26 (46.4%)	24 (39.3%)			
Fully mastered	25 (44.6%)	33 (54.1%)			
In total	56 (100%)	61 (100%)			

6.3 Analysis of Results

Table 6.12 Cross-tabulation analysis of emotional development of young children with different genders

The highest stage of emotional development	Boys (%)	Girls (%)	Df	X^2	P
Phase 1: Show self-discipline and interest in the world	0 (0)	0 (0)	7	9.92	0.19
Phase 2: Develop relationships	3 (5.1%)	2 (3.1%)			
Phase 3: Use of emotional emotions in an interactive, purposeful way	4 (6.8%)	6 (9.4%)			
Phase 4a: Use interactive emotional signals or gestures to communicate	10 (16.9%)	6 (9.4%)			
Phase 4b: Use interactive emotional signals or gestures to solve problems	9 (15.3%)	3 (4.7%)			
Phase 5a: Use symbols or concepts to convey intentions or feelings	14 (23.7%)	12 (18.8%)			
Phase 5b: Use symbols or ideas to express the need beyond basic needs	6 (10.2%)	15 (23.4%)			
Phase 6: Build a logical bridge between emotions and concepts	10 (16.9%)	15 (23.4%)			
Not at the above phases	3 (5.1%)	5 (7.8%)			
In total	59 (100%)	64 (100%)			

T-tests showed that there was no significant gender difference in the frequency of emotion recognition, emotional understanding, and emotional regulation strategies used by 2–3 years old.

6.3.4 Correlations Between Emotion Recognition, Emotional Understanding, Emotion Regulation Strategies, and Development of Social Emotions

The relationship between emotional recognition, emotional understanding, emotional regulation strategies, and social–emotional development of 2–3 years old was analyzed, as shown in Table 6.13. There was a significant positive correlation between sensitive naming ability and expressive naming ability ($r = 0.41^{**}$). There was a very significant positive correlation between emotional understanding ability and expressive naming ability ($r = 0.37^{**}$); there was a significant positive correlation between emotional understanding ability and sensibility naming ability ($r = 0.23+$); there was a very significant negative correlation between the frequency of use of active activities strategy and self-conflict strategy frequency ($r = -0.22^{**}$); there was a very significant negative correlation between the use of active activities strategy frequency and the use of distraction strategy frequency ($r = -0.56^{***}$). There was a significant negative correlation between the frequency of using seeking help

Table 6.13 Correlation of emotion recognition, emotion understanding, emotion regulation strategies, and social–emotional development

	Expressive naming	Sensitive naming	Emotional under-standing	Active activities	Seeking help	Self-comfort	Seeking comfort	Distraction	Venting	Social mood develop-ment
Sensitive naming	0.41**									
Emotional understanding	0.37**	0.23+								
Active activities	0.07	−0.04	−0.03							
Seeking help	−0.09	−0.30*	−0.04	−0.11						
Self-comfort	−0.08	0.16	−0.00	−0.22**	−0.17*					
Seeking comfort	0.07	0.02	0.32*	0.02	0.21*	−0.04				
Distraction	−0.10	0.12	−0.04	−0.56***	−0.53***	0.24**	−0.30***			
Venting	0.23	0.03	−0.14	−0.09	0.33***	−0.06	0.09	−0.26**		
Social mood development	0.18	0.03	−0.14	0.09	−0.13	−0.03	−0.11	−0.02	0.02	
Sensory processing capability	0.12	0.10	−0.04	0.13	−0.15	−0.04	0.01	−0.03	−0.09	0.76**

Note +$P < 0.1$, *$P < 0.05$, **$P < 0.01$, ***$P < 0.001$

strategy and sensitive naming ability (r = −0.30*); there was a significant positive correlation between the frequency of seeking help strategies and the frequency of seeking comfort from others (r = 0.21*), and the use of help-seeking strategies; there was an extremely significant negative relationship between frequency and distracting strategy frequency (r = −0.53***); there was a very significant positive correlation between frequency and action venting strategies using seeking help strategies (r = 0.36***). There was a very significant positive correlation between self-consolation strategy frequency and distracting strategy frequency (r = 0.24**). There was an extremely significant negative correlation between the frequency of seeking comfort for others and the frequency of distraction strategies (r = −0.30***). There was a very significant negative correlation between the frequency of the distraction strategy and the frequency of the action vent strategy (r = −0.26**). There was a very significant positive correlation between the level of social–emotional development and sensory processing ability (r = 0.76**).

6.4 Discussion

6.4.1 Overall Analysis of the Emotional Development of Young Children

The results of this study showed that the comprehensive score of social–emotional development level of 2–3 years old concentrated between 80 and 105; when it comes to the processing capability, about half of the children had fully mastered the sensory processing capability, while the vast majority of the other half of the children had just mastered this ability, and only a small proportion of the young children felt it difficult; the highest stage of mastering social emotions was phase 5a–6, followed by phase 3–4b and phase 2.

The scores and distribution of social–emotional development and the social emotions of 2–3 years old were already in development and there were individual differences; differences in the level of development in sensory processing capabilities indicated that approximately 50% of 2–3 years old have had mature or substantially mature sensitivities to color, sound, touch, or action and can perform emotional perception and response based on these cues. It is because 2–3 years old are getting familiar with the rules of social expression and thus have a keen sense and reaction due to brain development, the development of cognitive abilities, and the expansion of social contacts. On the contrary, those who face challenges are lag in acquisition of social expression rules due to individual differences in cognitive development or limited social contact; the result of the highest stage of acquisition of social emotions is related to the cognitive development of 2–3 years old, who, in the preoperational phase, know to use symbols and conceptual representations, but still use direct, interactive ways to express emotions.

The study found that 2–3 years old already have the ability to identify emotions. Among them, the expressive naming ability was relatively low compared to the total score, the sensibility naming ability was relatively higher compared to the total score, and the individual differences were relatively large; children's expressive naming scores were lower than sensibility naming scores; emotional understanding ability was not high, and individual differences were small. This is consistent with the fact that the facial expressions of children and human figures before the age of 3 were not well recognized and named (Widen and Russell 2003). Emotion recognition and understanding development have the foundation of cognitive development. Only when the child's cognitive ability and language knowledge develop to a certain stage can the child accurately identify and name the expression, and accurately judge the task response in a certain situation. Social experience is equally important. For example, Brown and Dunn (1996) found that 6 years old who can better understand emotional conflicts often discuss with parents about the causes of emotions. In the quiz, some parents explained, their children seldom took a bus and could not understand the word "monster". The lower expressive naming scores than the sensible naming scores were related to the development limitations of language vocabulary and linguistic expression ability of 2–3 years old. Vicari et al. (2000) studied the perception of emotional facial expressions among school-aged children and found that there was a clear difference in emotional cognition and other areas of cognition (cognitive fields with high correlation with visual space and semantic vocabulary competence). De Rosnay and Harris (2002) studied the individual differences in emotional understanding of 3–6 years old and found that early attachment had a significant impact on children's emotional understanding. Obviously, there are many factors that affect children's emotional recognition and understanding, and thus more detailed and in-depth research is needed.

Frequency of emotional regulation strategies used by 2–3 years old declines, according to active activities, distractions, seeking help, self-comfort, seeking comfort, and venting. Through clustering analysis, the emotion regulation strategies used by young children in frustration scenarios were divided into three types: active, seeking help, and abstracted. This showed that 2–3-year-old children were more active or distracted in the 3-min experimental context. In the early stage of the experimental situation, young children were attracted by the task and would inevitably focus on the task. However, soon after that, they encountered setbacks. Besides, as it is difficult for 2–3 years old to maintain their attention for a long time, their attention was shifted to others due to diminished attraction, patience, attraction to the surrounding; few children turned to venting, because they live and receive kindergarten education in a caring environment; adults are always in mild mood when they are facing children, and there are less venting examples; more children used strategies of seeking help, self-comfort, and seeking comfort, because 2–3 years old are less capable and participate in activities accompanied by adults in daily life; children of this age haven't developed to be shameful due to failure to fulfill tasks and their attachment with parents make them believe and rely on helps and supports from their parents.

Therefore, as caregivers and educators of young children, parents should fully recognize that the social emotions of 2–3 years old are already in development, and that some young children's social mood has reached a higher stage. Parents shall have full confidence in their young children; parents need to create a safe and rich environment for children so that they can develop their child's sensory processing capabilities. In this way, children can gradually grasp the rules of social expression in social contact, expand their social contact, allow young children to explore in society, and develop children's social experiences. The development of young children's emotional ability and their cognitive development, and language skills should be simultaneously developed; at the same time, we must respect the individual differences in children, and patiently care for the development of each child.

6.4.2 Age and Gender Differences in Emotional Development of Young Children

The emotional development of children older than 30 months was significantly higher than that of children younger than 30 months. There was no significant difference in sensory processing ability among different age groups; there was no significant difference in sensory processing ability and mood development for different genders. The emotional development of young children was significantly higher than that of young children, but it was not related to gender. This indicated that emotional development was closely related to age. High-age children have a higher level of cognitive development, so they can use symbols and concepts to achieve the purpose of emotional and feeling expression, while young children in low age group can't use symbols and concepts to achieve the purpose of emotional and feeling expression. They prefer expressing ideas and intentions through intuitive interactions because of limitations in cognitive development and social experience. There was no significant age and gender difference in sensory processing capabilities, which was more related to the individual's sensitivity to external stimuli.

There was no significant gender difference in the emotional recognition and understanding of children aged 2–3 years. It is not consistent with studies of Liang et al. (2011) who found that girls' emotional recognition ability was significantly better than that of boys. And the study of Yao et al. (2004) who used tests and questionnaires to 3–5 years old and found that the girl's ability to infer other people's emotions was higher than that of boys of the same age. It conforms to the study of Zhan (2005) who used facial expression recognition and storytelling to measure 3–5 years old and found that there was no significant gender difference in children's emotional cognitive abilities. The contradiction of this result may be related to the measurement methods used by different researchers and the difference in the ages of the subjects. There was no significant gender difference in emotional recognition and comprehension of children aged 2–3 years. This may be explained by their correlation with cognitive development. The differentiation and identification of the comic book was adopted in the study. The processing of facial expressions by young children, the correct understanding of the situation, and the migration of life experience are the keys to the correct response of young children; therefore, there is less gender relatedness.

When it comes to emotion regulation, the frequency of using active activity strategies for children older than 30 months was significantly higher than that for children younger than 30 months, and the frequency of using help-seeking strategies was significantly lower than that of children younger than 30 months of age. There was no significant difference between the two groups of children in the use frequency of other strategies; there was no significant gender difference in the frequency of emotional regulation strategies used by 2–3 years old. Older children have a deeper understanding of experimental tasks. They understand the task requirements and follow the tasks, and their attention is more sustained. Meanwhile, children of high age have greater motivation for self-determination and achievement, have higher self-esteem, and therefore show more enthusiasm in the task. They carefully adopt strategies of seeking help from others; to the contrary, children in the young age group cannot understand the task requirements and it is difficult to maintain their attention for a long time. Their motivation for success is not high, and shameful emotions are not completely developed. Therefore, they often show other reactions after a period of activity and seek more help from others. Emotional regulation strategies used have no significant gender differences. It might because that 2–3 years old are less sexualized, and the gender features are still nondistinctive and unstable.

6.4.3 Correlation Analysis of Emotion Recognition, Emotion Understanding, Emotion Regulation Strategies, and Social Mood Development

There was a very significant positive correlation between social–emotional development level and sensory processing ability. Part of the reasons is children who can only further use emotional signals to express based on the perception of sound, color, and motion.

There was a very significant positive correlation between sensitive naming ability and expressive naming ability. There was a very significant positive correlation between emotional understanding ability and expressive naming ability. There was a significant positive correlation between emotional understanding ability and sensitive naming ability. This shows that the expressive naming capacity of young children is based on sensitive naming ability. Only young children can identify basic emotions before they can further name their emotions; emotion understanding is based on the development of emotion recognition, only on the basis of understanding the basic emotional connotation can the young children be able to distinguish the emotions of the characters in different situations.

6.4 Discussion

There was a very significant negative correlation between the frequency of using active activity strategies and the frequency of self-comfort strategies. There was an extremely significant negative correlation between the frequency of using active activity strategies and the frequency of using distracting strategies. The main reason is that positive activities and self-comfort are strategies to solve the problem of orientation, and they are disassociated with distraction. Young children with more activities paid more attention to tasks. They cared about how to open jars and devoted more attention to task resolution. Therefore, they rarely comforted themselves or distracted. To the contrary, children with less activities paid less attention to tasks. As the self-esteem of 2–3 years old has developed, they like to show that they are competent in front of adults, and therefore they will be more self-comforting to protect their self-esteem when they encounter the "open" dilemma. Besides, as the task itself was not attractive to young children, and the children's interest in the task after the frustration of couldn't open cans was reduced, their attention was more likely to be dispersed or transferred, and thus they were more likely to be distracted.

There was a significant negative correlation between the frequency of using seeking help strategy and the naming capability of disability and frequency of distraction strategies ($R = -0.30*$, $R = -0.53***$). There was a significant positive correlation between the frequency of using help-seeking strategies and the frequency of seeking comfort strategies and action vent strategies ($R = 0.21*$, $R = 0.36***$). Reasons are that seeking help, seeking comfort, and venting are all task-solving based. Young children who focused on tasks were more likely to behave like this and were less distracted. However, for young children with higher sensibility, they were more impressed by the experimenter's demand on opening the bottle by themselves, and they had a clearer understanding of facial expressions of the parents at present. Therefore, they were less likely to adopt seeking help strategy.

There was a very significant positive correlation between the frequency of the distraction strategy and the frequency of the self-comfort strategy ($R = 0.24**$). There was a very significant negative correlation between the frequency of distraction strategies and the frequency of seeking comfort strategies and the frequency of action venting strategies ($R = -0.30***$, $R = -0.26**$). This was mainly because young children with more distractions paid less attention to tasks. However, young children needed a reasonable excuse to balance their feelings of guilt and shame because they couldn't fulfill specified requirements, so that young children could be distracted by not paying attention to the tasks. Therefore, children with more distractions would have more self-consolation behavior. Because children with more distractions did not pay much attention to the task, they were less concerned with how to solve difficulties. Therefore, it was naturally less problematic to seek solutions such as seeking comfort and venting. To the contrary, children who more often seek comfort and vent through actions were more problem solving-based and thus less distracting-based.

6.5 Conclusion

In this study, the emotional development of 145 2–3 years old in Beijing was investigated using parent–child-reported social mood questionnaires, emotional recognition and understanding of picture tests, and emotion-suppressing frustration context experiments. The results showed that, for 2–3 years old:

(1) It was normally distributed in social mood development; when it comes to the processing capability, about half of the children had fully mastered the sensory processing capability, while the vast majority of the other half of the children had just mastered this ability, and only a small proportion of the young children felt it difficult; there was no significant difference between groups of different age and gender. The distribution of the highest stage of mastering social emotions was that most children were in phase 5a–6 followed by phase 3–4b and phase 2. The emotional development of children older than 30 months was significantly higher than that of children younger than 30 months. There was no significant difference between genders; there was a very significant positive correlation between social–emotional development and sensory processing capabilities.
(2) Emotion recognition and emotional comprehension had developed, with a low level and no significant difference in genders. Sensitivity naming ability was higher than expressive naming ability, and there was a very significant positive correlation between them; there was a significant positive correlation between emotional understanding ability and emotion recognition ability.
(3) The frequency of emotional regulation strategies decreased according to active activities, distractions, seeking help, self-comfort, seeking comfort, and venting; through clustering analysis, the emotional regulation strategies used in the children's frustration situation experiment were divided into three types: active, seeking help, and abstracted.
(4) In terms of emotional regulation, the frequency of using active activity strategies for children older than 30 months was significantly higher than that of children younger than 30 months, and the frequency of using help-seeking strategies was significantly lower for children younger than 30 months of age. There was no significant difference between the two groups of children in the use frequency of other strategies; there was no significant gender difference in the frequency of emotional regulation strategies used by 2–3 years old.
(5) There was a very significant negative correlation between the frequency of using active activity strategies and the frequency of self-comfort strategies. There was an extremely significant negative correlation between the frequency of using active strategies and the frequency of using distracting strategies; there was a significant negative correlation between the frequency of using seeking help strategies and sensitive naming ability and the frequency of distracting strategies. There was a significant positive correlation between the frequency of seeking help strategies and the frequency of seeking comfort, the strategy of venting; there was a very significant positive correlation between the frequency of the distraction strategy and the frequency of the self-comfort strategy. There was

a very significant negative correlation between the frequency of the distraction strategy and the frequency of seeking comfort for others and the frequency of the action vent strategy.

References

Branson, D., & Demchak, M. (2011). Toddler teachers' use of teaching pyramid practices. *Topics in Early Childhood Special Education, 30*(4), 196–208.
Brown, J. R., & Dunn, J. (1996). Continuities in emotion understanding from three to six years. *Child Development, 67*(3), 789–802.
Day, K. L., & Smith, C. L. (2013). Understanding the role of private speech in children's emotion regulation. *Early Childhood Research Quarterly, 28*(2), 405–414.
Denham, S. A. (1986). Social cognition, prosocial behavior, and emotion in preschoolers: Contextual validation. *Child Development, 57*(1), 194–201.
Denham, S. A., Blair, K. A., DeMulder, E., Levitas, J., Sawyer, K., Auerbach-Major, S., et al. (2003). Preschool emotional competence: Pathway to social competence. *Child Development, 74*(1), 238–256.
De Rosnay, M., & Harris, P. L. (2002). Individual differences in children's understanding of emotion: The roles of attachment and language. *Attachment & Human Development, 4*(1), 39–54.
Funder, D. C., Block, J. H., & Block, J. (1983). Delay of gratification: Some longitudinal personality correlates. *Journal of Personality and Social Psychology, 44*(6), 1198–1213.
Hua, Z. (2015). The pyramid model and its implications for preschool teachers' social emotional education. *Course Education Research, 3*, 18–19.
Izard, C. E. (1980). The young infant's ability to produce discrete emotions expressions. *Developmental Psychology, 16*(2), 132–140.
Ji, L. (2013). The influence of social emotional ability on children's life. Interview with Wei Yu—The prime minster of education. *Shanghai Education, 10*, 26–27.
Kogan, N. P. (1997). *Attachment and emotion regulation in mothers and infants*. Doctoral dissertation. Yale University, New Haven, US.
Liang, Z., Zhang, G., Chen, H., & Zhang, P. (2011). Preschooler' s emotion understanding development and its relation with parental meta-emotion philosophy. *Psychological Development and Education, 27*(3), 233–240.
Ministry of Education. (2001). Outline for kindergarten education guidance (Trial). *Education of Shandong, 30*, 4–7.
Pons, F., & Harris, P. L. (2000). *Test of emotion comprehension-TEC*. Doctoral dissertation. Oxford University, Oxford, UK.
Pons, F., Harris, P. L., & de Rosnay, M. (2004). Emotion comprehension between 3 and 11 years: Developmental periods and hierarchical organization. *European Journal of Developmental Psychology, 1*(2), 127–152.
Pons, F., Lawson, J., Harris, P. L., & de Rosnay, M. (2003). Individual differences in children's emotion understanding: Effects of age and language. *Scandinavian Journal of Psychology, 44*, 347–353.
Qian, X. (2014). *Event of 14-year-old boy kills 1 year old and half-sister warns second child's parents*. [OE/BL]. http://www.rmzxb.com.cn/yl/rp/2014/08/13/362579.shtml.
Saarni, C. (1984). An observational study of children's attempts to monitor their expressive behavior. *Child Development, 55*(4), 1504–1513.
Saarni, C. (1999). *The development of emotional competence*. New York, NY: Guilford Press.
Tang, Z., & Xue, X. (2015). A review of studies on children's social emotional ability. *Course Education Research, 21*, 15–16.

Tian, H., Yang, Y., & Li, J. (2009). A review of researches on children's emotional and social ability. *The Science Education Article Collects, 14,* 76–77.

Vicari, S., Reilly, J. S., Pasqualetti, P., Vizzotto, A., & Caltagirone, C. (2000). Recognition of facial expressions of emotions in school-age children: the intersection of perceptual and semantic categories. *Acta Paediatrica, 89*(7), 836–845.

Wang, J., & Chen, H. (1998). Emotion regulation strategies of 2 years old in stressful conditions. *Acta Psychologica Sinica, 30*(3), 289–297.

Wang, X. (2010). Research on the development of children's emotional comprehension ability. *Educational Study, 1,* 10–12.

Wei, Y. (2015). *Reading Notes on Brain and Education (9)—Learning Standards for Training Students' Social Emotional Ability.* [EV/OL]. http://blog.ci123.com/weiyu/entry/10054.

Widen, S. C., & Russell, J. A. (2003). A closer look at preschoolers' freely produced labels for facial expressions. *Developmental Psychology, 39*(1), 114–128.

Yao, D., Chen, Y., & Qiao, Y. (2004). The study on the age characteristics, development trend and gender difference of emotional ability in children aged 3 to 5 years old. *Psychological Development and Education, 20*(2), 12–16.

Zhan, N. (2005). Research on the developmental characteristics of children's emotional cognitive ability. *Studies in Early Childhood Education, 7,* 46–48.

Zhao, J., Shen, J., & Zhang, W. (2006). Relationship among children's emotion understanding, prosocial behavior and peer-acceptance. *Psychology Development and Education, 22*(1), 1–6.

Zhuo, M. (2008). *Study on emotion understanding development of 2–9 years old.* Doctoral dissertation. Zhejiang University, Hangzho.

Part II
Family Environment and Infants and Toddlers' Development

Chapter 7
Relationship Between Grandparent–Parent Co-parenting, Infant Temperament, and Emotional Adjustment

7.1 Introduction

Family, which is the most direct micro-environment for infant development, plays an irreplaceable role in infant emotional development. In October 2015, China's Ministry of Education printed *Guiding Opinions of the Ministry of Education on Strengthening Family Education*, guiding local governments to actively play the important role of family education in the growth process of children. The *Guiding Opinions* addressed that "family is the basic cell of society, and family education concerns the lifelong development of children, the very interests of all families and the future of the country and nation." Meanwhile, it further clarifies the entity responsibility of parents in the family education and suggested them to systematically improve the scientific ideas and methods of family education, try to grasp the law of family education, teaching children according to their natural ability, respect children's reasonable needs and personality, and create necessary conditions and life situations suitable for children's growth. The printing of *Guiding Opinions* shows the Chinese government began to attach great importance to the important role of family education in the process of individual growth. For infants aged 2–3, family is the most important environment for their growth and development, and grandparent—parent co-parenting, which forms the general background of family education is an important component of family system.

Not until the full implementation of two-child policy in 2015, the one-child policy, implemented in China since the 1980s has led to the significant change of Chinese family intergenerational hierarchy and the formation of the 4–2–1 family structure model (4 grandparents, 2 parents, and 1 child) (Zhan 2004). The reality of having only one child makes family members pay more attention to the responsibilities of infant care and education. In addition, with the development of era, the traditional intra-household labor division of "men's work centers around outside, women's work centers around the home" has quietly changed. A growing number of women have joined the labor market, and two-career families have become more and more common. In the face of the double pressure from work and life, parents need other people, such as grandparents or domestic helpers, to participate in caring for the children. On the other hand, because of the adequate retirement time and the emphasis on the traditional family ethics, grandparents tend to regard caring for grandchildren as a self-conscious responsibility and an increasing number of them get involved in the grandchildren care (Xing et al. 2015). A survey shows that approximately 60% grandparents in Chinese families get involved in the raising and caring for young children, which indicates that grandparent–parent co-parenting is a common parenting mode in China (Pei 2005).

The concept of grandparent–parent co-parenting was developed based on the concept of co-parenting. Van and Hawkins (2004) believed that co-parenting relationship involves two or more caregivers who jointly look after a child. When a child is co-parented, any behaviors and ideas that may improve or damage the parenting results of another caregivers falls into the category of co-parenting (Van and Hawkins 2004). According to Van et al. the definition of grandparent–parent co-parenting in this study is that in an original family or a family with a newborn baby, the parents transfer part of the parenting responsibility to the grandparents, and the grandparents share the parenting responsibility with the parents.

As grandparents' involvement in infant rearing becomes increasingly common, researchers began to pay attention to the influence of such parenting mode on children's emotional adjustment. Emotional adjustment mainly refers to a series of processes of which children trigger, maintain and adjust emotional responses (including positive and negative responses) (Grolnick et al. 2010). Barnett et al. (2012) studied the grandmother–mother co-parenting in 85 American families with low socioeconomic status and found that the more language conflicts there are between grandmothers and mothers, the more emotional adjustment problems children have at the age of 3 (Barnett et al. 2012). However, some researchers have found that grandparents' involvement in infant rearing has no negative effect on children's emotional adjustment. According to the study of Solomon and Marx (1995), except academic performance, children brought up by their grandparents are very similar to those brought up by their parents (Solomon and Marx 1995). Both of the two types of children are less likely to have emotional adjustment problems than children from single-parent families. According to the study of Jones and Hansen (1996), in such disadvantaged families, such as single-parent family and low-income families, the existence of grandparents has a positive meaning for the development of infant emotions and self-esteem. The above researches indicate that whether the influence of grandparents' involvement in infant rearing on their emotional adjustment is negative or positive has not been decided in the academic circle.

With the in-depth research, researchers further explored the internal mechanism of co-parenting influencing infant emotional adjustment, believing that infants' individual characteristics regulating the influence of grandparent–parent co-parenting on infant emotional adjustment. This idea is supported by the co-parenting ecological

7.1 Introduction

model (Feinberg 2003). This theory points out that co-parenting not only indirectly affect the infants' adjustment through the parents' adjustment and parents' parenting mode, but also directly affect the infants' adjustment. In addition, the infants' characteristics (such as temperament) can also exert a direct impact on the infants' adjustment, which reminds researchers that infant temperament may play a role in regulating grandparent–parent co-parenting and emotional adjustment. Temperament is the steady difference between individuals in terms of reactivity and self-regulation based on the physiological basis (Rothbart 1981). In fact, the possible regulating effect of infant temperament on grandparent–parent co-parenting and infant emotional adjustment is, to some extent, supported by some researches. According to the research of Lengua et al. (2000), in the negative parenting environment, children with higher impulsivity are more likely to have adjustment problems, while positive emotions can reduce the possibility of children having adjustment problems. At the same time, Eisenberg et al. (2005) believed effortful control, as a part of temperament, is closely related to the infants' emotional control and expression and behavior responses (Eisenberg et al. 2010). At present, there are few researches discussing the mechanism of infant temperament in the influence of grandparent–parent co-parenting on the infant emotional adjustment.

To sum up, the existing researches have the following characteristics. Firstly, The difference of the research background of grandparent–parent co-parenting between China and foreign countries is enormous, so that the research conclusions of foreign countries may not be applicable to the situation in China. In foreign studies, the families in which grandparents are involved in children rearing are usually special families. For example, the parents are divorced or unable or unwilling to assume the childrearing obligation due to imprisonment or drug abuse. But in China, grandparents' involvement in childrearing is common in normal families. Different family backgrounds may also induce the different research results. Second, grandparent—parent co-parenting is a common parenting mode in China. Children younger than 3 years old are mainly looked after by grandparents and parents because they haven't attended kindergartens. The family environment formed by parental grandparent–parent co-parenting mode has a greater impact on their development in various aspects. At present, the domestic researches on grandparent–parent co-parenting mainly focus on literature review and status quo, and there is a shortage of researches on the influence of grandparent–parent co-parenting on the development of children aged 2–3. Third, there is no clear conclusion on whether the influence of grandparent–parent co-parenting on children's emotional adjustment is positive or negative in the academic circle. Based on that, this study will, with the co-parenting ecological model as the theoretical basis, investigate the influence of grandparent–parent co-parenting on infant emotional adjustment, and explore the mechanism of infant temperament in it.

7.2 Methods

7.2.1 Participants

A total of 145 infants and their parents participated in the study, including 17 parents without grandparents' involvement in their children's parenting; 14 parents said others (such as nannies, other relatives) other than grandparents took care of their children, and the remaining 114 children (78.6%)were co-parented by their grandparents and parents, including 57 boys and 57 girls with a mean month age of 33.23 (SD = 3.48). The father or mother of the infants completed the questionnaire. The age of mothers ranges from 20 to 44 with an average age of 32.29 (SD = 3.67). The age of fathers ranges from 25 to 46 with an average age of 34.08 (SD = 4.65). The age of grandparents ranges from 44 to 73 with an average age of 58.85 (SD = 4.95).

7.2.2 Measures

7.2.2.1 The Family Experiences Questionnaire (FEQ)

The Family Experiences Questionnaire (FEQ) adapted by Van and Hawkins (2004) was used to measure grandparent–parent co-parenting in present study. There were 29 items in the original scale, which were divided into four dimensions: co-parenting solidarity, co-parenting support, co-parenting impairment and sharing parenting responsibility. It should be pointed out that the expressions of items were carefully checked and the inappropriate expressions were modified or removed from the beginning, because the original FEQ was used to measure co-parenting between fathers and mothers. The revised FEQ contains 24 items in 4 dimensions: co-parenting solidarity, co-parenting support, co-parenting impairment, and sharing parenting responsibility. The dimension of co-parenting solidarity contains 7 items including "Co-parenting deepens my emotion with the elders; the dimension of co-parenting support contains 5 items, including "When there is nothing I can do to parent my child, the elders can always give me support and help"; the dimension of co-parenting impairment contains 6 items, including "The elders don't believe in my ability as a parent"; the dimension of sharing parenting responsibility contains 6 items, including "To rear the child, the elders are willing to make personal sacrifices." The scale was completed by children's father or mother and the items were rated on 7-point Likert types scale to indicate the status of grandparent–parent co-parenting, with higher scores reflecting more harmonious the grandparent–parent co-parenting relationship. *Cronbach's* α of each dimension in this measure ranges from 0.71 to 0.86.

7.2 Methods

7.2.2.2 Early Childhood Behavior Questionnaire (ECBQ)

Considering that there are too many items in the original scale of Early Childhood Behavior Questionnaire (ECBQ), this study employed the shortened version of ECBQ to measure the infant temperament (Putnam et al. 2006), which is suitable for toddlers aged 18–36 months. The shortened ECBQ contains 36 items, which are divided into 3 dimensions: negative emotion, extroversion, and effortful control. The dimension of negative emotion contains 12 items, including "When a strange gets close to your child in public places (such as shop), how much is your child clingy to the parents?"; the dimension of extroversion contains 12 items including "When there is an opportunity to choose one from several activities, how quickly can your child make a decision and do it?"; the dimension of effortful control contains 12 items including "When you say no to your child, to what extent your child will not do what is not allowed?" The scale was completed by child's father or mother and the items were rated on 7-point Likert types scale, to indicate the frequency of infant's behaviors, with higher scores reflecting more frequently the infant acted like this in the past two weeks. *Cronbach's α* of each dimension in this study ranges from 0.71 to 0.78.

7.2.2.3 Bayley Scales of Infant Development (3rd Edition) (Social–Emotional Scale)

This questionnaire is the same as the one in Chap. 6, so it is not described here.

7.2.2.4 Emotion Regulation Experiment

The experimental method is the same as the one in Chap. 6, so it is not described here.

Factor analysis was used in this study to calculate the composite score of infant emotional regulation strategies. An exploratory factor analysis was carried out on being active in the activities, asking for help, self-comforting, seeking comfort from others, distraction and venting through actions to get the composite score of infant emotional regulation strategies. After a common factor was extracted according to the standard that eigenvalue is larger than 1, 2 factors could be obtained, whose accumulating contribution rate is 57.0%. After the orthogonal rotation, the item load ranges from 0.46 to 0.90 (see Table 7.1). Finally, the following formula was obtained:

Emotional regulation strategies = (asking for help * 0.83 + venting through actions * 0.70 + seeking comfort from others * 0.46 − being active in the activities * 0.90 + distraction * 0.75 + self-comforting * 0.52)/0.57.

Table 7.1 Factor analysis of infant emotional regulation strategies

Element	Factor 1	Factor 2
Asking for help	0.83	
Venting through actions	0.70	
Seeking comfort from others	0.46	
Being active in the activities		−0.90
Distraction		0.75
Self-comforting		0.52

$*p < 0.05, **p < 0.01, ***p < 0.001$

7.3 Relationship Among Grandparent–Parent Co-parenting and Infant Temperament and Emotional Adjustment

7.3.1 Correlations Among the Study Variables

Correlation analysis showed that the correlation among most of variables reached a significant level, as shown in Table 7.2. First, except the correlation between co-parenting impairment and co-parenting solidarity, and the correlation between co-parenting impairment and co-parenting support, the association among other dimensions of grandparent–parent co-parenting were significant. It shows that The Family Experiences Questionnaire has good psychometric indexes. Second, in the correlation analysis of grandparent–parent co-parenting and infant emotional adjustment, co-parenting impairment was negatively associated with social emotions and positively correlated with emotional adjustment strategy. In the analysis of the correlation between infant temperament and emotional adjustment, the infants' social emotions were negatively associated negative emotion, and positively correlated with extroversion and effortful control; and the emotional regulation strategies was positively associated negative emotion and negatively correlated with effortful control.

7.3.2 Multiple Regression Analyses

A series of hierarchical regressions evaluated the contribution of grandparent–parent co-parenting and infant temperament to the predication of infants' social emotions. The first set of regressions included sex and age as proximal control variables; The centralized scores of negative emotion, extroversion, effortful control and grandparent–parent co-parenting were included on the second step and the interaction term of centralized score of negative emotion and that of grandparent–parent co-parenting, the interaction term of centralized score of extroversion and that of grandparent–parent co-parenting, and the interaction term of centralized score of effortful control and

7.3 Relationship Among Grandparent–Parent …

Table 7.2 Correlations among grandparent-parent co-parenting and infant temperament and emotional adjustment

	1	2	3	4	5	6	7	8
1. Co-parenting support	0.68***							
2. Co-parenting impairment	−0.14	−0.05						
3. Sharing parenting responsibility	0.42***	0.27**	−0.38***					
4. Negative emotion	−0.12	−0.05	0.39***	−0.02				
5. Extroversion	0.18*	0.1	−0.24*	0.16	0.05			
6. Effortful control	0.15	0.19*	−0.27**	0.27**	−0.30**	0.29**		
7. Social emotions	0.12	0.16	−0.35**	0.1	−0.24*	0.49***	0.49***	
8. Emotional regulation strategies	0.04	−0.13	0.23*	−0.01	0.19*	−0.06	−0.18*	−0.13

*$p < 0.05$, **$p < 0.01$, ***$p < 0.001$

that of grandparent–parent co-parenting were included in the third step. The regression analysis results are shown in Table 7.3. After the effect of the variables on Level 1 was controlled, negative emotion and extroversion had a significant predictive effect on infants' social emotions, while effortful control and grandfather–parent co-parenting had no significant predictive effect; the interaction between effortful control and grandparent–parent co-parenting could significantly predict the infants' social emotions. In other words, effortful control of infants can regulate the influence of grandparent–parent co-parenting on infants' social emotions.

Simple slope test was employed to further analyze the regulating effect of infants' effortful control on the relationship between grandparent–parent co-parenting and infants' social emotions. The method of adding a standard deviation to or subtracting a standard deviation from the mean was used to classify the infants' effortful control into two groups: high-score group and low-score group; and the influences of grandparent–parent co-parenting of the two groups on the social emotions were surveyed respectively. The result showed that the grandparent–parent co-parenting had a significant positive predictive effect on infants' social emotions in the low-score group, with $\beta = 0.71, t = 2.24, p < 0.05$, while the grandparent–parent co-parenting in the high-score group didn't have a significant predictive effect on infants' social emotions, with $\beta = 0.39, t = 1.45, p > 0.05$ (Fig. 7.1).

After the effect of the variables on Level 1 was controlled, negative emotion, extroversion and effortful control of infants didn't have a significant predictive effect on infants' emotional regulation strategies, while the interactions between effortful control and grandfather-parent co-parenting had no significant predictive effect; and none of the significant interaction effects between negative emotion, extroversion, effortful control and grandparent–parent co-parenting were found.

7.4 Discussions

7.4.1 Relationship Between Grandparent–Parent Co-parenting and Infant Emotional Adjustment

This study shows a significant negative correlation between the co-parenting impairment and the development level of infants' social emotions. In other words, the higher degree of criticism parents receive from grandparents for raising children, the lower level of social emotions the infants has, which is basically consistent with the results of previous researches and also conforms to our practical experience (Barnett et al. 2012). For infants aged 2–3, family is the main environment for their growth and the main place for their early emotional development. According to the family system theory, in the whole family system, the involvement of other caregivers except mother (such as father, grandparents, members of the extended family or nonfamily members) can extent the mother–child relationship to a tripartite relationship, and only when three parties establish a good and stable relationships and the family

7.4 Discussions

Table 7.3 Regulating effect of infant temperament on the influence of grandparent-parent co-parenting on infant emotional adjustment

		Variables entered the equation	R	R^2	ΔR^2	F	β	T
Social emotions	Level 1 (Enter)		0.13	0.02	−0.02	0.46		
		Month					−0.05	−0.42
		Sex					−0.13	−1.16
	Level 2 (Enter)		0.64	0.41	0.34	5.98***		
		Centralized score of negative emotion					−0.28	−2.20*
		Centralized score of extroversion					0.57	4.05***
		Centralized score of effortful control					−0.03	−0.19
		Centralized score of total score of co-parenting					0.12	1.03
	Level 3 (Enter)		0.69	0.47	0.38	4.88***		
		Total score of co-parenting * negative emotion					0.17	1.37
		Total score of co-parenting * extroversion					−0.12	−0.81
		Total score of co-parenting * effortful control					0.35	2.20*

(continued)

Table 7.3 (continued)

		Variables entered the equation	R	R^2	ΔR^2	F	β	T
Emotional regulation strategies	Level 1 (Enter)		0.32	0.10	0.08	4.08*		
		Month					−0.20	−1.69*
		Sex					0.10	0.89
	Level 2 (Enter)		0.37	0.14	0.06	1.82		
		Centralized score of negative emotion					0.09	0.65
		Centralized score of extroversion					0.08	0.59
		Centralized score of effortful control					−0.16	−1.09
		Centralized score of total score of co-parenting					−0.12	−0.92
	Level 3 (Enter)		0.40	0.16	0.05	1.42		
		Total score of co-parenting * negative emotion					0.01	0.10
		Total score of co-parenting * extroversion					−0.16	−1.15
		Total score of co-parenting * effortful control					0.19	1.28

*$p < 0.05$, **$p < 0.01$, ***$p < 0.001$

7.4 Discussions

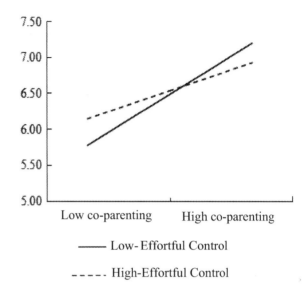

Fig. 7.1 Regulating effect of infant temperament on the relationship between grandparent–parent co-parenting on infant emotional adjustment

system is in a state of balance, can the infant development be promoted effectively (Minuchin 1985). Due to the different parenting concepts and practices, differences are inevitably existed in the process of raising children between grandparents and parents. In the case of the parenting concepts or practices between grandparents and parents are inconsistent, if grandparents always stick to their own ideas, especially when grandparents blindly blame the parents for their mistakes when taking care of the child, become angry and even doubt their parenting ability, the co-parenting relationship will become strained, which will affect the overall emotional atmosphere of the family and is not conducive to the healthy development of infants' social emotions.

This study also found that there was a significant positive correlation between grandparent–parent co-parenting impairment and infant emotional regulation strategies. According to the item loads of six emotional regulation strategies obtained from the factor analysis result and the calculation formula of emotional regulation strategies of infants determined based on that, the infants who have the higher score of emotional regulation strategies are less active in the activities and ask for help, distract, and vent through actions more frequently. The existing researches show that the venting strategy and alternative activities of infants parented by grandparents are significantly higher than those parented by parents, which shows that the grandparents may be more indulgent with children and tend to allow the children to vent their negative emotions through actions or shift their attention when encountering unpleasant things, but paying no attention to the cultivation of children's habits and attentiveness (Zhao 2012). However, the parents may be stricter with their children by requiring them to control their temper and pay more attention to cultivating their attentiveness and perseverance. In the families with a high co-parenting impairment level, the grandparents may be stubborn and even scold parents for different parenting ideas. Moreover, they seldom solve the conflicts in the way of consultation and communication. As a result, the infants' emotional regulation strategies cannot be improved. In addition, some researchers point out that the interpersonal interaction between caregivers and infants is an important reason for the formation of individual differences in emotional regulation. And it is the caregivers who provide the development structures and frameworks for the infants' emotional regulation ability (Denham 1998). Grandparents' emotional responses, solutions, and perspectives in dealing with things may provide children with the cognitive reference of emotional regulation strategies.

7.4.2 Regulating Effect of Infant Temperament on the Relationship Between Grandparent–Parent Co-parenting on Infant Emotional Adjustment

Based on the co-parenting ecological model, this study investigated the regulating effect of infant temperament on the relationship between the grandparent–parent co-parenting and infant emotional adjustment. According to the regression equation model, infants' effortful control can regulate the influence of grandparent–parent co-parenting on infants' social emotions. In the further simple slope test, it was discovered that when the score of infants' effortful control is low, grandparent–parent co-parenting has a significant positive predictive effect on infants' social emotions; when the score of infants' effortful control is high, grandparent–parent co-parenting doesn't have a significant positive predictive effect on infants' social emotions. This result provides empirical evidence for the co-parenting ecological model. The low effortful control level of infants means that the infants have a poor ability to actively suppress their advantages or instinctive behavior, but launch and maintain disadvantaged reactions or behavior. When the co-parenting solidarity between grandparents and parents in a family is strong and they could support each other and share the parenting responsibility, and thus construct a good co-parenting relationship, the low effortful control of infant may make the grandparents and parents unite closely, form a "united front", strive to help the infant to suppress the infant's instinctive impulse and teach the infant to learn to control their emotions and behavior together, which will then promote the development of infant's social emotions. When the infants' effortful control level is high, the grandparents and parent may pay less attention to the development of the infant's ability to suppress the impulse and regulate their emotions in the parenting process, and won't take extra measures to promote the infant's emotional development, which contributes to the study result that grandparent–parent co-parenting doesn't have a significant predictive effect on the infants' social emotions.

7.4.3 Implications

First, grandparents and parents should respect each other's parenting concepts and methods to create a harmonious family atmosphere in the co-parenting process. In three-generation families, due to differences between the grandparents and parents in the growth environment, education level, ideology, and personality, they may have difference in education concept, education mode, and requirements on children's living habits. When the conflicts and disagreements happen on the parenting issues, grandparents and parents should avoid conflicts in front of children. For example, when parents make mistakes due to their lack of parenting experience, instead of scolding them blindly, grandparents should try to help them to parent children better. On the contrary, when the grandparents spoil the infants too much or are indulgent with the infant, the parents should remind the grandparents when their child is not present. If grandparents and parents can regularly analyze and discuss children's growth and make an agreement on educational concepts and behaviors, a warm and harmonious growth environment will be created for children.

Second, we should take a rational view of grandparent–parent co-parenting, and avoid exaggerating the disadvantages of grandparents' involvement in infant parenting. In this study, it was found that for infants with low effortful control level, positive grandparent–parent co-parenting relationship could effectively promote the development of infants' social emotions. When infant's problems such as low-level effortful control were found, the grandparents and fathers should unite and support each other, and work hard together to help the infant learn to suppress impulses and regulate emotions, which is conducive to the formation of a good family environment and can support the healthy development of infants' social emotions.

Third, the community should pay attention to carrying out education guidance for the grandparent–parent co-parenting families. The community can help the grandparents improve their parenting concepts, solve the practical difficulties and problems for parents in the co-parenting process, help the parents to analyze the reasons for the problems and guide the parents' parenting practice by offering family education guidance lectures, consulting, and other forms of activities, so as to form a positive grandparent–parent co-parenting relationship and promote the healthy and happy growth of infants. For example, Australia and Hong Kong have designed and carried out GTP (Grandparents Triple P) for grandparents involved in co-parenting based on Triple P program (Triple P—Positive Parenting Program). GTP is specially designed to take advantage of the users' information input to meet the needs of grandparents involved in children rearing. The content and process of the program is communicated to users by means of the grandparents from focus groups regularly providing the main problems of the infants they look after, which include that grandparents want to obtain information about effective parenting strategies, strategies for improving communication with children's parents, and strategies for dealing with stress, guilt, and depression. Therefore, the content of GTP program includes these three priority areas determined by grandparents: (1) positive parenting strategies; (2) establishing a positive parenting team with the parents; and (3) the strategies of dealing with helplessness. In addition, the GTP program delivers the content grandparents report to complete in a team environment. According to the results of grandparents' groups participating in the GTP intervention program, compared with the control group (the grandparents who did not participate in the GTP intervention program), the grandparents who participated in the GTP program reported an obvious improvement in the children behavioral problems, parenting effectiveness, grandparents' depression, anxiety and pressure in a short term, and they also improved the relationship with the parents. In addition, although the parents were not involved in the program, they also reported a significant reduction in children behavioral problems. The study also showed that these short-term effects remained for the next 6 months (Kirby and Sanders 2014). Therefore, an intervention program similar to GTP is necessary for grandparent–parent co-parenting families in China.

7.5 Conclusions

1. Grandparent–parent co-parenting impairment has a significant negative correlation with infants' social emotions, and a significant positive correlation with their emotional regulation strategies.
2. Effortful control of infants can regulate the influence of grandparent–parent co-parenting on infants' social emotions. For infants with low effortful control level, grandparent–parent co-parenting can significantly positively predict the infants' social emotions. For infants with high effortful control level, grandparent–parent co-parenting has no significant effect on their social emotions.
3. Infant temperament has no significant regulating effect on the relationship between grandparent–parent co-parenting and infants' emotional regulation strategies.

References

Barnett, M. A., Mills-Koonce, W., Gustafsson, H., & Cox, M. (2012). Mother-grandmother conflict, negative parenting, and young children's social development in multigenerational families. *Family Relations, 61*(5), 864–877.
Denham, S. A. (1998). *Emotional development in young children*. Guilford Press.
Eisenberg, Nancy, Zhou, Qing, Spinrad, Tracy L., Valiente, Carlos, Fabes, Richard A., & Liew, Jeffrey. (2010). Relations among positive parenting, children's effortful control, and externalizing problems: a three-wave longitudinal study. *Child Development, 76*(5), 1055–1071.
Feinberg, M. E. (2003). The internal structure and ecological context of coparenting: a framework for research and intervention. *Parenting, 3*(2), 95–131.
Grolnick, W. S., Bridges, L. J., & Connell, J. P. (2010). Emotion regulation in two-year-olds: strategies and emotional expression in four contexts. *Child Development, 67*(3), 928–941.
Jones, M. R., & Hansen, C. (1996). Caregiving behaviors which predict adjustment of children raised by grandparents. *Adoption*, 12.

References

Kirby, J. N., & Sanders, M. R. (2014). The acceptability of parenting strategies for grandparents providing care to their grandchildren. *Prevention Science, 15*(5), 777–787.

Lengua, L. J., Wolchik, S. A., Sandler, I. N., & West, S. G. (2000). The additive and interactive effects of parenting and temperament in predicting adjustment problems of children of divorce. *Journal of Clinical Child Psychology, 29*(2), 232–244.

Minuchin, P. (1985). Families and individual development: provocations from the field of family therapy. *Child Development, 56*(2), 289–302.

Pei, L. Y. (2005). *Characteristics of grandparenting and its influence on infant development.* (Doctoral dissertation, Shandong Normal University).

Putnam, S. P., Gartstein, M. A., & Rothbart, M. K. (2006). Measurement of fine-grained aspects of toddler temperament: the early childhood behavior questionnaire. *Infant Behavior & Development, 29*(3), 386–401.

Rothbart, M. K. (1981). Measurement of temperament in infancy. *Child Development, 52*(2), 569–578.

Solomon, J. C., & Marx, J. (1995). "to grandmother's house we go": Health and school adjustment of children raised solely by grandparents. *Gerontologist, 35*(3), 386–394.

Van Egeren, L. A., & Hawkins, D. P. (2004). Coming to terms with coparenting: implications of definition and measurement. *Journal of Adult Development, 11*(3), 165–178.

Xing, S. F., Wang, Z. Y., University, C. N., & Psychology, D. O. (2015). Multiple attachment relationships and their effects on children's development against the background of multiple caregiving. *Journal of Capital Normal University*.

Zhan, H. J. (2004). Socialization or social structure: investigating predictors of attitudes toward filial responsibility among chinese urban youth from one- and multiple-child families. *International Journal of Aging and Human Development, 59*(2), 105.

Zhao, Z. (2012). The study on the differences between urban and rural grandparenting preschoolers' emotion regulation strategy development. *Psychological Research*.

Chapter 8
The Influence of Home Literacy Environment on Print Awareness of Children Aged 2–4 in Urban China

8.1 Introduction

Studies have shown that young children have developed literacy abilities in their daily lives before they accept formally literacy instructions. Eight-month-old babies can take books, turn pages, say something about books, and pretend to read books. As the environmental print in the urban environment increases, children are surrounded by environmental print on daily life. For example, when a young child sees an arch like the letter M, he thinks this arch is McDonald's (Pullen and Justice 2003). Print awareness is one of the most important predictors of children's reading ability development (Lomax and McGee 1987). Studies have shown that the print awareness in early childhood is an important prerequisite for the development of letter–sound relationship and has a close relationship with early literacy and the development of reading ability in later schools (Evans and Saint-Aubin 2010).

The home literacy environment is an important factor affecting early childhood literacy. Melhuish et al.'s (2010) research shows that the home learning environment makes an important contribution to children's preschool learning experience, and this impact is sustained. Durkin (1966) had studied some first-grade children who from the common view of maturation, were too young mentally and physically to read were readers upon entrance to school, these children had similar home experiences, they were read to extensively by their parents. Durkin (1966) and Teale (1986) implies that the literacy development of children begins before formal schooling, and is affected by the quantity and quality of the home literacy environment. Parents, teachers, and the surrounding environment play an important role in the development of early childhood literacy (Li and Dong 2004).

However, the existing researches on the home literacy environment and children's print awareness are mostly of children and families in English background. Due to the differences in linguistic features and cultural values, children's early language learning preparations vary in different language backgrounds. English is a phonetic script, and phonological awareness is the most important predictor of children's literacy development (Pullen and Justice 2003). Chinese script is represented by Chinese characters and each character is a square-shaped configuration with condensed strokes (Lily et al. 2008). Chinese characters have strong graphic, visual, and integral characteristics, the appearance of a Chinese character expresses meaning (Chen and Tang 1998). Chinese learning emphasizes the importance of visual ability rather than the ability to speak, which is the key difference between learning Chinese characters and English script. However, there has been relatively little research on the relationship between children's home literacy environment and the development of children's print awareness under the cultural context of China.

The purpose of this study is threefold:

(1) To determine the basic conditions and characteristics of the development of the 2–4-year-old children's print awareness.
(2) To determine the status and characteristics of the 2–4-year-old children's home literacy environment.
(3) To determine the factors of home literacy environment that influence the development of children's print awareness.

8.2 Literature Review

8.2.1 Definition and Measurement of Print Awareness

Upon the analysis of the existing research, it was found that there are two main ways to define print awareness: 1. Define directly. For example, print awareness refers to children's ability to recognize the form and function of written language and to understand the relationship between spoken and written language (Mason 1980; Hiebert 1981; Goodman 1986; Justice and Ezell 2001). Justice and Ezell (2001) pointed out that the print awareness refers to the children's ability to interact with the written language and to think about the written language, to understand the form and function of the printed text. Some researchers suggest print awareness refer to children's knowledge about print and book reading conventions such as print directionality and the sequencing of book elements including cover, title page, and so on (Chaney 1992; Hiebert 1981, Mason 1980). 2. Define the components of print awareness. For example, Justice and Ezell (2004) believes that print awareness includes five aspects: (1) print is an object that can draw children's attention; (2) print carry meaning; (3) print is organized in a special way; (4) Print units can be distinguished and named; (5) print units can be combined to form other print units. Evans and Saint-Aubin (2005) believes that print awareness includes an understanding of the book reading conventions (e.g., knowing to read from left to right, that a book has cover title page and so on), understanding words as discrete units following orthographic conventions, knowledge of alphabet (e.g., ability to differentiate letters from numbers), and knowledge of metaliterary terms.

Based on existing research, the definition of print awareness of Chinese script can be given from five aspects: (1) attention to the print: attention to the environmental print, focus on print appeared in storybook, and so on; (2) the function of print: understanding symbols and Chinese characters can express a certain meaning, knowing that the print has a function of record, can record spoken language; understanding the correspondence between written and spoken language; (3) the form of print: the ability to distinguish between pictures and Chinese characters, knowing that there is space between Chinese characters; (4) the convention of print: knowing print follows orthographic conventions, understanding strokes are basic elements of component of Chinese characters, and components are combined to make Chinese characters according to a certain way and can guess the meaning of Chinese characters based on components and other cues. Knowledge about of reading convention of print, such as print is read from left to right and top to bottom; (5) Interaction and recognition of print in the environment: can read out some symbols or logos in the environment and guess the print according to the environment.

The assessment of print awareness in this study includes three essential areas, that is: understanding of print function, understanding of print form, and attention to print.

1. Understanding of print function refers to (1) print carries meaning; (2) there is a correspondence between spoken and written language;
2. Understanding of print form refers to (1) complete perception of print, that is, can distinguish Chinese characters from pictures and other symbols (e.g., numbers, English letters, logos); (2) Structural perception of print can understand the Chinese characters are composed of strokes according to orthographic conventions. (3) know that there is space between Chinese characters;
3. Attention to print refers to Pay attention to the print in the reading process, and show interest in scribbles, drawings, and invented spellings.

At present, the study methods of print awareness mainly use behavioral measurement, eye movement research, parents' reporting, and systematic observation. There have been studies in China to measure children's structural perception of print, Liu (2012) studied 152 children in kindergartens through vocabulary judgment tasks, the task of vocabulary judgment includes 11 types of violations of normal Chinese characters.

8.2.2 Home Literacy Environment and Early Print Awareness

According to existing research, there is no unified definition of the home literacy environment. Based on the current study, it is mainly defined in two ways. 1. Direct definition. For example, Sénéchal and colleagues (1998) believes that the home literacy environment includes all the literacy-related activities and experience of young children in the home. 2. Define the composition of the home literacy environment. Sénéch (1998) studied the effect of home literacy experience on the development of oral and written language in children aged 4–5 years. The literacy environment for young children is divided into two parts: storybook exposure and parents' literacy instruction.

Existing studies on literacy environment in the home has found that the home literacy environment includes seven aspects: (1) Basic family information, including parents' academic background and economic income. Levy et al. (2006) investigated the home literacy environment through questionnaires and explored its positive impact on early childhood reading development. The questionnaire includes family information such as family language, background of parents' education, income before tax. (2) Role model of literacy by parents. Dickinson and De Temple (1998) believed that adults could play an exemplary role doing literacy-related activity in front of children. By observing parents' behavior, children are interested in literacy and try to imitate parents. (3) Availability of literacy materials, including:story books appropriate for the age of the child, paper and pens for drawing or writing. (4) Parents' literacy instructions for young children. (5) Parent–child verbal interaction, such as table discussions, reading discussions. Hess and Holloway (1984) found that the home environment influences the development of reading through five aspects, that is: (1) emphasis on literacy; (2) providing reading guidance for children, responding to children's reading interests, encouraging children to achieve excellent literacy abilities; (3) providing and making full use of literacy materials; (4) reading with children; (5) language interaction, including table discussions and reading discussions. Rodriguez and Tamis Lemonda (2011) tracked 1852 low-income children, measured each child's home learning environment from birth to 5 years old for 4 times, and obtained the trajectory of changes in each child's home learning environment during the first 5 years. Measurement of the home learning environment includes the participation of young children in literacy activities, the quality of the interaction between mothers and children, and the learning materials available to young children. (6) parents' belief and attitudes towards early childhood literacy. Wu (2009) believes that parents' attitudes towards early childhood literacy include six aspects: parents' literacy role, parent–child reading emotional experience, direct reading instruction, values for early reading, attribution of Reading obstruction, and language developmental plasticity. (7) Children's early literacy activities such as how often children read independently at home. Shu et al. (2002) compiled a parents' questionnaire to collect relevant cultural backgrounds and cultural behaviors of children and discussed the relationship between family cultural background and children's reading development. The family cultural background questionnaire is divided into four aspects: 1 parents' educational background; 2 home reading resources; 3 parent–child activities related to reading; 4 children's independent cultural behavior, such as the frequency of independent reading at home, watching TV every day.

Studies have found that the relationship between literacy home, literacy environment and children's print awareness. Ezell and Justice's (2000) findings confirmed that parents' teaching strategies for young children in the home literacy environment had a positive effect on the development of children's print awareness. Subjects are randomly assigned to an experimental or control group. Parents of control group did not accept the shared book reading strategies, while parents of the experimental group accepted strategies which included the use of verbal and nonverbal references to print(e.g., discussing and questioning the print in the storybook; pointing to words in a storybook and underlining words while reading). Conclusions were made after 4 weeks of study: if parents are given relevant advice before reading activities, and have some print focus behaviors while reading, print awareness in several essential areas of children would be improved. Liu et al. (2018) studied Chinese characters and suggested that literacy home environment includes: (1) literacy resources at home; (2) formal home literacy experience such as the frequency of teaching Chinese pinyin, teaching read and write Chinese characters. (3) informal home literacy experience, such as the frequency of reading for children at weekends and on weekdays. According to the research results, the relationship between home literacy environment and reading Chinese characters is not as straightforward as researches in alphabetic languages.

8.3 Method

8.3.1 Participants

This study selected 100 2–4-year-old children and their parents from three kindergartens as research subjects. All children were native Mandarin speakers. Effective subjects were 90 children, of whom 55 were children in 2–3 years of age and 35 children were aged 3–4 years. Of the subjects, 45 were boys and 45 were girls, with a minimum age of 28 months and a maximum age of 51 months. A total of 90 questionnaires on home literacy environment were sent out to children's parents. There were 85 effective recoveries, with a recovery rate of 94.4%, as shown in Table 8.1.

Table 8.1 Participants' information

School age group		Less than 36 months old	Over 36 months old	Total number
Number	Male	16	29	45
	Female	18	27	45
	Total number	34	56	90
	Average month ages	33.7	41.05	38.7
	Standard deviation	2.20	3.37	4.59

8.3.2 *Measurements*

8.3.2.1 Assessment of Visual Cognitive Processing Capability

The purposes of measuring visual cognitive processing capabilities are 1. exploring the relationship between children's visual cognitive processing ability and print awareness; 2. accurately analyzing the relationship between the development of children's print awareness and home literacy environment, using visual cognitive processing capability as the control variable. Evaluation of cognitive processing capabilities consists of visual memory tasks and visual recognition tasks.

8.3.2.2 Assessment of Print Awareness of Children

Print awareness includes three areas that are 1. understanding of print function; 2. understanding of print form; 3. attention to print the assessment of overall print awareness is made up of the performances on the level of understanding of print function, understanding of print form, and attention to print.

The study measured print awareness of children in 4 different ways: 1. by sharing reading; 2. through Chinese character recognition; 3. through writing; 4. through parents' questionnaires on children's literacy behaviors.

Measurement of the print function consists of part of reading and writing tasks. Measurement of the print form consists of the other part of reading and writing tasks as well as Chinese character recognition tasks. Measurement of attention to print is through parents' questionnaires on children's literacy behaviors, as shown in Table 8.2.

Reading Sharing

Reading sharing task is adapted from Concepts about Print test (Clay and New 1972), to be available for Chinese children. Under the premise of ensuring reading coherence, choose the picture book "My Dad" (written by Lina Bramp), and further, reduce and adjust the contents of the picture book to achieve the intended aim.

The children were asked questions when reading the picture books, to illustrate children's understanding level of the form and function of print. Reading tasks include 6 questions, and children would be scored according to their answers. The highest score is 3, no answer or Error is 0. The children were asked to: (1) answer where is the book title; (2) finger point to print while reading the title, the recorder shall notice whether the children finger pointed to the Chinese characters of book title word by word; (3) answer how many Chinese characters of the book title. This task is to find out whether the subjects know the space between Chinese characters; (4) answer where to start reading on the first page; (5) point out where the Chinese characters

8.3 Method

Table 8.2 Print awareness assessment

Components of print awareness	Contents	Tasks			
		Reading task	Writing task	Chinese character recognition task	Parents' questionnaire
Print function	1. Print carries meanings	Pointing out the book title; Where to start reading; Pointing out where the print that the protagonist said is	Express what you wrote	/	/
	2. Relationship between spoken and written language	Finger point to print while reading the title	/	/	/
Print form	1. Distinguish print from pictures, and other symbols	/	Written form	Task of complete perception of print	/
				Task of structural perception of print	/
	2. Space between Chinese characters	Telling the number of Chinese characters of the book title	Space between Chinese characters	/	/
Attention to print		/	/	/	Parents' questionnaires on children's literacy behaviors

of the baby giraffe talked are on the second page; (6) guess what the baby giraffe would tell his dad in the last page.

Chinese Character Recognition

The task is to examine children's understanding of print form and the tasks include a complete perception of print and structural perception of print. The materials required of tasks about the complete perception of print that is self-made drawing, there are several sketches, Chinese characters, numbers, English letters and logos in the self-made drawing. Children were asked to discriminate the Chinese character from the other symbols.

The examination of structural perception of print was adopted from the Liu's (2012) research, which studied 152 children in kindergartens through vocabulary judgment tasks, she inspected children's understanding and development of visual awareness, orthographic awareness, and other aspects of print awareness. Materials required for the testing about structural perception of print includes 10 non-Chinese characters cards that violate the component convention, 10 non-Chinese characters cards are divided into 5 categories (1) number within Chinese character; (2) letter within Chinese character; (3) loosely arranged structure; (4) non-block structure (5) mirror structure. The subjects are asked to judge whether that is a normal Chinese character.

Writing

This study contains three writing tasks to examine the children's understanding level of print function and form. The first writing task was arranged after reading the picture book "My Dad" and the subjects were asked to write down what the baby had said. The other two writing tasks are arranged in the final part of the test: writing down what they like to eat and their own names. The three writing tasks examine the following two aspects: (1) knowledge about space between Chinese characters, which examines the understanding of print form. (2) answer what they had written, which examining the understanding of print function. Scores were given according to the writing performance, with the highest score of 3 points and the lowest score of 0 point.

Parents' Questionnaires on Children's Literacy-Related Behaviors

The self-made questionnaires examine children's attention to the print. The questionnaires consist of 9 aspects of children's literacy-related behaviors, that are the child asks the parents to read, write, and point out the Chinese characters he/she is interested in, behaviors that the child is interested in Chinese characters, behaviors that the child pretends to read and write, and behaviors that the child reads independently. There are 5 levels according to time span and frequency.

8.3.2.3 Home Literacy Environment Questionnaire

The home literacy questionnaire consists of two parts. The first part is basic family information, including the tested child's name, gender and birth date, as well as parents' educational level and occupations. The second part contains 4 aspects: 1. availability of literacy-related material provided at home; 2. role model of literacy by parents; 3. parents' advice on enhancement of print awareness; 4. parents' attitudes toward early literacy. The internal consistency of the four dimensions, respectively, was 0.74, 0.72, 0.81, and 0.79, and the internal consistency of the entire questionnaire was 0.84.

8.4 Research Results and Analysis

8.4.1 Analysis on the Basic Conditions and Characteristics of the Development of the 2–4-Year-Old Children's Print Awareness

8.4.1.1 Understanding of Print Function

66% of participants can point out the book's title correctly; 56.6% of participants can finger point to print while reading the title; 37% of participants can point out the Chinese characters in the picture book when they were asked "where to start reading"; 32.1% of participants can point out where the print that the protagonist said is; 60.8% of participants can at least express once what had written for the three writing tasks as shown in Table 8.3.

Table 8.3 Conditions and characteristics of print function development

	Correctly pointed out the title (%)	Correctly read the book title (%)	Knew where to start reading (%)	Pointed out where the print that the protagonist says is (%)	Express what had written (%)
Percentage of participants	68	56.6	37	32.1	60.8

Table 8.4 Count the print of book title

Count the print of book title	Failure to count word by word (%)	Can count word by word (%)
Percentage of participants	12.1	87.9

Table 8.5 Performance about knowing space between Chinese character

Space between Chinese characters	Never appear (%)	Appear once (%)	Appear for twice (%)	Appear for 3 times (%)
Percentage of participants	41.4	34.5	20.7	3.4

8.4.1.2 Understanding of Print Form

Knowledge About the Space Between Chinese Characters

In the reading process, 87.9% of the subjects have known that there is space between Chinese characters, and can correctly count how many Chinese characters the title has. Only 12.1% of the subjects cannot count. This shows that in the reading process, children from 2 to 4 years old basically know that there is a space between Chinese characters. In three writing tasks, about 58.6% of participants leave spaces between what they have written in at least one of the three writing tasks, while 41.4% not even once. It can be seen that in writing tasks, children's performance about understanding of space between Chinese characters was worse than reading tasks as shown in Tables 8.4 and 8.5.

Distinguish Chinese Characters from Picture, and Other Symbols

In terms of the complete perception of print, more than 90% of the participants were able to distinguish Chinese characters from pictures, and different kinds of symbols, it means children basically have the ability of complete perception of print.

In terms of structural perception of print, performed relatively poor, when the children were asked to judge whether noncharacters are normal Chinese character or not, they performed relatively worse than in terms of the complete perception of print. That means children are weaker in the structural perception of print. In this study, we show five different types of non-Chinese characters, 16% of the children didn't think "number within Chinese character" were normal Chinese characters, with the highest correct rejection rate among the five types.

However, there were only 5% of the children didn't think "mirror structure" was normal Chinese characters, with the lowest correct rejection rate, as shown in Table 8.6.

8.4 Research Results and Analysis

Table 8.6 Text structure awareness

	Loosely arranged structure (%)	Non-block structure (%)	Number within Chinese character (%)	Letter within Chinese character (%)	Mirror structure (%)
Correct rejection rate	12	10	16	10	5

8.4.1.3 Assessment on Level of Attention to Print

Children's attention to print was examined through Parents' questionnaires on children's activities of early literacy. There are 9 items assessing children's state of attention to print, each item with five ranking options, respectively, are "never", "seldom", "sometimes", "usually", "almost every day".

The items: "ask adults to write down something important," "pretend writing while playing games," "find similarity or difference in some Chinese characters" and "ask adults to read by touch" mostly focus on "never" option, the percentage of children, respectively, are 70.6, 47.1, 44.7, 37.6%.

The items: usually "pretend reading," "ask adults to read for them," "ask adults to read out Chinese characters they are interested in" and "initiatively point out or read out characters they are familiar with," mostly focus on "usually" option, the percentage of children, respectively, are 43.5%, 41.2%, 31.8%. 50.6% of the children spent less than 15 min in reading alone, as shown in Table 8.7.

8.4.1.4 Print Awareness Developmental Trend by Month

To analyze children's print awareness developmental trend by month, the average total score of all children in each month on a different aspect of print awareness was calculated. Take the factor of months as independent variables, the average of total score of all children in each month as dependent variable. According to independent variables and dependent variable, a scatter diagram was drawn which was fitted according to the logarithmic curve as can be seen from Fig. 8.1: the understanding level of print function develops with months' increase.

It can be seen from Fig. 8.2 that the understanding level of print form develops with months' increase.

From Fig. 8.3, the fitting curve is almost a horizontal straight line and does not show an obvious trend. Attention to does not change significantly with the month's increases.

As can be seen from Fig. 8.4: Print awareness develops with months' increase.

Table 8.7 Children's literacy-related activities

	Nearly never (%)	Seldom (%)	Sometimes (%)	Usually (%)	Almost everyday (%)
Ask adults to write down something important	70.6	22.4	2.9	1.2	0
Pretend writing while playing games	47.1	18.8	14.1	17.6	2.4
Find similarity or difference in some Chinese characters	44.7	27.1	20	7.1	1.2
Ask adults to read and point to the print	37.6	16.5	25.9	14.1	5.9
Pretend reading	12.9	16.5	22.4	43.5	4.7
Ask adults to read for them	2.4	1.2	15.3	41.2	40
Ask adults to read out Chinese character they are interested in	11.8	15.3	30.6	31.8	10.6
Initiatively point out or read out characters they are familiar with	22.4	21.2	23.5	29.4	3.5
	Nearly never (%)	Less than 15 min (%)	15–30 min (%)	30 min to 1 h (%)	Over 1 h (%)
Time of reading alone	5.9	50.6	37.6	5.9	0

8.4 Research Results and Analysis

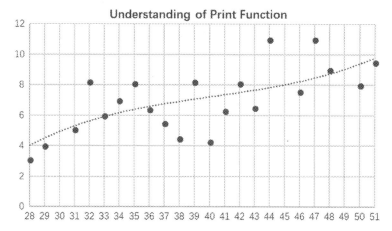

Fig. 8.1 The developmental trend of understanding of print function with months increased (the factor of months as independent variables, the average of total score of all children on the understanding of print function in each month as dependent variable)

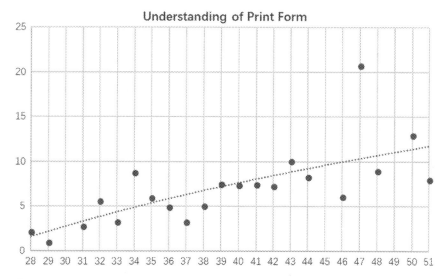

Fig. 8.2 The developmental trend of understanding of print form with months increased (the factor of months as independent variables, the average of total score of all children on the understanding of print form in each month as dependent variable)

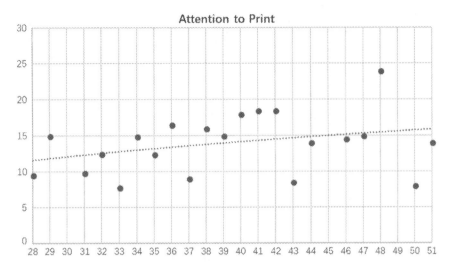

Fig. 8.3 The developmental trend of attention to print with months increased (the factor of months as independent variables, the average of total score of all children on attention to print in each month as dependent variable)

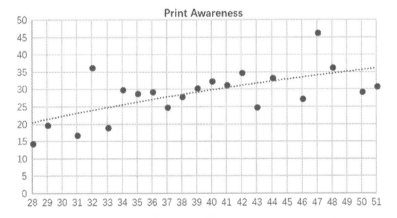

Fig. 8.4 The developmental trend of overall print awareness with months increased (the factor of months as independent variables, the average of total score of all children on overall print awareness in each month as dependent variable, the total score of overall print awareness is added by the score of understanding level of print from, understanding level of print function and level of attention to print)

8.4 Research Results and Analysis

Table 8.8 Relationship between visual cognitive processing and print awareness

	Print function	Print form	Attention to print	Print awareness
Visual cognitive processing	0.389**	0.323**	0.345**	0.516**

**means significant relevance at the level of 0.01

Table 8.9 Relationship between age, gender, and print awareness

	Print function	Print form	Attention to print	Print awareness
Months	0.074	0.258*	0.084	0.205*
Gender	0.139	0.115	0.030	0.117

*means significant relevant at the level of 0.05

8.4.1.5 The Relationship Between Visual Cognitive Processing Ability and Print Awareness

The visual cognitive processing was significantly correlated with the understanding of print function, understanding of print form, attention to print. The respective correlation coefficients were 0.389 ($p < 0.01$), 0.323 ($p < 0.01$), and 0.345 ($p < 0.01$), 0.516 ($p < 0.01$), as shown in Table 8.8.

8.4.1.6 Relationship Between Months, Gender, and Print Awareness

With visual cognitive processing as a control variable, the variables of understanding of print function, understanding of print form, attention to print, and overall print awareness were analyzed in relation to the Variables of months and gender, respectively. As shown in Table 8.9, the months are significantly correlated with an understanding of print form, and overall print awareness. The respective correlation coefficients were 0.258 ($p < 0.01$) and 0.205 ($p < 0.01$). (2) There was no significant correlation between gender and any other factors.

8.4.2 The Status and Characteristics of the 2–4-Year-Old Children's Home Literacy Environment

8.4.2.1 Availability of Literacy-Related Material Provided at Home

41.2% of families have more than 80 Chinese children books. 51.8% of families have less than 10 children book of other languages, 43.5% of families have less than 10 Chinese music CD, while 64.7% of families have less than 10 music CD of other languages. 62.4% of families provide children with access to 1–3 pens that can be

Table 8.10 Availability of literacy-related material provided at home

	Less than 20 books (%)	21–40 books (%)	41–60 books (%)	61–80 books (%)	More than 80 books (%)
Chinese children's books	4.7	21.2	17.6	15.3	41.2

	Less than 10 books (%)	10–20 books (%)	21–30 books (%)	31–100 books (%)	100 books or above (%)
Children's books of other languages	51.8	28.2	5.9	1.2	12.9

	Less than 10 (%)	11–20 (%)	21–30 (%)	31–40 (%)	More than 40 (%)
Chinese music CD of other languages	**43.5**	24.7	14.1	3.5	14.1
	64.7	16.5	8.2	1.2	9.4

	Nearly never (%)	1–3 (%)	4–7 (%)	8–10 (%)	Over 10 (%)
Available pen	0	**62.4**	35.3	1.2	1.2
Available paper	2.4	**43.5**	31.8	9.4	12.9

	Less than 10 (%)	11–20 books (%)	21–50 books (%)	51–100 books (%)	100 books or above (%)
Chinese books for adults	10.6	12.9	17.6	22.4	**36.5**
Books for adults of other languages	**47.1**	22.4	24.7	2.4	3.5

freely used, while 43.5% of families provide children with access to 1–3 papers that can be freely used. 36.5% of families have over 100 Chinese books for adults, while 47.1% of families have less than 10 books for adults of other languages. There are fewer books of other languages at home, as shown in Table 8.10.

8.4.2.2 Parents' Literacy–Related Role Models

The proportion of parents spend less than 30 min in reading and watching TV at home are both 40%. 35.4% of parents spend 0.5–1 h on surfing the Internet and using mobile phones at home. 38.8% of parents seldom write with pens at home.

8.4 Research Results and Analysis

Table 8.11 Parents' role models

	Nearly never (%)	Less than 30 min (%)	0.5–1 h (%)	1–2 h (%)	2 h or above (%)
Parents read books at home	9.4	**40.0**	35.3	12.9	2.4
Parents watch TV at home	28.3	**40.0**	20.0	8.2	3.5
Parents surf the internet at home	17.6	25.9	**35.4**	12.9	8.2
Parents watch mobile phones at home	0	23.5	**35.4**	32.9	8.2

	Nearly never (%)	Seldom (%)	Sometimes (%)	Usually (%)	Every day or almost everyday (%)
Frequency of writing with pen at home	4.7	**38.8**	32.9	15.4	8.2

That means, traditional writing and reading mode changes with the invention of modern scientific and technological products as shown in Table 8.11.

8.4.2.3 Parents' Instructional Strategies for Promoting Children's Print Awareness

56.5% of parents spent 15–30 min in reading picture books for their children every day, 22.4% of parents spent 30 min to an hour in doing so, while 7.1% of parents spent more than 1 h. So, 86% of parents spent more than 15 min in reading for their children every day. This shows that parents pay much attention to children's early reading experience.

In the reading process, parents often use strategies that enrich their children's early reading experiences to improve their children's print awareness. 41.2% of parents usually "read environmental print for children," 45.9% of parents usually "remind children to pay attention to common Chinese characters." In the process of reading 56.5% of parents usually "ask children questions," and 50.6% of parents usually "discuss with children," 41.2% of parents seldom point to print, 45.9% of parents seldom discuss print. 68.2% of parents "nearly never" or seldom discuss Chinese characters. Apparently, parents do not often discuss Chinese characters with children.

Parents are less likely to adopt strategies that enrich their children's early writing experience. The proportion of parents "nearly never" and "seldom" encourage their children to write while playing games were 44.7% and 22.4%, respectively, which indicates that parents rarely encourage children to pretend to write in games. The proportion of parents "nearly never" and "seldom" write notes with their children were 57.6% and 23.5%, respectively. 43.5% of parents seldom write with pens in front of their children at home, indicating that parents rarely write or encourage writing with their children in life, for example, parents ask children to write shopping lists, travel goods, and so on as shown in Table 8.12.

8.4.2.4 Parents' Attitudes Toward Early Literacy

Parents' attitudes toward the recognition of Chinese characters and early literacy of young children are more scientific and reasonable. The proportion of parents completely agree on "parents should teach Chinese characters actively when children are interested in them," "the children's experience in scribbles is helpful to the writing in the future," "children's experience in scribbles is helpful to the future writing," "Reading with children help children's future reading," "children's interest in print is more important than how many Chinese characters they recognize "are 60.0%, 42.3%, 65.9%, and 70.6%, respectively. As the Table 8.13 shown, the majority of parents believe that it is more important to develop children's interests in print, instead of amount of Chinese characters they recognize. Comparatively, few people believe that children's experience in scribbles is helpful to the future writing.

8.4.3 *Influence of Home Literacy Environment on the Development of Print Awareness in Children Aged 2–4-Year-Old*

In this study, multiple regression analysis was conducted on the factors of family literacy environment, months, visual cognitive processing ability, and print awareness.

8.4.3.1 Multiple Regression Analysis of Home Literacy Environment, Months, Visual Cognitive Processing Ability, and Understanding of Print Function

The effect of visual cognitive processing ability on an understanding of print function was significant (F = 3.523, $p < 0.01$).

The sum of the three independent variables, including home literacy environment, months, and visual cognitive processing ability, had a predictive variation ratio of 19.6% ($R^2_{adj} = 0.196$) on the understanding of print function. The influence of months, parents' educational level, home literacy environment, availability of literacy materials, role modeling, parents' instructional strategies for promoting children's

8.4 Research Results and Analysis

Table 8.12 Parent's strategies

	Nearly never (%)	Less than 15 min (%)	15 min to 0.5 h (%)	0.5–1 h (%)	Over 1 h (%)
Time of story telling	3.5	11.8	**52.9**	27.1	4.7
Time of reading picture books for children	1.2	12.9	**56.5**	22.4	7.1

	Nearly never (%)	Less than 30 min (%)	0.5–1 h (%)	1–2 h (%)	Over 2 h (%)
Time of reading in front of children	23.5	**49.4**	22.4	3.5	1.2

	Never (%)	Seldom (%)	Sometimes (%)	Usually (%)	Everyday (%)
Writing in front of children at home	8.2	43.5	28.2	17.6	2.4
Reading print in the environment for children	2.4	16.5	24.7	**41.2**	15.3
Remind children to pay attention to common Chinese characters	1.2	9.4	18.8	**45.9**	24.7
Discuss Chinese characters with children	**34.1**	**34.1**	18.8	12.9	0
Ask children questions while reading	1.2	7.1	22.4	**56.5**	12.9
Discuss while reading	3.5	10.6	27.1	**50.6**	8.2
Point to print while reading	9.4	17.6	**41.2**	25.9	5.9
Discuss print while reading	20.0	15.3	**45.9**	16.5	2.4
Encourage children to write while playing games	**44.7**	22.4	17.6	14.1	12
Encourage children to write notes together	**57.6**	23.5	16.5	2.4	0

Table 8.13 Parents' attitude toward early literacy

	Do not agree (%)	Do not totally agree (%)	Do not know (%)	Generally agree (%)	Complete agree (%)
Parents should teach Chinese characters actively when children are interested in them	0	4.7	5.9	29.4	**60.0**
Children's experience in scribbles is helpful to the future writing	0	11.8	11.8	34.1	**42.3**
Reading with children help children's future reading	0	0	2.4	31.8	**65.9**
Children's interest in print is more important than how many Chinese characters they recognize	0	0	0	29.4	**70.6**

print awareness, parents' attitude toward early literacy had no significant influence on the understanding of print function as shown in Table 8.14.

8.4.3.2 Multiple Regression Analysis of Home Literacy Environment, Months, Visual Cognitive Processing Ability and Understanding of Print Form

From the multiple regression analysis results in Table 8.15, the influence of months on the understanding of print form was significant (F = 2.665, $p < 0.01$). The predictive effects of the sum of the independent variables of the home literacy environment, months, and visual cognitive processing ability on the understanding of print form reach 13.8% ($R^2_{adj} = 0.138$). There are no significant influences of parents' education

8.4 Research Results and Analysis

Table 8.14 Regression analysis of textual function awareness

	B	t	F	R^2	R^2_{adj}	Sig.
			3.523	0.273	0.196	0.002
Months	0.073	1.083				0.282
Visual cognitive processing	0.398**	3.222**				0.002
Availability of literacy material	−0.054	−0.976				0.332
Role model	−0.022	−0.208				0.835
Parents' strategies	−0.065	−1.197				0.235
Parents' attitudes	−0.161	−1.092				0.278
Mother's educational level	0.414	1.011				0.315
Father's educational level	0.659	1.927				0.058

**means significant relevance at the level of 0.01

Table 8.15 Regression analysis of the understanding of print form

	B	t	F	R^2	R^2_{adj}	Sig.
			2.665	0.221	0.138	0.012
Months	0.300**	2.822**				0.006
Visual cognitive processing	0.350	1.797				0.076
Availability of literacy material	0.098	1.133				0.261
Role model	−0.073	−0.430				0.669
Parents' strategies	−0.037	−0.430				0.669
Parents' attitudes	−0.084	−0.361				0.719
Mother's educational level	0.872	1.348				0.182
Father's educational level	0.130	0.240				0.811

**means significant relevance at the level of 0.01

level in home literacy environment, availability of literacy materials material, role modeling of parents, parents' instructional strategies for promoting children's literacy awareness, parents' attitude toward early literacy on an understanding of print form.

8.4.3.3 Multiple Regression Analysis of Home Literacy Environment, Months, Visual Cognitive Processing Ability and Attention to Print

The visual cognitive processing ability and the parent's instructional strategies for promoting children's literacy awareness had a significant influence on attention to print (F = 8.842, $p < 0.05$). The predictive effects of the sum of all independent variables on the attention to print reach 43.0% ($R^2_{adj} = 0.430$), of which, the predic-

Table 8.16 Regression analysis of attention to print

	B	t	F	R^2	R^2_{adj}	Sig.
			8.842	0.483	0.430	0.000
Months	0.050	0.436				0.664
Visual cognitive processing	0.514*	2.457*				0.016
Availability of Literacy material	0.084	0.906				0.368
Role model	−0.293	−1.615				0.111
Parents' strategies	0.590***	6.433***				0.000
Parents' attitudes	−0.018	−0.074				0.941
Mother's educational level	0.831	1.198				0.235
Father's educational level	−0.106	−0.183				0.855

*means significant relevance at the level of 0.05
***means significant relevance at the level of 0.001

tive effect of the instructional strategies of parents for promoting children's literacy awareness is 35.5%, as shown in Table 8.16.

8.4.3.4 Multiple Regression Analysis on Home Literacy Environment, Months, Visual Cognitive Processing Ability and Print Awareness

Months, the visual cognitive processing ability, parents' instructional strategies for promoting children's print awareness at home, and mother's educational background have a significant influence on print awareness ($F = 8.331, p < 0.05$). The predictive effect of all independent variables on print awareness is 41.4% ($R^2_{adj} = 0.414$), of which, the predictive effect of months is 8.23%, the predictive effect of the visual cognitive processing ability is 19.27%, and the predictive effect of the parents' instructional strategies is 15.68%. The predictive effect of mother's educational level is 5.76%, as shown in Table 8.17.

8.5 Discussions and Suggestions

From the results of the study, children from 2 to 4 years old already have certain print awareness, includes an understanding of print functions, understanding of print form, and attention to print. This shows that the individual's print awareness has developed in the early stages of life, and to a certain extent, the idea of emergent literacy has been verified. In recent years, there are schoolizing practices in some Chinese kindergartens. As to literacy and language, teachers tend to teach children to practice Pin-Yin and Chinese characters in the way of rote memory, which might work

8.5 Discussions and Suggestions

Table 8.17 Regression analysis on print awareness

	B	t	F	R^2	R^2_{adj}	Sig.
			8.331	0.471	0.414	0.000
Months	0.422*	2.599*				0.011
Visual cognitive processing	1.262***	4.233***				0.000
Availability of Literacy material	0.129	0.972				0.334
Role model	−0.388	−1.500				0.138
Parents' strategies	0.488***	3.737***				0.000
Parents' attitudes	−0.264	−0.740				0.461
Mother's educational level	2.117*	2.140*				0.036
Father's educational level	0.683	0.827				0.411

*means significant relevance at the level of 0.05
**means significant relevance at the level of 0.01
***means significant relevance at the level of 0.001

in cost of young children's interests. Therefore, some people had such misconception that "recognition of Chinese characters is harmful to children." Actually, children live in the environment full of print, they will spontaneously recognize some words and generate interests in scribbles, drawings, and invented spellings. As long as the parents' instructional strategies are in line with the children's learning characteristics, and follow the laws of children's physical and mental development, teaching Chinese is helpful to children's future literacy development.

However, the development of children's print awareness in all dimensions is not synchronized. For example, a complete perception of print develops more quickly than the structural perception of print. 90% of children aged 2–4 can distinguish between print and pictures, but almost none of them have the structural perception of print.

Children's interest in "reading" is higher than that of "writing". 43.5% of children "usually" pretend to read, 41.2% of children "usually" ask adults to read for them, and 31.8% of children "usually" ask adults to read Chinese characters they are interested in. 70.6% of children "nearly never" ask adults to write down something important, while 47.1% of children "nearly never" pretend to write while playing games.

The study has found that the understanding of print form, understanding of print function, and the overall print awareness develop when months' increase, and attention to print did not change with months. At the same time, parents' instructional strategies for promoting children's literacy awareness have a significant impact on children's attention to print ($F = 8.842, p < 0.05$). This shows that children's attention to print is mainly influenced by adult's instructional strategies. Multiple regression analysis showed that the visual cognitive processing ability, parents' instructional strategies for promoting children's literacy awareness, months, and the mother's education had a significant influence on print awareness. However, the home literacy environment, parents' role models, parents' attitudes toward literacy, and father's educational level had no significant effect on print awareness. Compared with fathers, the educational level of mothers has a greater effect on the development of children's print awareness.

The visual cognitive processing ability, the instructional strategies to promote children's literacy awareness, months, and the mother's educational level predictive effect on the development of print awareness were 19.27%, 15.68%, 8.23%, and 5.76, respectively. Among them, visual cognitive processing capability has the most obvious predictive effect. In the home literacy environment, only parents' instructional strategies to promote children's writing awareness have a significant impact on the development of print awareness. Availabilities of literacy-related materials, parents' role models, and parents' attitudes are not significant, which is inconsistent with the findings of existing related studies. Part of the reasons for not having a significant relationship may be due to the study of children's age is between 2 and 4 years, the age span is too big, Because the younger the child is, the greater is the influence of natural maturity. In the regression analysis between the home literacy environment and the level of print awareness, although the factor of months has been taken as the control variable, the contribution of months to print awareness is too large. As a result, the contribution of home literacy environment to the level of print awareness is very limited, and it is easy to lead to the regression result is not significant.

Through the analysis of parents' instructional strategies to promote children's print awareness, it is found that parents pay more attention to their children's early reading experience, compared to children's writing experience. About 40–50% of parents "often" ask children questions and discuss with children while reading. About 40–50% of parents "nearly never" encourage their children to "write in games" and "write notes together." Besides, according to the questionnaire on parents' attitudes toward early literacy, 11.8% of parents "do not totally agree" with the opinion that "scribble contributes to future writing." This means that parents do not pay enough attention to the value of writing experience for children's future writing ability development.

Through this study, it is suggested that parents should pay more attention to the children's experience of early writing, provide children with enough writing materials, and encourage children to scribble and drawing. Parents should write more in front of their children during daily life such as making shopping lists in advance and write down important events with pens and paper. If the child is interested about writing, the parents should invite them to write together. The purpose of encouraging children to write is not to ask children to write accurate characters, but to enrich their children's writing experience, to understand the function of print, and to increase their interest in writing.

References

Chaney, C. (1992). Language development, metalinguistic skills, and print awareness in 3-year-old children. *Applied Psycholinguistics, 13,* 485–514.

Clay, M., & New, A. (1972). *The early detection of reading difficulties: A diagnostic survey with recovery procedures.* Heinemann.

Dickinson, D. K., & De Temple, J. (1998). Putting parents in the picture: Maternal reports of preschoolers' literacy as a predictor of early reading. *Early Childhood Research Quarterly, 13*(2), 241–261.

Durkin, D. (1966). *Children who read early.* New York: Teachers College Press.

Evans, M. A., & Saint-Aubin, J. (2005). What children are looking at during shared storybook reading: Evidence from eye movement monitoring. *Psychological Science, 16*(11), 913–920.

Evans, M. A., & Saint-Aubin, J. (2010). *An eye for print: Child and adult attention to print during shared book reading.* ON: Springer.

Ezell, H. K., & Justice, L. M. (2000). Increasing the print focus of adult–child shared book reading through observational learning. *American Journal of Speech-Language Pathology, 9*(1), 36.

Goodman, Y. M. (1986). Children coming to know literacy. In W. Teale & E. Sulzby (Eds.), *Emergent literacy.* Norwood, NJ: Ablex.

Hiebert, E. H. (1981). Developmental patterns and interrelationships of preschool children's print awareness. *Reading Research Quarterly, 16,* 236–260.

Justice, L. M., & Ezell, H. K. (2001). Word and print awareness in 4-year-old children. *Child Language Teaching and Therapy, 17*(3), 207–225.

Justice, L. M., & Ezell, H. K. (2004). Print referencing: an emergent literacy enhancement strategy and its clinical applications. *Language, Speech, and Hearing Services in Schools, 35*(2), 185–193.

Levy, B. A., Gong, Z., Hessels, S., Evans, M. A., & Jared, D. (2006). Understanding print: early reading development and the contributions of home literacy experiences. *Journal of Experimental Child Psychology, 931,* 63–93.

Li, Y., & Dong, Q. (2004). A research of environmental influential factors in preschooler's literacy development. *Psychological Science, 03,* 531–535.

Lily, C., Cheng, Z. J., & Chan, L. F. (2008). Chinese preschool children's literacy development: From emergent to conventional writing. *Early Years, 28*(2), 135–148.

Liu, N. (2012). *A study on the development of preschool children's writing awareness* (pp. 18–20). Tianjin Normal University.

Liu, C., Georgiou, G. K., & Manolitsis, G. (2018). Modeling the relationships of parents' expectations, family's SES, and home literacy environment with emergent literacy skills and word reading in Chinese. *Early Childhood Research Quarterly, 43,* 1–10.

Lomax, R. G., & McGee, L. M. (1987). Young children's concepts about print and reading: Toward a model of word reading acquisition. *Reading Research Quarterly,* 237–256.

Mason, J. M. (1980). When do children begin to read: an exploration of four-year-old children's letter and word reading competencies. *Reading Research Quarterly 15,* 203–227.

Melhuish, E. C., Mai, B. P., Sylva, K., Sammons, P., Siraj-Blatchford, I., & Taggart, B. (2010). Effects of the home learning environment and preschool center experience upon literacy and numeracy development in early primary school. *Journal of Social Issues, 641,* 95–114.

Pullen, P. C., & Justice, L. M. (2003). Enhancing phonological awareness, print awareness, and oral language skills in preschool children. *Intervention in School and Clinic, 39*(2), 87–98.

Rodriguez, E. T., & Tamis Lemonda, C. S. (2011). Trajectories of the home learning environment across the first 5 years: Associations with children's vocabulary and literacy skills at prekindergarten. *Child Development, 82*(4).

Saracho, O. N. (1997). Using the home environment to support emergent literacy. *Early Child Development and Care, 127–128,* 201–216.

Shu, H., Li, W., & Yu, Y. (2002). The role of home literacy environment in children's reading development. *Psychological Science, 02,* 136–139.

Teale, W. H. (1986). Home background and young children's literacy development. In *Emergent literacy: Writing and reading*.

Wu, X. (2009). *The development of preschool children's character recognition and writing and its relationship with parents' literacy beliefs and behaviors* (p. 83). East China Normal University.

Sénéchal, M., LeFevre, J., Thomas, E. M., & Daley, K. E. (1998). Differential effects of home literacy experiences on the development of oral and written language. *Reading Research Quarterly, 33*(1), 96–116.

Chapter 9
Study on the State and Influencing Factors of Family Art Education for Children Aged 0–3 in China

9.1 Introduction

Beginning of art education is part and parcel in babies and toddlers. Family is the cradle of art education. The artistic influence of early childhood not only directly determines the interests and aesthetic preferences of infants and young children in artistic activities, but also continuously influences the artistic experience as they become adults. According to experiences in real life, some parents think they are at a loss to their children's artistic education. They turn to kindergarten education when their children are 3 years old. Some held that art training in educational institutions is real art education, and there is no connection between families and art education for infants and toddlers. At the same time, according to media services, some parents give infants and young children artistic training in ways to develop artistic stars or show-business celebrities, bringing great harm to the physical and mental health of them. In addition, many studies have clearly pointed out that Chinese parents have a tendency to utilitarianism in early childhood education. In that case, what is the state of art education for infants and young children in China nowadays? Whether parents attach importance to young children's art education? Whether there is an obvious utilitarian tendency?

Early family education research focuses on reading, language skills, learning quality, sociability, mental health, behavior, and moral education. It discusses more about relations between family education and childhood development such as family environment, mode of education, education investment and parenting behaviors. Little attention was paid to art learning and aesthetic development, and the relationship between family education and them. Besides, in the past, the study on children's art education mainly focused on art learning of preschool children aged 3–6 including a study on curriculum, teaching methods and parental involvement, and little study on organization and roles of museum art education. However, little research has been done on family art education of children, let alone families with children aged less than 3.

In the field of researches on family art education for children, research has been made on family art education for children aged 3–6. For example, there are studies on urban and rural kindergarten parents in Taiwan, in ways to find attitudes and understanding of children's art education. Class and gender of children have a significant influence on parents' understanding; it is found that professions, educational background, gender, age of parents, classes and the gender of young children have a significant influence on parents' awareness. Most parents think that their children can attend art classes when they are 3 years old and they do so (Hsiao 2015). Besides, a study investigating family art education for children aged 3–6 in Changsha, Hunan Province, China, points out that such family art education are utilitarian and subordinate; when it comes to family art education, it is close to children's life. However, drama and opera are less favored (Li 2009). Another survey with target groups of parents with children in kindergartens in Taiyuan, Shanxi Province, China, found that most parents recognized the importance of art education but still tended to be utilitarian; most parents recognize the importance of family art education, but are not familiar with family art education (Shen and Lian 2008).

Family art education for children aged 3–6 are analyzed in whole and in a detailed manner. Studies point out that, in art education of 3–6-year-old children, there is a lack of awareness of preschool children's family art education. There are less time for activities, single form of activities, and misunderstanding of children's drawings, insufficient collection and arrangement of fine art works (Zhou 2011). Besides, some studies analyzed the problems of art guidance by elders, from the perspective of family education subjects (Jiang 2013). In addition, studies on reasons for after-school arts learning institutions for young children found that, most parents consider young children to be able to participate in after-school art education institutions when they are 4 years old, and hold that art learning has a significant impact on children's painting (Hsiao and Kuo 2013).

As for research methods, most studies used a combination of questionnaires and interviews, and interviewed parents with children aged 3–6. A small part of researches employed methods of personal backtracking and narrative research. In some studies, university students who study art are asked to recall their parents' attitudes towards their artistic activities when they were 3–7 years old. Artistic activities and art materials are collected and questionnaires are filled out to delve into children's family art education (Green 1975). Another study using the method of narrative research pointed out features of children's family art education, the way of "story telling of family art education in children's upbringing—summarizing of changes in family art education—proposing suggestions on family art education" (Wang 2014).

To sum up, studies on family art education for children aged 3–6 pointed out that, there are problems such as utilitarian, monotonicity or incompleteness, lack of methods and forms, lack of time and materials, unscientific assessment, parents' lack of self-confidence in their ability to art education, partiality in educational ideas. No studies answered whether such problems exist in families with children aged less than 3. Besides, studies have confirmed that many parents think that their children need to have access to art learning when their children are 3 years old, and learn in after-school education institutions after they are aged 4. No studies answered whether family art education for infants and children took on more responsibilities or whether parents paid less attention to children's art learning. There is an ongoing process of children's art learning and development. If family art education is not valued or problematic, it will have a greater negative impact on infants and toddlers aged 0–3. It is needed to be solved. In this view, this study analyzes contemporary art education for young children aged less than 3 in China.

9.2 Research Design

9.2.1 Research Problems

What is the state of art education in the family for young children aged less than 3 in contemporary China? What about its objectives, contents, organization, evaluation, time, and environment? Whether there are influences of family background on family art education for young children? What are the differences or similarities of family art education for young children aged 0–3 when compared to the previous study on family art education for children aged 3–6?

9.2.2 Participants

Taking into account the feasibility and convenience of data collection, parents with children aged 3 are asked to recall family art education in pre-kindergarten years and fill out questionnaires when their children enrolled into kindergarten in the beginning. One study has found that age, education background, income, and occupation of parents are related to their art education ideas (Hsiao and Pai 2014). In kindergartens with a geographic difference, social backgrounds of parents are quite different. To this end, the study chose kindergartens in different regions to have a questionnaire survey, in ways to cover parents of different social backgrounds. Finally, the study selected 6 classes aged 3 in 2 kindergartens in urban areas, 2 in township and 2 in rural in Beijing in September 2013. In each class, 15 children were selected at random. Questionnaires were filled out by parents to collect data. A study distributed a total of 270 questionnaires, 176 of which were received, with a response rate of 65%.

9.2.3 Research Methods

The study collected data via *Questionnaire on Family Art Education for Children*. According to the previous research framework on family art education for children aged 3–6, researcher first designed interview outline consisting of objectives, content, organization, and evaluation in art education and interviewed over 20 parents with children aged 0–3. Then, according to parents' feedback during the interview, time of art education and educational environment were added into the study. *Questionnaire on Family Art Education for Children* was well designed. After testing more than 50 parents with children aged 0–3, four questions that were not well-differentiated were deleted and the questionnaire was revised. Finally, the questionnaire of 66 items consisting of objectives, contents, organization, evaluation, time and environment came into being. Answers to each question is divided into five response categories, that is, "very consistent", "quite consistent", "normal", "less consistent", and "not consistent". The reliability and validity of the questionnaire were satisfactory. The overall Krenbach a coefficient of the questionnaire was 0.924. The correlation between the six dimensions and the total score were at a significant level (r of objectives $= 0.578**$, r of contents $= 0.901**$, r of forms $= 0.709**$, r of evaluation $= 0.404**$, r of time $= 0.531**$, r of environment $= 0.817**$, $p < 0.01$).

9.3 Research Results

9.3.1 The State of Family Art Education for Children Aged 0–3

9.3.1.1 Educational Objectives Are not Utilitarian, but Slightly Going with Crowd

As listed in Table 9.1, educational objectives are not utilitarian. Considering the mean of items regarding with educational objectives, they are up to 3 points when it comes to recognition of nonutilitarian items that consists of ontological objectives and tool-based objectives of art education. The survey found that the majority of parents turn to let children experience different art forms as much as possible, develop children's hobbies and potentials in art, cultivate children's imagination, creativity and aesthetic perception, nurture children spirituality, and improve children's overall quality. Ontological objective of art education focus on inner experience and value provided by art. Most parents also hope that family art education helps to cultivate children's sociability, body shaping, temperament and giving children a way of pressure relief. However, these tool-based objectives are different from the utilitarian objectives, which show the active role of art itself in children's development in other fields naturally. Some art educational objectives scored 2–3, which shows that some parents recognize them and displays that parts of parents go with crowd in setting art educational objectives, such as "encouraging children to have fun to have something to do," "learning something for compensating the pity of parents' childhood and avoiding the pity of children himself/herself in the future," "competing with other children and avoiding to be lagged behind," and "following the trends of art learning."

9.3 Research Results

Table 9.1 Parents' objectives of family art education for children aged 0–3

No.	Description	N	Mean value	Standard deviation
9	Cultivate children's imagination and creativity	176	4.18	0.805
10	Cultivate children's sociability	176	4.05	0.850
3	Provide children with quality education in ways to improve the overall quality	176	4.04	0.884
2	Develop aesthetic perception, music and rhythm, and cultivate sentiment	176	4.04	0.871
7	Shape body and develop temperament	176	3.99	3.190
1	Have wider exposure to art, develop hobbies, and be artistic	176	3.97	0.871
6	Learn a bit of music theory	176	3.36	1.005
8	Pressure relief	176	3.28	0.979
5	Encourage children to have fun, have something to do	176	2.97	1.044
4	Learning something for compensating the pity of parents' childhood and avoiding the pity of children himself/herself in the future	176	2.51	1.195
11	Compete with other children and avoid to be lagged behind	176	2.29	1.091
12	Follow the trends of art learning	176	2.28	1.062

9.3.1.2 There Are Artistic Tendencies and Family Differences in Selection of Art Education Content

When it comes to types of art, art consists of architectural art, garden art, practical arts, calligraphy art, painting art, sculpture art, photography art, music art, dance art, drama art, opera art, cinema art, and television art (Ma 2011). The paper delves into artistic appreciation, creation, and selection for families with children. As can be seen from Chart 9.1, photography, music, television, and painting are widely exposed to and preferred by infants and toddlers at home. Parents often "appreciate photos with their children," "have children take pictures for family folks or friends or take pictures for family folks or friends with children," "accompany their children to watch their favorite television programs," and "discuss with children about their impressive television episodes," "encourage children to appreciate some music that suits them," "sing with children," "appreciate painting works with children," and "provide children with tools to draw pictures."

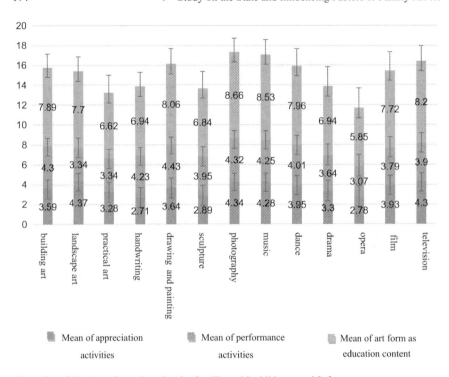

Chart 9.1 Selection of art education for families with children aged 0–3

On the contrary, parents rarely give children access to drama, practical arts, sculpture, and calligraphy and theater arts. Besides, selection of art education differs with families, due to poor mean value and big standard deviation in the 5 art options, especially standard deviation of drama (SD = 2.003) and opera (SD = 1.952) that is much higher than that of photography (SD = 1.401), and music (SD = 1.519). Many parents fail to "guide their children to pay attention to dramas in everyday life" and have less chance of "humming impressive drama with their children". However, very few parents who like dramas will be intended to guide and do with their children. When it comes to theater art, some parents "encourage their children to watch role-plays or dramas," and "have role-plays with them according to needs of their children (such as having a role-play according to episodes of Journey to the West together)." However, there are still many families that lack conditions or awareness. Calligraphy is different from drama and opera. Parents, generally speaking, do not "ask their children to appreciate calligraphy" but "write and paint with their children." Calligraphy appreciation posts the lowest score in art appreciation, but with a higher score of performance.

In this regard, there are obvious and universal artistic tendencies in the selection of family art education. Emphasis is placed on photography, music, television and graphic arts, with less emphasis on drama, practical art, sculpture, calligraphy, and

9.3 Research Results

opera. Besides, there are family differences in selection of art education, especially in terms of dramas and operas.

9.3.1.3 Education Form Is Heavily Family-Based but Slightly Use of Public Education Resource

Here, education form refers to the way of art education. Family art education can be held within the family, happen in public place with the help of public education resource, and be organized at home by the relevant expert. The survey found that young parents rely mainly on their families to educate children at home, including having arts activities, providing materials and equipment, and decorating the environment. Arts education in public places is little provided for children. There are huge family differences in this regard. Some families take their children "to attend art classes," or "often take children to concerts or musicals," or have children "attend community-based art events," while some families do not. Few parents ask a relevant expert to provide education for their children at home, as the mean value of only 1.57 (Table 9.2).

9.3.1.4 Educational Evaluation Focuses Not on Mastery of Knowledge and Skills but on Emotional Attitude and Learning Quality

Art educational evaluation aims at evaluating the process and results of art learning. According to the question of "What's your priority in art education for children?", "caring about grading," and "caring about mastering of art knowledge and skills" are evaluations of art skills, "caring about moods in art learning" and "caring about

Table 9.2 Types of family art education for children

No.	Description	Mean value	Standard deviation
39	I pay for a relevant expert to provide art education at home for my kid	1.57	0.839
45	I often take my child to visit art exhibitions	2.05	0.987
47	I often take my kid to attend community-based art events	2.31	1.150
44	My kid has attended art classes	2.52	1.481
43	I usually take my kid to the concert or musicals	2.84	1.181
41	I decorate our home to provide a pleasant environment for my kid	3.31	1.018
40	I teach my child art by virtue of books, TV programs, and VCDs	3.64	1.086
42	I often sing, paint and tell stories with my children at home	4.36	0.758

whether children like learning" are evaluations of emotional attitudes. "Caring about insistence" and "caring about imagination and creativity" are evaluations of learning qualities. According to these three evaluation indexes, scores of knowledge and skill evaluation (M = 5.4091, SD = 2.04317) <scores of learning qualities (M = 8.7841, SD = 1.42186) <scores of emotion and attitude evaluation (M = 8.8466, SD = 1.36666). In addition, scores of knowledge and skill evaluation are much lower than scores of emotion and attitude evaluation. There are huge cognitive differences among parents; scores of learning qualities are close to scores of emotion and attitude evaluation, and parents accept these two evaluation indexes. It indicates that parents, in evaluating art learning of kids, pay less emphasis on the mastering of art knowledge and skills, put more emphasis on emotional experience during art learning and improvement in learning qualities.

9.3.1.5 More Than 80% of Families Have Reasonable Art Education Time and Schedule, About 20% of Families Lack of Art Activities

The study delves into hours of art education in families with children at weekdays and on weekends, and days of art activities per week, in ways to find time and schedule of family art education for infants. According to surveys, 43.2% of parents have art interactions with children half an hour a day on weekdays. 55.1% of them provide art activities 1–1.5 h a day at weekends. In a week, 35.8% of families with children spend 1 or 2 days in art education; 27.8% of families spend 3–4 days per week; 5.1% of families spend 5–6 days per week; 11.4% of families have art education per day; 44.3% of families spend 3–4 days in art education for children per week. About half of the families in China schedule it the way. It is worth noting that there are still 19.9% of families that never provide art learning for children in a week (Table 9.3).

In terms of schedules of art learning in a week, many families increase spending on art learning at weekends, 4% of the families spending 2 h or above in art learning in a day reduce spending in this regard on weekends. 43.2% of families spend one day and a half-hour in art learning at weekdays. The ratio reduces by 18.8% on weekends; on the contrary, only 30.7% of families spending 1–1.5 h in art learning at weekdays. The ratio increases by 24.4% on weekends. 17.6% of families never provide art learning for kids at weekdays. The ratio reduces by 1.7% on weekends. It indicates that scheduling of family art education for infants gets more reasonable on weekends.

9.3.1.6 Abundance of Emotional Support, but Lack of Material Support in Art Educational Environment

Educational environment includes the physical and spiritual environment, including space, materials, facilities, as well as adult demonstration, guidance, help, and encouragement. According to the listing of mean values as listed in Table 9.5, par-

9.3 Research Results

Table 9.3 Time and schedule of family art education for infants

Hours of art activities at weekdays	Frequency	Percentage	Hours of art activities on weekends	Frequency	Percentage	Days of art activities per week	Frequency	Percentage
More than 2 h	15	8.5	More than 2 h	8	4.5	Every day	20	11.4
1.5 h	13	7.4	1.5 h	38	21.6	5–6 days	9	5.1
1 h	41	23.3	1 h	59	33.5	3–4 days	49	27.8
Half an hour	76	43.2	Half an hour	43	24.4	1–2 days	63	35.8
Little	31	17.6	Little	28	15.9	Little	35	19.9

ents give more mental support to kids, in particular, they encourage their children in a good way ("when kids show their art works, I will communicate with them and praise them") and provide help ("when kids have some difficulties in art activities, I will find methods with children"). Parents provide guidance ("when kids have art activities, I will provide some advice") and demonstration. It indicates that parents are not active enough in art education for children. They provide encouragement and help until children ask for help; few parents are active in providing guide and demonstration for children.

Due to different material and facilities required in art activities, the study does not list requirements in investigation and comparison. The study only investigates space closely related to education activities ("I have a fixed place for art activities for children") and facility use ("I keep my children's artworks according to some orders"). The paper finds that family art education for infants lacks material support. Many families fail to provide a fixed venue for art activities, nor keep and store artworks of children well. It, undoubtedly, does harm to family art education for infants (Tables 9.4 and 9.5).

9.3.2 Influences of Family Background on Family Art Education for Infants

With variance analysis method, the study analyzes influences of family background on family art education for young children, such as degree, profession, household monthly income, geography, number of children and gender, and finds significant influences of some of family information on total scores of family art education for young children in some directions.

Table 9.4 Family art education environment for infants

No.	Description	Mean value	Standard deviation
56	I have a fixed venue for art activities	3.06	1.112
58	I (other family members) provide art activities at home	3.16	1.150
57	I keep my children's artworks according to some orders	3.26	1.094
61	I provide some advice when children are involved in art learning	3.84	1.019
60	I find solutions with children when they have difficulties in art learning	4.22	0.834
59	I communicate with children and praise them when they are showing their artworks	4.23	0.845

9.3 Research Results

Table 9.5 Influence of parents' degrees on family art education for children aged 0-3

Variable	Degree of the father	N	Mean value	F	Degree of the mother	N	Mean value	F
Total education score	Middle school	11	13.45	0.000***	Middle school	10	13.40	0.000***
	High school (technical secondary school)	26	13.77		High school (technical secondary school)	28	13.96	
	Junior college	39	13.97		Junior college	31	13.65	
	Undergraduate	69	15.75		Undergraduate	83	15.65	
	Master	27	16.74		Master	20	17.25	
	Doctor	4	16.25		Doctor	4	15.75	
Educational evaluation	Middle school	11	27.27	0.004**	Middle school	10	27.00	0.004**
	High school (technical secondary school)	26	27.50		High school (technical secondary school)	28	27.57	
	Junior college	39	28.13		Junior college	31	28.26	
	Undergraduate	69	29.20		Undergraduate	83	29.06	
	Master	27	29.89		Master	20	30.10	
	Doctor	4	31.00		Doctor	4	31.50	
Time of education	Middle school	11	9.18	0.006**	Middle school	10	9.60	0.015*
	High school (technical secondary school)	26	11.69		High school (technical secondary school)	28	11.32	
	Junior college	39	11.03		Junior college	31	10.74	
	Undergraduate	69	11.43		Undergraduate	83	11.66	
	Master	27	13.26		Master	20	13.50	
	Doctor	4	13.25		Doctor	4	12.75	

(continued)

Table 9.5 (continued)

Variable	Degree of the father	N	Mean value	F	Degree of the mother	N	Mean value	F
Educational environment	Middle school	11	19.36	0.019*	Middle school	10	18.80	0.001**
	High school (technical secondary school)	26	20.19		High school (technical secondary school)	28	20.93	
	Junior college	39	21.03		Junior college	31	19.84	
	Undergraduate	69	22.45		Undergraduate	83	22.53	
	Master	27	23.33		Master	20	24.05	
	Doctor	4	23.25		Doctor	4	22.50	

*$p < 0.05$, **$p < 0.01$, ***$p < 0.001$

9.3 Research Results

9.3.2.1 With Differences in Parents' Degree, Total Grades of Family Art Education, Educational Evaluation, Time of Education, and Educational Environment Differ Significantly

With the promotion of parents' degree, scores of total grades of family art education for infants and toddlers, educational evaluation, time of education, and educational environment increase. But, if the father and the mother are PhDs, comparing with Masters, total scores of art education, scores of time of education and educational environment reduce, and educational evaluation score rises a little bit. In addition, if parents have only associate degrees, comparing with high school level, score of time of education reduces.

9.3.2.2 With Difference in Parents' Occupations, Total Grades of Family Art Education, Educational Objectives and Educational Environment Differ Significantly. Father's Occupation Has Great Influences on Family Art Education Evaluation

In a family where the father is a leader in an enterprise and a public institution, children score highest in the mean value of art education, educational objectives, educational evaluation, and educational environment, with largest standard deviation. It indicates that such families provide good family art education, with huge internal differences. If the father is a self-employed entrepreneur, children score lowest in family art education; if the father is a staff in service industry, children score lowest in objectives and art educational evaluation; if the father is a technician, teacher, or artist, children score lowest in art educational environment.

In a family where the mother is a leader in an enterprise and a public institution, children score highest in art education and educational environment. If the mother is a self-employed entrepreneur, children score lowest in family art education; if the mother is a staff in service industry, children score lowest in educational objectives and educational environment. Different from categories of the father's occupation, the study delves into families where the mother is a housewife according to research objects. Such families have the highest score of educational objectives, with the hugest standard deviation. Besides, total family education score is not high in such a family. To compare with the father's occupation, if the mother is a technician, teacher or artist, children do not score lowest in family art educational environment.

In a nutshell, if parents are leaders in an enterprise and a public institution, children receive good art education, have better educational objectives and educational environment. If parents are self-employed entrepreneurs or staff in the service industry, children receive the worst family art education (Tables 9.6 and 9.7).

Table 9.6 Influences of father's occupation on family art education for children aged 0–3

Variable	Father's occupation	N	Mean value	Standard deviation	F
Total grades of family art education	Leader in an enterprise and a public institution	20	17.30	2.774	0.000***
	Staff in an enterprise and a public institution	67	15.15	2.536	
	Staff in the service industry	9	14.22	1.302	
	Worker	16	14.88	2.655	
	Technician, teacher or artist	31	14.74	2.394	
	Self-employed entrepreneur	21	13.52	2.159	
	Other	12	15.58	2.575	
Educational objectives	Leader in an enterprise and a public institution	20	46.60	9.730	0.030*
	Staff in an enterprise and a public institution	67	43.37	5.069	
	Staff in service industry	9	41.11	2.804	
	Worker	16	44.44	4.633	
	Technician, teacher, or artist	31	42.03	4.151	
	Self-employed entrepreneur	21	44.67	4.066	
	Other	12	46.17	4.282	
Educational evaluation	Leader in an enterprise and a public institution	20	30.70	3.114	0.007**
	Staff in an enterprise and a public institution	67	29.06	2.587	
	Staff in the service industry	9	26.89	1.691	
	Worker	16	28.56	2.581	
	Technician, teacher, or artist	31	28.32	3.919	
	Self-employed entrepreneur	21	27.52	2.337	

(continued)

9.3 Research Results

Table 9.6 (continued)

Variable	Father's occupation	N	Mean value	Standard deviation	F
	Other	12	28.50	2.844	
Educational environment	Leader in an enterprise and a public institution	20	24.05	4.817	0.002**
	Staff in an enterprise and a public institution	67	22.34	4.385	
	Staff in service industry	9	21.89	3.257	
	Worker	16	20.81	3.563	
	Technician, teacher, or artist	31	19.26	3.540	
	Self-employed entrepreneur	21	20.95	4.500	
	Other	12	23.75	4.330	

$*p < 0.05$, $**p < 0.01$, $***p < 0.001$

Table 9.7 Influences of mother's occupation on family art education for children aged 0–3

	Mother's occupation	N	Mean value	Standard deviation	F
Total grades of family art education	Leader in an enterprise and a public institution	7	17.14	2.734	0.031*
	Staff in an enterprise and a public institution	57	15.18	2.323	
	Staff in service industry	18	13.72	2.218	
	Worker	13	14.69	2.626	
	Technician, teacher, or artist	37	15.78	2.869	
	Self-employed entrepreneur	6	13.50	1.761	
	Housewife	16	14.56	2.421	
	Other	22	15.18	2.889	
Educational objectives	Leader in an enterprise and a public institution	7	45.57	6.133	0.044*
	Staff in an enterprise and a public institution	57	44.42	4.705	

(continued)

Table 9.7 (continued)

	Mother's occupation	N	Mean value	Standard deviation	F
	Staff in service industry	18	41.94	3.654	
	Worker	13	43.85	5.640	
	Technician, teacher, or artist	37	42.70	4.841	
	Self-employed entrepreneur	6	44.17	5.345	
	Housewife	16	47.63	9.715	
	Other	22	42.32	4.571	
Educational environment	Leader in an enterprise and a public institution	7	25.29	7.319	0.005**
	Staff in an enterprise and a public institution	57	22.60	4.255	
	Staff in service industry	18	18.67	4.298	
	Worker	13	19.92	3.685	
	Technician, teacher, or artist	37	21.54	3.132	
	Self-employed entrepreneur	6	20.33	1.506	
	Housewife	16	23.00	3.899	
	Other	22	21.95	5.269	

$*p < 0.05$, $**p < 0.01$, $***p < 0.001$

9.3.2.3 With Difference in Household Monthly Income, Total Grades of Family Art Education, Educational Evaluation and Educational Environment Differ Significantly

On the whole, as household monthly income increases, total grades of family art education, scores of educational evaluation and educational environment increase. When household monthly income increases from 3,000–5,000 yuan to 5,000–8,000 yuan, total grades of family art education and score of educational evaluation reduce a little bit (see Table 9.8).

9.3 Research Results

Table 9.8 Influences of household monthly income on family art education for children aged 0–3

	Household monthly income	N	Mean value	Standard deviation	F
Total grades of family art education	Less than 3,000 yuan	2	11.50	0.707	0.000***
	3,000–5,000 yuan	19	14.53	2.294	
	5,000–8,000 yuan	60	13.88	2.009	
	8,000–12,000 yuan	32	14.75	2.463	
	More than 12,000 yuan	63	16.68	2.500	
Educational evaluation	Less than 3,000 yuan	2	29.50	6.364	0.001**
	3,000–5,000 yuan	19	27.89	2.904	
	5,000–8,000 yuan	60	27.70	2.294	
	8,000–12,000 yuan	32	28.88	3.581	
	More than 12,000 yuan	63	29.89	2.829	
Educational environment	Less than 3,000 yuan	2	19.50	7.778	0.004**
	3,000–5,000 yuan	19	19.89	4.175	
	5,000–8,000 yuan	60	20.90	3.917	
	8,000–12,000 yuan	32	21.47	4.472	
	More than 12,000 yuan	63	23.37	4.371	

$*p < 0.05$, $**p < 0.01$, $***p < 0.001$

9.3.2.4 With Geography Difference, Total Grades of Family Art Education, Content of Education, Educational Evaluation, Time of Education and Educational Environment Differ Significantly

Urban families provide the best art education, with the highest scores in all directions. Apart from high ranking in time of education, rural families score lowest in other items. When it comes to the time of education, suburb families score lowest. Township families rank next to suburb families when it comes to overall education and evaluation; while suburb families rank second to township families in terms of the content of education, environment and time of education. Generally speaking, urban families scored highest when it comes to family art education, content of education, evaluation, and environment. Suburb families and township families ranked second, while rural families lagged behind (Table 9.9).

Table 9.9 Children's family art education in different places

Variable	Geography	N	Mean value	Standard deviation	F
Total grades of family art education	City	92	15.75	2.768	0.004**
	Suburb	61	14.48	2.433	
	Town	10	14.30	0.823	
	Village	13	13.85	1.908	
Content of education	City	92	100.34	12.021	0.019*
	Suburb	61	96.20	17.113	
	Town	10	99.20	12.336	
	Village	13	87.85	14.820	
Educational evaluation	City	92	29.45	2.876	0.002**
	Suburb	61	28.36	3.173	
	Town	10	27.10	1.729	
	Village	13	26.77	1.922	
Time of education	City	92	12.18	2.851	0.017*
	Suburb	61	10.54	3.374	
	Town	10	11.40	3.596	
	Village	13	12.08	3.685	
Educational environment	City	92	22.91	4.298	0.003**
	Suburb	61	20.49	4.411	
	Town	10	21.20	2.616	
	Village	13	20.00	4.041	

$*p < 0.05$, $**p < 0.01$, $***p < 0.001$

9.3.2.5 Number of Children Has Significant Influences on Family Art Education Environment. Educational Environment in Families with Two Children Have Higher Mean Value Compared to Families with Only One Child

See Table 9.10.

Table 9.10 Influence of number of children on family art educational environment

	Number of children	N	Mean value	Standard deviation	F
Family art educational environment	1	141	21.64	4.177	0.041*
	2	32	22.47	5.370	

$*p < 0.05$

9.3 Research Results

Table 9.11 Influence of gender of children on family art education

Variable	Gender	N	Mean value	Standard deviation	F
Content of art education	Male	103	97.61	12.868	0.029*
	Female	72	98.19	16.681	

*$p < 0.05$

9.3.2.6 Gender of Children Has a Great Impact on Family Art Education Selection. Families with Girls Score Higher in the Content of Art Education

See Table 9.11.

9.4 Discussion

The study finds, objectives of family art education for children aged 0–3 are not utilitarian. This is different from previous research. A study on family art education for children aged 3–6 found that parents' educational objectives are utilitarian (Li 2009). Mean value of utilitarianism of educational objectives is about 2. Actually, the value of 2 means that parents hold such objectives do not fit them, and that parents have a negative attitude towards utilitarianism of educational objectives. According to the study, during estimation, parents are found to reject utilitarian educational objectives. To this end, according to the standard of lack of distinction, the study deletes, in a formal questionnaire, 4 subjects of utilitarian educational objectives. According to survey results, parents agree on nonutilitarian educational objectives, and pay emphasis on emotional attitude and learning quality in terms of educational evaluation. It indicates from both positive and negative sides, objectives of family art education for children aged 0–3 are not utilitarian. Of course, it is related to research object, research scope, and samples. The research delves into art education for children aged less than 3, different from families with children aged 3–6 in previous research. In addition, the study collects parents in Beijing. The data is quite different from parents in other parts of China. The study finds, if fathers and mothers are staff in service industry, objectives score lowest; if fathers and mothers are leaders in enterprises and public institutions or staff in an enterprise and a public institution, objectives score highest or have higher scores. In the study, few fathers and mothers are in service industry, 0.05% and 1%, respectively; most of the fathers and the mothers are in enterprises and public institutions, 48.9% and 36%, respectively.

Parents have a propensity toward some art forms in art education. Most of them provide their children with film, music, television, and drawing classes, but slightly with drama, practical crafts, sculpture, calligraphy, and opera classes. Obviously, the popular art form is closely related to family life, and is easy to approach. Less favored arts seldom are accessible in daily household life, or do not draw the attention of parents. Besides, there are huge differences among families when considering less favored arts. First, with difference in geography, there is obvious difference in the content of family art education for children. Urban families score highest, suburb families rank second, township families rank third, rural families rank fourth. Families in different places have different art activities. When it comes to "dramas," urban and suburb families obviously have more access to art activities than township and rural families. In addition, families in different places live in different ways, which influence attitudes toward arts and emphasis on art. For example, suburb families have easier access to art resources, but they tend to lack art activities in different categories at leisure times for business. So, the score of the content of education obtained by suburb families is lower than that of township families. Second, families with girls have better scores in art education selection. They have wider art forms to choose, with a higher frequency of art appreciation and expression activity. Having girls have more access to arts is widely accepted by the Chinese, which is influenced by gender division. Families with children aged 0–3 have the same performance on the content of education with families owning children aged 3–6 according to previous research results. For example, in Changsha, parents are not interested in drama and opera learning for children (Li 2009). Gender of children has a great influence on selection of photography and dance learning (Li 2009). As for parents in Taiwan, gender of children has a significant role in attitudes of parents towards children's art functions and media (Hsiao 2015). In fact, different arts have unique charms and values. Social arts and cultures require inheritance and involvement of children. All children are necessary to have full access to art in their childhood, in ways to be emotionally rich. Lack of opportunities for art learning due to lack of resources and conditions, adults' awareness or intentional restriction, is educational unjust and social unjust. The study does not hold that each child has to learn all the arts. However, parents are suggested to encourage children to have access to different arts, to broaden horizon, and gradually find what children are interested in.

In the family educational environment, families provide better emotional support but lack material support. When children ask for help, parents can encourage and help them. To the contrary, parents seldom provide active advice to children or intentionally demonstrate to children. It indicates that parents are negatively involved in family art education for young children. On a positive side, families give more freedom for children to show, and do not intervene in children's art development. In terms of potential influences, negative involvement in family art education for young children may reduce the role of family art education in children's art learning. In terms of material support, many families fail to provide fixed venues for children to have art activities, nor can they keep and store children's artworks. First, it is related to space limitations. The study finds, as household monthly income increases, family art educational environment scores higher. Second, it is related to educational awareness and educational input of parents. Score of family art educational environment increases as parents' degrees improve, apart from the transition of parents' degrees from masters to PhDs. If fathers and mothers are in enterprises and public institutes, family art educational environment scores higher. In particular, if the father is a technician, teacher, or artist, family art educational environment scores lowest. When it comes to geography, urban and township families educational environment scores better. Mean value of family educational environment in families with two children is higher than that in families with only one child. Obviously, only with scientific education awareness, adequate education input and family financial support can family art education environment for young children improve.

9.5 Conclusion and Suggestion

As a whole, families provide good art education for children. (1) There are explicit and nonutilitarian educational objectives. Parents focus on ontological and tool-based objectives of art education, experience in art activities, and active roles of arts activities in other areas; (2) families have a propensity toward art forms in content selection. Families generally favor art forms that are closely linked to daily life and are easy to operate, such as photography, music, television, and painting; (3) Education rely on family-based activity; (4) Educational evaluation focuses not on the mastery of knowledge and skills, but on emotional attitude and learning quality; (5) 80% of family schedule art education activity well. About half of the families provide art activities for their children 3–4 days a week. Parents have art interactions with children half an hour a day on weekdays. They provide art activities 1–1.5 h a day at weekends. Most of the families in China nowadays schedule family art education following this way. (6) Families provide emotional support for children's art learning enough. Parents encourage and help in time when children ask for help or initiate in the course of art learning. In addition, few parents provide advice or set an example for children in an active way.

It is worth noting that

(1) Some families go with crowd when it comes to set art education objective for children. Part of parents provide art education for their children in ways to spend time, make up for regrets, prepare for competition, and chase trends. Objectives of family art education are significantly affected by parents' occupation. This reminds us to intervene in objectives of art education in specific families according to their parents' occupation and to promote the value and significance of art education.
(2) In terms of the content of education, parents rarely give children access to drama, practical crafts, sculpture, calligraphy, and opera. In addition, the propensity of art education has obvious family differences. This is significantly influenced by the geography of family and gender of children. To compare scores of types of education, urban families rank first, suburb families rank second, township families rank third, and rural families lag behind; families with baby girls score higher than those with baby boys. The study suggests that the government and public education departments provide accessible artistic activities, especially drama and opera, for children in township and rural areas. In addition, the study suggests parents learn more about art, recognize the close relationship between

practical crafts, sculpture, and calligraphy and people's daily life, and help children to find art in their daily life with the sense of aesthetic.
(3) In terms of educational ways, parents rarely take children to be involved in public education including participating in community activities, attending training courses, go to a show or visit art exhibitions in public education institutions. Reasons behind it are unsuitability of having public education activities, and lack of public places and activities for children aged 0–3. The study urges for more access to art activities and places nearby, in ways to prompt parents to get their children involved.
(4) When it comes to the time of education, nearly 20% of families barely have time for artistic activities for their children. This is obviously unreasonable. Provision of artistic activities for children is not only related to whether parents recognize the importance of artistic education, but also whether parents have time to do so. The study suggests that publicity and public education assistance should be provided to families who have no time for children's art activities. On the one hand, it emphasizes the importance of art education for children to parents; on the other hand, it encourages parents to send their children to attend art activities in public education places for giving their children regular art learning time.
(5) Many efforts shall be made in providing a better material environment of family art education for children. Many families cannot provide fixed venues for children to have artistic activities, nor can they properly keep and manage the artistic works of them. Educational environment score is significantly influenced by five factors, that is, parents' education background, occupation, household monthly income, geography and number of children. To improve the environment of family art education for children, efforts shall be made in improving family environment, parents' educational awareness, and educational input.

References

Green, N. H. (1975). Some effects of parental injunctions on the visual art education of children and adults. *Art Education, 28*(1), 11–17.
Hsiao, C. Y., & Pai, T. C. (2014). Taiwanese parents' beliefs regarding young children's art education and the actual art achievements of children. *Canadian Center of Science and Education, 7*(9), 24–36.
Hsiao, C. Y. (2015). Current kindergarten parents' attitudes toward and beliefs about children's art education in majority cities and counties of Taiwan. *International Education Studies, 8*(4), 80–94.
Hsiao, C. Y., & Kuo, T. Y. (2013). Investigating kindergarten parents' selection of after-school art education settings in Taiwan. *Journal of Education and Learning, 2*(4), 208–218.
Jiang, X. (2013). *A case study on children's family art education by the grandparents* (abstract), M.A. Thesis, Hunan Normal University.
Li, J. (2009). *A survey on the state of family art education in families with children in Changsha* (pp. 43–44), M.A. Thesis, Hunan Normal University.

References

Ma, X. (2011). *A case study on children's family art education* (pp. 43–62), M.A. Thesis, Nanjing Normal University.

Shen, X., & Lian, P. (2008). A Survey on Family Art Education in Families with Children in Taiyuan. *New Course (Primary School Edition), 2*, 50.

Wang, Y. (2014). *Narrative research on children's family art education* (abstract), M.A. Thesis, Shanxi Normal University.

Zhou, Y. (2011). *A survey on pre-school children's family art education* (abstract), M.A. Thesis, Hunan Normal University.

Part III
Policies and Challenges

Chapter 10
Growth Prediction of Population Aged 0–3 Under the Universal Two-Child Policy: A Study Case of Beijing

10.1 Research Background

10.1.1 Rollout of Universal Two-Child Policy to Tackle Aging Population Crisis

In order to control the size and structure of population, China started to carry out the one-child policy since the 1970 and 1980s, stipulating only one child for every couple to control the pileup of population and concentrate on construction of economy and national industrialization. The strict implementation of the one-child policy resulted in an upsurge of national economic growth rate as well as a rapid decline of birth rate. So, China stepped into a high equilibrium path of high-saving and economic growth. However, the childbearing culture was impacted deeply in economic and social transitions, so that China gradually fell into the trap of lowest low fertility of population. The Fifth Plenary Session of the 18th CPC Central Committee concluded on October 29, 2015, decided that "adhering to the basic state policy of family planning, and improving the population developing strategy; implementing the policy in all-round way that every couple may have two-child, and actively addressing aging trend". This is another important adjustment of population policy after the decision on implementation of the "two-child fertility policy" for couples where either the husband or the wife is from a single-child family was made at the Third Plenary Session of the 18th CPC Central Committee since 2013.

10.1.2 Unknown Population-Changing Trend Under the Influence of Factors

After the two-child policy for couples where either the husband or the wife is from a one-child family was started, the expected "small baby boom" did not appear. The data from many actual surveys show that China's younger population aged 0–14 years in 2014 accounted for 16.5% of total population, lower than 6.29 percentage points in the sixth census in 2000, an far below the world average level of 26% (Guo 2014), while the population at the age of over 60 was in a rising proportion. Three reasons are that the childbearing will was overestimated; the childbearing intention which was rendered into the bearing behavior was interfered by many social factors; and the insufficient guarantee of public service system made the childbearing group lose confidence to deliver their children. Then, what is the trend of population growth after the rollout of the universal two-child policy? What challenges will be posed in the new demographic situation to the relevant supporting measures such as public services? The policy-related prediction research is particularly necessary in order to cope with and adjust the social impact of population changes in a timely manner, and lay a favorable realistic foundation for improving public services and other supporting measures.

10.1.3 Beijing–A Typical Case for the Research on Population Growth and Policy Demands

As the center of China's politics, culture, science and education, and international exchanges, Beijing took first to implement population adjustment policies, and accepted the feedback of implementation effect of these policies. For a long time, the household population in Beijing has maintained a low fertility rate of around 1%, and the birth rate of the permanent population has been lower than 10% since 2000. However, according to the survey on fertility intention of the population at the childbearing age released by Beijing Family Planning Commission, only about 50–60% of only-child families were willing to have two children (Beijing Population and Family Planning Commission 2014). Therefore, if a universal two-child policy can bring changes in population structure, it will first show the effect in Beijing. In addition, the childbearing people have more open mind in Beijing, which has the leading economic development as a national political and economic center. Their policy demand for the birth of two children will be clearer. Therefore, Beijing city is a better case as a research object on population prediction and the supporting public service demands under the universal two-child policy.

(1) The changing characteristics of the population aged 0–3 years old in Beijing during 2000–2014
① Description of demographic data change

The birth demographic data (Table 10.1) can be obtained according to the *Beijing Statistical Yearbook* (2000–2015). Since the founding of the People's Republic of China, the total fertility rate of permanent residents in Beijing has shown a great volatility, and it dropped to below 1% as a level of the lowest low fertility rate (Table 10.1), continuing to be lower than the national level.

10.1 Research Background

Table 10.1 Changes of fertility rate and birth number of permanent and registered residents in Beijing during 2000–2014

Year	Permanent residents Number of birth (10,000)	Birth rate (‰)	Registered residents Number of birth (10,000)	Birth rate (‰)	National birth rate (‰)
2000	8.08	6.20	7.20	6.50	14.03
2001	8.38	6.10	6.00	5.35	13.38
2002	9.26	6.60	6.00	5.28	12.86
2003	7.34	5.06	4.50	3.92	12.41
2004	8.99	6.13	6.60	5.68	12.29
2005	9.53	6.29	7.50	6.35	12.40
2006	9.76	6.22	7.70	6.43	12.09
2007	13.37	8.16	9.90	8.16	12.10
2008	13.59	7.89	10.60	8.62	12.14
2009	13.90	7.66	10.90	8.75	11.95
2010	13.90	7.27	10.20	8.11	11.90
2011	16.50	8.29	12.50	9.78	11.93
2012	18.49	9.05	14.50	11.18	12.10
2013	18.69	8.93	13.60	10.40	12.08
2014	20.80	9.82	17.20	10.90	12.37

Data source: Beijing Statistical Yearbook (2000–2015)

Since 2000, the birth rate of Beijing's household registered population has been declining from 6.5% in 2000 to 3.92% in 2003, the lowest in more than 10 years. It then continued to rise to 11.18% in 2012, but slightly dropped to 10.4% in 2013. The main reasons are: (1) Most people were just in the childbearing stage with the effect of the baby boom during the 1970–80s; (2) The childbearing behavior was on the rise with the effect of the two-child policy for only-child couples was on the rise; (3) The fertility rate increased with implementation of the "household registration with father" policy in 2003 to a certain extent. In addition, the "dragon baby" effect might also be one of the factors for the small birth peak in 2012.

According to the number of newborns in Beijing during 2000–2014 from the *Beijing Statistical Yearbook*, the population aged 0–3 years old and total population during 2003–2015 in Beijing are obtained, respectively, by the age recursive formula in the population prediction software (Table 10.2). It can be seen that in the past decade or more, the infants aged 0–3 years old in Beijing had basically maintained an upward trend in number, and a small peak of population aged 0–3 years old had been formed, respectively, in 2014 and 2015. People from all walks of life generally believed that the implementation of the two-child policy for couples where either the husband or the wife is from a single-child family would bring about a sudden outbreak of potential fertility, which led to a small climax in birth. But as a matter of fact, within 3 months after the policy came out, the two-child applications in Beijing showed a short and concentrated release. However, since the highest value

Table 10.2 Data of population aged 0–3 years old in Beijing during 2003–2015

Year	Population aged 0 (10,000)	Population aged 1 (10,000)	Population aged 2 (10,000)	Population aged 3 (10,000)	Population aged 0–3 (10,000)
2003	7.34	9.26	8.38	8.08	33.06
2004	8.99	7.34	9.26	8.38	33.97
2005	9.53	8.99	7.34	9.26	35.12
2006	9.76	9.53	8.99	7.34	35.62
2007	13.37	9.76	9.53	8.99	41.65
2008	14.08	13.37	9.76	9.53	46.74
2009	14.63	14.08	13.37	9.76	51.84
2010	13.47	14.63	14.08	13.37	55.55
2011	16.50	13.47	14.63	14.08	58.68
2012	18.50	16.50	13.47	14.63	63.10
2013	18.68	18.50	16.50	13.47	67.15
2014	20.80	18.68	18.50	16.50	74.48
2015	17.20	20.80	18.68	18.50	75.18

Data source: Beijing Statistical Yearbook (2000–2015)

of 4690 cases in April, the number of two-child applications has been declining, far lower than people's expectations. This might be because of too low fertility intention and fertility-declining culture as well as the off-year effect of the Year of the Goat. Therefore, the trends can be found in Beijing's fertility data over the past 10 years (Fig. 10.1).

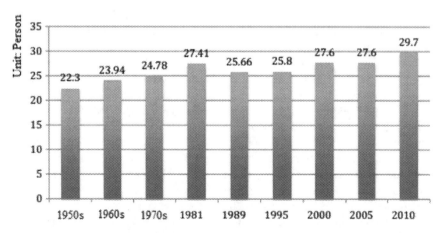

Fig. 10.1 Initial childbearing ages of women at the childbearing age since the 1950s in Beijing. *Data source* Ma Xiaohong, Hu Yuping, and Yin Deting. Modern Beijing Population (A, B), China Renmin University Press, 2014:78

② Changes of age at first birth in Beijing

The mean age at childbearing is an important indicator reflecting the status and pattern of woman childbearing, and it is an average age of the women who bear first child. From the Fig. 10.1, it can be seen that the age at first birth for women at the childbearing age in Beijing had risen since the 1950s, and has risen again after a small decline in the 1980s. By 2010, the mean age of women at the first-birth age in Beijing had reached 29.7 years, and the average childbearing age of the registered population was even higher, up to 30.4 years old. The population aged 0–3 years old was mainly affected by the fertility rate, whereas the fertility rate was influenced by the initial childbearing age of women at childbearing age.

10.2 Literature Reviews

Before the release of the two-child policy, the studies were carried out on population problems with the implementation of the two-child policy for couples where either the husband or the wife is from a single-child family. The more research results focused on the possible population changes as well as analysis and calculation on the number of newborns once above two-child policy was carried out.

A survey showed that the families which gave birth to the second children and were in line with the childbearing policy after the policy adjustment would account for more than 30% of total single families, forming a small baby boom during 2015–2017, but no great increase at the fertility level. According to their results, the newborns also accounted for only 10% of total number of births at the boom with the come out of the policy. By using the theory and quantitative analysis model, a study conducted the discussion on the possible birth "pile-up" phenomenon and its fertility release patterns in the adjustment of the two-child policy for couples where either the husband or the wife is from a single-child family. Their results found that the national pileup scale reached around 26,120,000 couples with the implementation of this policy, and the pileup phenomenon will disappear basically by 2040; these pileup couples and their fertility release mainly occurred in the cities and eastern regions; the pileup couples in married couples increased first and then decreased in proportion, and they would account for around 7.9% at the baby boom in the implementation of the policy. In the first 5 years, the cumulative release amount of the fertility made up 30–37% of the total level.

Based on relevant data, Shi Renbing (2014) estimated the "stock" and "increment" of possible fertility potential of the couples who had one child but met the requirements of the two-child policy for couples where either the husband or the wife is from a single-child family. He believed that the national fertility potential stock was around 20,470,000 in 2013, while the total release amount of this stock came to 10,210,000–12,260,000 by the "release proportion". At the same time, he suggested that due to the lag of policy response, the number of births would not increase significantly in 2014, but the policy-related birth increment of around 3,470,000–4,170,000 might be released in 2015, which was equivalent to the 21.3–25.5% of the national birth rate in 2012. As a result, the "pile-up" of birth would be remarkable. Of course, he also held that policy adjustment has different effects on childbearing women at different age groups in the urban and rural areas with different birth policies, as well as the areas with different fertility transformation.

Some scholars also based on the condition of the specific areas, estimated the baby boom with the rollout of the policy didn't occur in 2015 but in 2016. In addition to above estimates, some scholars discussed the demographic consequences with immediate implementation of the universal two-child policy, but they had a far cry from judgment and conclusions of the demographic consequences. Thus, the further discussion should be made on this issue.

By analyzing the implementation effect of the two-child policy for couples where either the husband or the wife is from a single-child family, Zhai et al. (2015) discussed the current situation of the population in China and predicted the future changing trend of population, holding that the national birth population was expected to nearly 18 million in 2015; with further adjustment of the new population policy, the fertility would still be in a certain rise in China. However, a small number of scholars believed that the total childbearing population with a fertility intention was more stable at 55% or so, and the single childbearing population with a fertility intention was less than 30%, but those who were not willing to have two children were up to 40%. There is a gap between fertility intention, birth planning, and childbearing behavior. In the past, it was wrong judging the ideal child number and the biased fertility intention as the actual fertility level.

A scholar through the simulation of system dynamics, held that even if the two-child policy was implemented fully, the number of the newly born two children couldn't materially alter the structure of the population in China, but overall "universal two-child" policy would be more conducive to population growth than the two-child policy for couples where either the husband or the wife is from a single-child family. He suggested that social problems such as high cost of childcare and complicated application procedures should be solved by improving supporting measures.

The important information revealed to us from above research results is that the implementation of the universal two-child policy will bring a certain amount of birth "pile-up", but has a relatively limited effect on the annual birth population, and most of the potential birth "increment" will be released in the next 3–5 years. At the same time, due to the time lag between the implementation of the two-child policy and successful pregnancy of couples in line with the only two-child policy, the most pileup of births didn't occur in 2014, 2015 and 2016, where the birth of the large-scale "increment" and more significant "pile-up" of birth might occur likely.

The population changes need to be further discussed and studied after the implementation of the universal two-child policy. The fertility level in Beijing has been converging with that of the developed countries, and the fertility rate will be in the lowest low level (total fertility rate is below 1.5), so that the low fertility trap appears (Beijing Population & Development Research Center 2014). Whether is the universal two-child policy able to bring about a little reverse trend for the population in

Beijing? How about population changes? How to meet the needs in public services after the population changes? These are the focuses for next research as well as a matter of great concerns.

10.3 Research Questions

The two-child policy for couples where either the husband or the wife is from a single-child family had been out in the cold in various places since its implementation, and the expected baby boom did not appear. This was quite different from the research prediction of many scholars. The reason is that the actual fertility intention was not as high as the one in the survey, and there was also a great distance between the fertility intention and the actual childbearing behavior. As the fertility intention was influenced by many objective factors, so the childbearing behavior deviated from the fertility intention.

Then, will the expanded fertility group be able to trigger more childbearing behavior after the universal two-child policy has been carried out in an all-round way? How will the population trend develop and change after the policy is adjusted? And what requirements and challenges will be posed in the field of public services? For the research on these problems, the relevant models and parameters are urgent to be established through scientific population prediction software and statistical methods. Only by this way, the general growth trend of population aged 0–3 years old can be scientifically predicted in the next few years.

Research hypothesis: Under the universal two-child background, the population trend will be affected by the limited pileup effect, and the fertility rate will be recovered slightly after releasing a certain fertility potential. However, it is still not enough to change the present situation of population aging under the existing economic and social and cultural conditions.

The study will carry out the further prediction using the model developed by Zhai et al. (2015) and referring to the research results of other scholars.

10.4 Research Design

10.4.1 Research Object: Population Aged 0–3 Years in Beijing

The change of population in Beijing under the situation of the new childbearing policy is the basis and background of the follow-up studies. We need to grasp the two points of the change trend and its distribution. The research will realize the prediction of population growth trend by employing the existing statistical data, drawing on the related research results of scholars, referring to the population prediction and survey results after the implementation of the two-child policy for couples where either the husband or the wife is from a single-child family, and setting relevant parameters by population prediction software. The universal two-child policy benefits more population compared with the two-child policy for couples where either the husband or the wife is from a single-child family. So, on the basis of the results of the research on the change of population who have only two children, the more in-depth analysis is needed on the fertility intention of the population who benefit from the new policy, as well as the possibility of their intentions into the actual childbearing behavior as a reference. On the other hand, considering that the fertility intention may vary in different districts and counties, we perform the study on population growth trend by different functional areas.

10.4.2 Research Method (Population Prediction)

(1) **Population prediction method and tool choice**

In the previous study, a scholar applied the method that directly assumed total woman fertility rate up to the replacement level after relaxation of the childbearing policy. This method made a rough estimate of the population only by their own knowledge and specific assumptions, ignoring the key issues such as the pileup release of second childbirth energy accumulated in the past after the change of family planning policy. A researcher innovatively applied the age-progressive model, while another one scholar employed the parity progression ratio model for estimation of changes of population and birth rate in the policy situation. To some extent, this method can make up for the limitation of the traditional population prediction under the new policy-adjusting situation, but it is relatively complex. It needs the detailed fertile woman/child structure data, and the prediction result is easily affected by data quality.

This study reasonably sets several parameters, such as total fertility rate, average life expectancy, sex ratio at birth and fertility pattern, using Padis-int population prediction software by referring to Zhai Zhenwu's simulation method of fertility policy adjustment, Wang Guangzhou's parity progression model, and Ma Xiaohong and Zhu Xianqiang's parameter-setting logic based on demographic data. Furthermore, it predicts the growth trend of population aged 0–3 years old in the future 10 years in Beijing using PADIS-INT software based on the existing survey and research results of fertility intention as well as the online statistical data from Beijing sixth census and Beijing and sampled county health and family planning commissions.

Based on the existing survey and research results of fertility intention as well as the online statistical data from Beijing sixth census and Beijing and sampled county health and family planning commissions, this study sets total fertility rate of permanent resident population, and roughly predicts the future changing trend of population by such migration factors as the policy-related fertility potential, new urbanization, and population flow.

10.4 Research Design

(2) Estimation of main prediction parameters

A. Total fertility rate

Low-TFR program: The Total Fertility Tate (TFR) of permanent population is up to 0.706 in Beijing in 2010, and it remains below the national level for a long time (Zhi and Xu 2016). Some studies have shown that total fertility rate is between 1.63 and 1.65 in recent years at home (Zhai 2015). Therefore, in this study, the minimum total fertility rate in the future is set as 1.28 as a reference and warning plan based on the related literature, as well as the number and fertility pattern of women of childbearing age in Beijing.

Mid-TFR program: considering the full implementation of two-child policy in the next 10 years, we will increase the total fertility rate from 0.7067 in 2010 to 1.5 in 2026 to maintain this fertility level based on the related survey, that is, more than 1600 samples of the Sampling Survey of Childbearing Intention for Only Children in Beijing carried out by Beijing Family Planning Commission in 2002. The statistical results show that only children aged 20–30 years old have an average fertility intention of 1.03 children, and some of them are the ones who are married with a child and have an average fertility intention of 1.31 children. We believe that it is possible to restore the total fertility rate of women of childbearing age to 1.5 in the next 10 years in Beijing.

High-TFR program: The total fertility rate is increased from 0.7067 in 2010 to 1.8 in 2026 based on the urban average fertility level in the past 10 years.

B. Average life expectancy

The sixth national census showed the average life expectancy of men was 78.28 years, and 82.21 for women in permanent population in Beijing in 2010. The man/woman average life span increased by 0.1 years on average from 2010 to 2026 based on the empirical value of average annual growth pace of average life expectancy at different levels of birth issued by the United Nations in low-, mid-, and high-TFR programs.

C. Sex ratio at birth

We determine the sex ratio at birth declined in six consecutive years from 2008 to 2014 using China's sex ratio at birth as the basic data based on the statistical data from the National Planning Commission. Considering the natural adjustment of sex ratio at birth with adjustment of fertility policy, we believe that the sex ratio at birth of resident population in Beijing will gradually fall back to a normal level in low-, mid-, and high-TFR programs.

D. Fertility pattern

According to the relevant literature, the sample survey data in 2014 are applied in this study, and the fertility pattern will remain unchanged for the next 22 years for low-, mid-, and high-TFR programs.

10.5 Results and Analysis

Any population prediction and analysis models need to be carried out in certain assumptions, and the same is true in this study. According to the birth data and the changing trend of population during 2000–2014 years, as well as the effect of the implementation of the two-child policy for couples where either the husband or the wife is from a single-child family and the support of relevant research results in Beijing, the population prediction in this study is based on the following assumptions:

(1) Assume the future fertility level is divided into three levels: low (TFR = 1.28), mid (TFR = 1.5), and high (TFR = 1.8) in the wake of implementation of the universal two-child policy;
(2) Assume that the age in childbirth peak slowly goes on to 28 years old or more at high-, mid-, and low-TFR programs. Three programs have difference in the key parameter—Total Fertility Rate (TFR). The different fertility rates occur with the changing trend of population affected by such factors as childbearing age and intention after the two-child policy is fully carried out. Therefore, according to the study by Wang (2016) and others, the total fertility rate is set to three levels to predict the population-changing trend under the universal two-child policy. As a reference group, the low-TFR program is an assumption made on the slowly rising fertility rate for realistic childbearing conditions; the mid-TFR program is an assumption made based on the possibility of slightly increased fertility rate; at the same time, the high-TFR program is a highest estimate of fertility level under the universal two-child policy according to the existing research results. Based on above assumptions and basic demographic data, the predicting results of the future growing trend of population aged 0–3 years old in Beijing are obtained as follows using the queue factor prediction model (Table 10.3).

10.5.1 Analysis of Dynamic Trend of Population Aged 0–3 Years During 2016–2026 in Beijing

In general, each age group at 0–3 years of age shows a consistent growth trend of population under the assumptions of fertility rate at three levels. In the next 5–10 years, the pileup of fertility potential (especially for one-child family which plans to give birth to the second child but does not meet the two-child policy for couples where either the husband or the wife is from a single-child family) will be gradually released; it will release a certain growth potential, forming less obvious small peak. However, after that, the effect of regulatory policy will shrink and the newborn population will gradually decline in 2020 or so, even lower than the current fertility level. The sum of the population of 0–3 years old in Beijing will begin to decrease in 2023. In the low-TFR program (TFR = 1.28), total population aged 0–3 years old in Beijing will slide to the current population level in 2026 after experiencing a short period of

10.5 Results and Analysis

Table 10.3 Predicting results of the future growing trend of population aged 0–3 years in Beijing in different programs

Year	0	1	2	3	Sum aged 0–3 years old
Low-TFR program (TFR = 1.28)					
2016	197,595	179,485	166,780	152,393	696,253
2017	212,943	197,532	179,431	166,756	756,662
2018	224,952	212,876	197,475	179,404	814,707
2019	231,922	224,880	212,814	197,446	867,062
2020	232,877	231,848	224,815	212,782	902,322
2021	213,008	232,803	231,780	224,782	902,373
2022	191,760	212,941	232,735	231,745	869,181
2023	170,241	191,700	212,879	232,700	807,520
2024	150,296	170,186	191,644	212,847	724,973
2025	132,649	150,248	170,136	191,616	644,649
2026	117,440	132,606	150,203	170,111	570,360
Mid-TFR program (TFR = 1.5)					
2016	207,153	179,485	166,780	152,393	705,811
2017	231,591	207,088	179,431	166,756	784,866
2018	251,951	231,516	207,027	179,404	869,898
2019	266,092	251,871	231,448	206,996	956,407
2020	272,616	266,008	251,797	231,413	1,021,834
2021	249,355	272,529	265,929	251,760	1,039,573
2022	224,478	249,276	272,449	265,890	1,012,093
2023	199,283	224,406	249,202	272,409	945,300
2024	175,929	199,220	224,341	249,165	848,655
2025	155,266	175,873	199,161	224,308	754,608
2026	137,457	155,215	175,821	199,132	667,625
High-TFR program (TFR = 1.8)					
2016	219,993	179,485	166,780	152,393	718,651
2017	256,659	219,923	179,431	166,756	822,769
2018	288,261	256,577	219,859	179,404	944,101
2019	312,062	288,169	256,500	219,826	1,076,557
2020	326,090	311,963	288,084	256,461	1,182,598
2021	298,265	325,987	311,872	288,042	1,224,166
2022	268,497	298,170	325,892	311,826	1,204,385
2023	238,342	268,413	298,083	325,843	1,130,681
2024	210,388	238,266	268,334	298,040	1,015,028
2025	185,651	210,320	238,196	268,294	902,461
2026	164,332	185,591	210,258	238,161	798,342

growth. Subsequently, the population inertia of the low fertility rate will continue, as shown in the Figs. 10.2, 10.3 and 10.4.

As shown above figures, the trend of population growth is basically the same under the prediction programs at three fertility levels. The difference is that the population situations of the mid-TFR (TFR = 1.5) and high-TFR (TFR = 1.8) programs show a greater change. Total population of 0–3 years old has gradually fallen in the wake of its peak in 2023, but it is not rapidly decreasing to the current population level, slightly higher than 5–10 million.

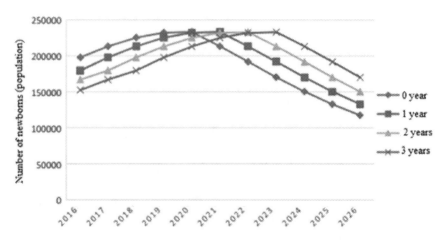

Fig. 10.2 Population growth trend under all low-TFR program (TFR = 1.28)

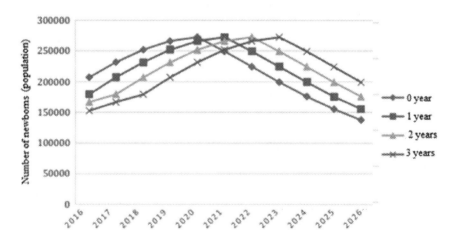

Fig. 10.3 Population growth trend under all mid-TFR program (TFR = 1.5)

10.5 Results and Analysis

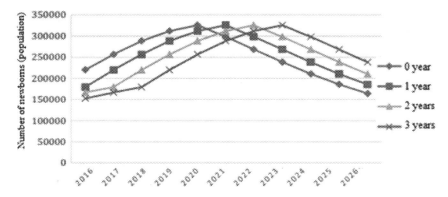

Fig. 10.4 Population growth trend under all high-TFR program (TFR = 1.8)

10.5.2 Analysis of the Trend and the Proportion of Total Population Aged 0–3 Years Old During 2016–2026 in Beijing

From Figs. 10.3, 10.4, and 10.5, we can see that the population of 0–3 years old in Beijing will experience a process of increase first and then decrease, presenting an "n" shape during 2016–2026. The main factor affecting the change of population aged 0–3 years old is total fertility rate. So, the size of total population in Beijing is stable under the prediction of three TFR programs. Under the influence of the universal two-child policy, the number of population aged 0–3 years old will be rebounded by the new fertility measures, and the proportion will also increase. However, with the gradual disappearance of the policy effect, it will face the population reduction period of the 0–3 years old population in Beijing.

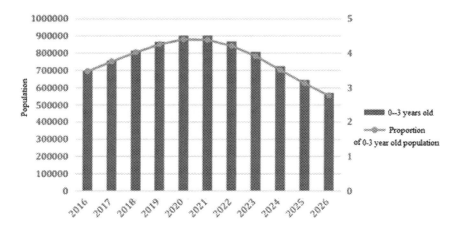

Fig. 10.5 Proportion of population aged 0–3 years old in all low-TFR program

In the low-TFR program, the 0–3 years old population will increase gradually to the peak in around 2021 from 3.47% in 2016 in proportion, accounting for 4.39% of the total population of all ages, and then a shrinking population comes. After that, the 0–3 years old population decline will be greater than the rise of the population growth; total population aged 0–3 years old is in a low proportion to 2.77% in 2026, still less than 3.47% in 2016. This is not conducive to coping with such social problems as aging population and shortage of labors in our country (Fig. 10.6).

In All mid-TFR program (Fig. 10.7), the 0–3 years old population keeps an increasing trend in the growth period with the all low-TFR program, but the extent of growth is larger than that of all low-TFR program. The proportion of the population under 3 will reach 5.01% in 2021. In a subsequent period of shrinking population, the population will reduce more than the population increase in the early period, but less than

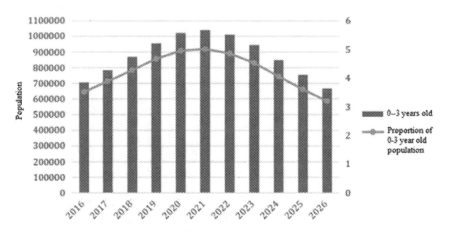

Fig. 10.6 Proportion of population aged 0–3 years old in all mid-TFR program

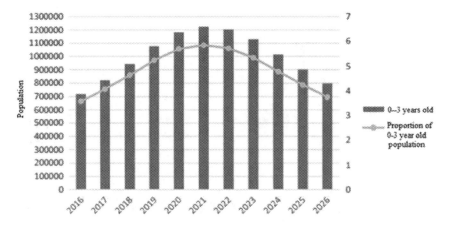

Fig. 10.7 Proportion of population aged 0–3 years old in all high-TFR program

10.5 Results and Analysis

the decline in the population shrinking period of all low-TFR program. By 2026, the total population of 0–3 years old will almost drop to the same level in 2016, accounting for around 3.20% of total population.

The population dynamic trend under the all mid-TFR program is more conservative relatively, but it is still far from being enough to cope with the current situation of serious imbalance in population structure.

In all high-TFR program, the increase in the population growth period is greater than the levels of All low-TFR and all mid-TFR programs, and is less than the population reduction in the later period. By 2021, the peak population aged 0–3 years old will reach 5.84% in proportion, far higher than all low-TFR and all mid-TFR programs. After a later period of shrinking population, the proportion of total population of 0–3 years old will fall to 3.7% in 2026, still higher than that in 2016.

Therefore, for the current population aging problem, the population growth situation presented in all high-TFR program can be addressed relatively, and more reasonable. But for the regulation of fertility rate accident, more incentive and supporting measures are needed in addition to the universal two-child policy to ensure the fertility behavior of the women of childbearing age.

10.5.3 Comparative Analysis of the Prediction of Population Changes Before and After the Two-Child Policy

In order to compare the rationality of demographic trends in three programs, the population trends are also predicted, respectively, under the two-child policy for couples where either the husband or the wife is from a single-child family and the two-child policy for only-child couples. The TFR is set as 0.70 and 1.12 in the two policies based on the actual fertility rates, and the following results are obtained by the comparison of three-level programs under the universal two-child policy.

As can be seen in the implementation of the two-child policy for only-child couples unchanged, total population of 0–3 years old in Beijing will continue to decline from 609,600 in 2016 to 307,000 in 2026. So this program is not conducive to adjustment of the population structure in China. For the two-child policy for couples where either the husband or the wife is from a single-child family carried out in the past few years, it brought a small increment of population aged 0–3 years old in Beijing from 688,600 in 2016 to the peak-800,000 in 2020, but followed by a more substantial population reduction to 493,000 by 2026. Therefore, the two-child policy for couples where either the husband or the wife is from a single-child family may be more favorable for controlling the size of population, but it is difficult to adjust the population structure and tackle the current aging problem (Fig. 10.8).

The growth trend of population aged 0–3 years old in three programs in the wake of universal two-child policy has been analyzed in detail in above paragraphs. Next, for the universal two-child policy, it is more conducive to the adjustment of birth rate to adjust the population structure in the future. The high-TFR program (TFR = 1.8)

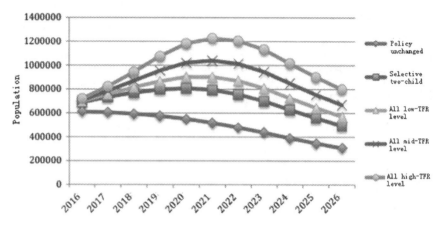

Fig. 10.8 Prediction and comparison of demographic dynamics in different policies

under the universal two children is only one that the increment of population in the first 5 years is greater than the reduction of population in the last 5 years. Though a small peak population in a short period of 5 years will bring a certain degree of population pressure to society, it is most conducive to alleviating the problem of increasingly serious population aging.

10.5.4 Summary

Through the prediction of population-changing trends during 2016–2026 in Beijing in high-, mid-, and low-TFR programs under the universal two-child policy, it is concluded that the total population of 0–3 years old in Beijing is increasing first and then decreasing in the three programs. In the low- and mid-TFR programs, the population reduction in the later stage is larger than the increment in the early stage, and the two programs are not the best way to adjust the current population structure and aging problem. In the high-TFR program, although the total population will decline after it reaches a peak in 2021, the decline is slightly less than the earlier rise. Therefore, the high-TFR population prediction program under the universal two-child policy is conducive to adjusting the current population structure, and helps alleviate the labor shortage caused by the population aging problem to a certain extent.

Under the overall implementation of the universal two-child policy, the main factor that affects the growth trend of population aged 0–3 years old population is the fertility rate. The fertility rate is greatly influenced by the childbearing willingness and behavior pattern of the fertility group. The women of childbearing age in Beijing are greatly reduced currently compared with the past, and the age of first birth is delayed until nearly 30 years old; infertility population will continue to increase.

10.5 Results and Analysis

So, we can see that the fertility group's childbearing behavior pattern in Beijing is constantly moving closer to that of western countries with a low fertility rate. Therefore, in the current reality, we should pay more attention to improving this depressive and slow childbearing behavior pattern, and helping fertility group transform their fertility intention into real childbearing behaviors, and reduce some obstacles. The universal two-child policy has opened up the threshold condition for the fertility group, but the more thresholds mean the enormous pressure to raising two children currently. This is the problem to be solved as a supporting measure for the two-child policy. On the other hand, after the opening of the two-child policy, Beijing will have a certain degree of fertility potential release in the next few years, which will bring certain challenges to all sectors of society, such as the medical and educational fields.

10.6 Discussion and Suggestions

10.6.1 Increase First and then Decrease of Population Aged 0–3 Years Old During 2016–2026 in Beijing

In this study, the conclusion is drawn through prediction that the population of 0–3 years old during 2016–2026 in Beijing will present a trend of increase first, and then decrease after the full implementation of the universal two-child policy; the changing trend of population at the age of 0–3 is mainly affected by the number of women of childbearing age and total fertility rate, and the total fertility rate is also affected by such factors as social economy, policy and the concept of fertility. Therefore, under the possible three fertility rate patterns, the 0–3 years old population in Beijing shows three dynamic change levels with a consistent changing trend but different changing sizes. Its growth size will not be too large, the peak population will appear around 2021, and then the population gradually gets into a reduction period. So, there will not be too much population pileup effect. However, for such a megacity of Beijing, it has diversified cultures with population migration as the external population is its main part (Gao and Zhang 2016). Moreover, it is carrying pressure from transportation, housing, education, health, employment, and public safety. Therefore, the number of new population will also bring pressure and challenge to the management of all levels in Beijing.

The trend of the increase first and then decrease of population aged 0–3 years old in Beijing can be said to be corresponding to the current level of economic development and the pattern of fertility behavior in Beijing. As an advanced area of China's economic and social development, Beijing completed the demographic transition as early as 1970s. It is converging with the developed countries in fertility level, fertility pattern, and childbearing willingness and behavior (Beijing Population & Development Research Center 2015). Since 30 years of reform and opening up, the woman childbearing age continue to be delayed with the leading role of rapid economic development and the policy of family planning, and they play different roles in the family and career, which leads to the change of the concept of marriage and childbearing gradually. In addition, the cost of child-rearing is rising in the current competitive society, and huge investment in both time and money is needed for child-rearing. This has become a biggest source of pressure for families to raise children in Beijing. Since the 1990s, a population development pattern of low natural growth and high mechanical growth comes into being in Beijing with its huge floating population scale (Gao and Zhang 2016). However, the fertility rate in Beijing is lower than the national level and below 1 for a long time. On the other hand, relative to the two-child policy for couples where either the husband or the wife is from a single-child family, the universal two-child policy is mainly aiming at the families with a child. For the women at the first-birth age of over 30, they are the main group aged 30–45 benefiting from the new policy measures in Beijing; but for women at the age of over 40, they are no longer suitable for birth giving for poor health condition, or have two children (60% of women at age of over 40 have two children according to the survey by the National Bureau of Statistics), or they have unstable fertility intention due to many social factors. Therefore, for Beijing, the overall implementation of the two-child policy may release a certain fertility potential, but the total fertility size is not optimistic. For a megacity with multi-culture and large population, the structure of the population may be more worthy of concern.

10.6.2 Full Understanding of the Reality that Beijing Is in a Low Fertility Level for a Long Time and in the Future

In the past 10 years, Beijing has always kept a trend that young population is declining and aged population is increasing in proportion, so that the aging of population is serious. Total fertility rate in Beijing has been below the population replacement level for nearly 40 years, and has been lower than the lowest low fertility level (the total fertility rate is below 1.5) for 20 years. It is undeniable that the low fertility phenomenon in the social development law is actually happening in Beijing. The implementation of the two-child policy for couples where either the husband or the wife is from a single-child family does not have a great impact on the population in Beijing, and the universal two-child policy would also not change Beijing's future population structure, but the overall liberalization of fertility policy will bring some incremental population, and this can alleviate such problems as the aging of population and labor shortage after a certain period of time. In the prediction of three programs in this research, the total fertility rate TFR = 1.8 or above can ensure the increase of population aged 0–3 in Beijing city in total proportion, and the reduced stage will not be lower than the current situation. This program helps alleviate the current severe population aging. Beijing should be prepared to cope with the social pressure caused by the expansion of population in the period of population growth.

In order to release the potential of fertility to the maximum, it should be the final direction of the policy to allow the people of childbearing age to choose their own birth pattern.

10.6.3 Learning the Experience from Low Fertility Countries in Formulating the Social Pro-breeding Policies

In order to control the population, most of the countries and regions of low fertility will basically adopt social pro-breeding policies. Though China has long fallen into the low fertility trap and taken corresponding measures such as revising the birth control policy to tackle related problems, we can learn some experience through analyzing the implementation effect of these pro-breeding policies.

For example, in maternity insurance and benefits, France, Finland, Australia, and East Asian countries such as Singapore offer a certain amount of compensation in materials and education funds to the newborn family for birth and rearing, and these funds are called maternity benefits and raising allowances. In the aspect of maternity leaves, French women giving birth to two children or above can enjoy 26 weeks (around 180 days) of maternity leave; those who deliver twins can enjoy 34 weeks of maternity leave. In addition, in some countries such as Germany, women can also enjoy childbearing women who have a certain paid parental leave (12–14 months); these leaves such as French unpaid parental leave (3 years) and father's leave are more conducive to childbearing families to overcome the enormous pressure from childbearing. In early education, Japan carried out the "Angel Plan" in 1994, taking one of the main measures is to implement childcare assistance for 0–3 years old children's education. In addition, Japan also alleviates family's educational burden through school aid and tuition waiver. But for China, it may be more urgent to solve the problem of shortage of educational resources at present.

References

Beijing Population & Development Research Center. (2014). *Beijing population and development research report*. Beijing: Social Sciences Academic Press.

Beijing Population & Development Research Center. (2015). *Beijing population and development research report*. Beijing: Social Sciences Academic Press.

Beijing Population & Family Planning Commission. (2014). *Beijing Health and Family Planning Commission's propaganda outline of initially implementing the two-child policy for couples where either the husband or he wife is from a single-child family*. Beijing Population and Family Planning Commission.

Gao, Y., & Zhang, X. (2016). Analysis of structure features and changing trend of population in China's megacities-taking a study case of Beijing. *Journal of Population Study, 02*, 18–28.

Guo, Z. (2014). *China's low fertility rate and sustainable population development*. Beijing: China Social Science Press.

Wang, G. (2016). Changes from the two-child policy for couples where either the husband or he wife is from a single-child family to the universal two-child policy. *The Forum of Leadership Science. 2*, 31–36.

Zhai, Z. (2015). How much is China's total fertility rate at the present stage? *Population Research: New Evidences from Household Registration Data, 11*(06), 23.

Zhi, D., & Xu, X. (2016). Structured changes of fertility rate and sharp growth of newborns—Based on Beijing APC model empirical study. *Statistical Research, 03,* 106–112.

Chapter 11
Parenting Characteristics and Problems of Urban Two Children Families Amid the Universal Two-Child Policy

11.1 Introduction

With the advent of the universal two-child policy, China is seeing a transition from one-children families to two-child families. The universal two-child policy is a good response to aging-related challenges and wins demographic dividend for more labor force. Most of the young people of childbearing age who are only children have difficulties in supporting the four elders in a family. Having a second child well resolves the challenge for the next generation and improves the quality of life in old age. As far as young children are concerned, the first children no longer feel lonely, as two children grow up together. It also improves sociability such as compassion, sharing, friendship and help (Sulian 2014; Le et al. 2016). However, two-child families also have difficulties in parenting. On February 21, 2016, at the launch of the nation's first "Two-Child Family Day" and the second-child family key data conference, parents pointed out that "it's difficult in raising a child, not alone raising two children". More than half of the families said that they are facing new problems such as jealousness of the first child and quarrels at bed time. Such has been reported for million times and must be concerning.

The universal two-child policy will affect family rearing. The previous monotonous education patterns hardly meet the needs of the second children. It is necessary to explore more according to the individuality of preschool children (Pei 2015). Family rearing plays a crucial role in the behavior problems of preschoolers. How parents and children get along with, development of habits and education methods influence preschool children's behaviors (Fengling 2003). In this regard, good family rearing reduces or avoids the occurrence of children's behavior problems, and plays an important role in children's development.

In terms of educational research under the two-child policy, most of the studies have analyzed the impact of the two-child policy on the changes of the educated population, the supply of preschool education resources, and the educational development strategy in China, and analysis and prediction from the perspectives of science, economics, sociology, and environmental science. Some studies have dealt with the countermeasures of family education misunderstanding under the comprehensive two-child policy, but lacks of empirical research. In addition, there is very little research into the micro-context of education to explore the impact of the two-child policy on the education of children in the real family. Some studies have down deep into the family of two children to explore the social impact of the birth of the two children, but they do not use case studies to explore the status of family care for the two children. In the study of family factors affecting the development of young children, the research objects mostly focus on the only child, and lacking of research on the family factors affecting the development of children in the second-child family. The research on the status quo of parenting methods has been studied in children, middle school students and college students and most of them explore the ways of parenting, cognitive development, social development, self-awareness, personality traits, self-reliance, and various diseases impacts. The diversity of research is reflected in the diversity of the types of subjects and the diversity of the impact on the development of the research objects, but neglects the study of parenting styles of different types of families (including single-child families, two-child families, families with many children, etc.). In the study on the fostering of only child and non-only child, most of the research is about the educational study of the only child, and a few studies involve a comparative study of the parenting style of the only child and the non-only child. However, studies have explored the differences in the way parenting between the only child and the non-only child in the horizontal, and the lack of a longitudinal study of the evolution of the family from the one-child family to the non-only-child family.

Summarizing the existing research find that the previous research rarely touches on the characteristics of the two-child family's parenting style and the related problems in the two-child policy, and lacks case studies. Therefore, this thesis studies the above issues.

The two-child families in this study had raised a child before the policy was implemented. With the advent of the universal two-child policy, parents raise the first and second children. The study has no limit of the gender of two children, but requires target groups of the second children born after the universal two-child policy was implemented.

In the study, family nourishment heavily refers to parenting tendency and the combination of children's emotional performance in the daily life of education and child-rearing through explicit actions (gestures), expression (moods), and language (intonation). It includes the concept of parenting, parenting attitudes and parenting behaviors. Caregivers in this study mainly refer to parents. If grandparents are involved in taking care of children, caregivers refer to parents and grandparents.

Among them, the concept of parenting includes parents' care for young children, meeting the needs of children, training of habits, abilities, and quality, peer interaction, and understanding, early education concept, views of traditional parenting, and caregiving by the elders. Parenting attitudes include: encouraging children to take part in challenging activities, respecting children's opinions and ideas, praising children, corporal punishment, interfering with children's activities, guiding ways

11.1 Introduction

to get along with, raising mentality and keeping their opinions with other family members. Nurturing behavior include paying attention to children's diet and feeding, ways to get along with children, distribution of caring for two children, intimate contact with children, body language and eye contact, and reading with children.

The study delves into rearing of the second children (concept, attitude, and behavior) before and after the birth of the second children, rearing influence on the second children, problems of and solutions to parenting of the second children. The study aims to arouse concern about the second-child family rearing, urges parents to realize the importance of family rearing to the second-children's growth and development. Second, by analyzing parenting problems and confusion in the five families with the second children, the study explains the reasons and give relevant suggestions. In addition, experience and common problems in raising the second children contribute to family rearing.

11.2 Research Methods

11.2.1 Target Groups

Target groups are parents, grandparents, the first child, and the second child in five urban two-child families in China amid the universal two-child policy. Three of the urban families are two-child families in Beijing and two are in urban Qingdao. In these two-child families, parents have a child before the implementation of the universal two-child policy. Amid the universal two-child policy, parents have the younger child. In the study, purposive sampling is utilized to choose target groups with certain parenting problems. With rural policies of "one child and half", there are few families with two children. The universal two-child policy has a greater influence on urban families, which is also the reason for choosing urban two-child families.

Before interviews and observation, the study delves into family information such as information of children (age and gender of the first child and the second child), information of parents (age, profession, degree, income, pedagogy background, the only child or not, and personality), and information of families (family income, main caregivers, and family atmosphere).

According to the first interview and observation, the five families are sorted in the following way: No. 1 family, No. 2 family, No. 3 family, No. 4 family, and No. 5 family. No. 1 family and No. 2 family are in Qingdao, while No. 3 family, No. 4 family, and No. 5 family are in Beijing.

According to Table 11.1, when it comes to age of two children, in these five families, the first child is aged 5–9. The youngest child is in middle class of kindergarten, while the eldest one is in grade three of primary school. The second child is aged 7 months–2 years and 10 months. The eldest one can receive preschool education. Age difference between the first child and second child is 2 years and 2 months–7 years. In terms of gender of two children, in these five families, two families have the

Table 11.1 Information of children in two-child families

	Children	No. 1 family	No. 2 family	No. 3 family	No. 4 family	No. 5 family
Nickname	The first child	Da Liang	Nuo Nuo	Duo Duo	Ni Ni	Ru Ru
	The second child	Er Liang	Cheng Cheng	Xi Xi	Mi Ni	En En
Age	The first child	5 years old	5 years old	9 years old	6 years old	5 years old
	The second child	2 years and 10 months	1 year old	2 years old	7 months	8 months
Gender	The first child	Female	Female	Male	Female	Female
	The second child	Female	Male	Female	Female	Male

younger and elder sisters, three families have a boy and a girl. Two families have an elder sister and elder brother. One family has an elder brother and a younger sister. In other words, four families have the elder sister, while the other one family has the elder brother.

According to Tables 11.2 and 11.3, parents of the five two-child families are aged 32–37. Apart from the mother in the No. 4 family who is a housewife and can be the main caregiver of children, parents of the four families work. In that case, grandparents become the main caregivers. In terms of degrees, parents of the five families have a junior college or above degrees. When it comes to incomes, the fathers earn more than the mothers, with yearly household income of over RMB 100,000. Two of the five families have a yearly household income of over RMB 200,000. On this very note, all of the five families have household incomes of above average level. As for pedagogy background, the mother of No. 3 family is a kindergarten teacher, the father of No. 5 family teaches astronomy at a university. Other parents have no pedagogy background. When it comes to parents as the only children, generally speaking, half of the parents are the only children. There are three families in which one of the parents is the only child, and the other one not. Only one family consists of parents as the only children. Only one of the parents are not the only children. All the family members get along in a harmonious manner, with a little quarrel. Parents of the No. 4 family never quarrel. All of the five families are democratic families. Four of the families discuss and decide on matters. Parents of the No. 2 family discuss and decide on matters.

In No. 1 family, the father is a navy man who is often on business trips and have only a quarter of a year at home. The mother works in a court. Usually, grandmother and grandfather take care of the second child aged 2 years and 10 months. Coming home

11.2 Research Methods

Table 11.2 Information of parents in two-child families

	Parents	No. 1 family	No. 2 family	No. 3 family	No. 4 family	No. 5 family
Age	Father	33	35	37	35	32
	Mother	32	35	36	35	32
Profession	Father	Solider	Professional	Professional	Private owner	University teacher
	Mother	Staff in a public institution	Professional	Kindergarten teacher	Housewife	Staff in a public institution
Degree	Father	Bachelor's degree	Bachelor's degree	Master's degree	Master's degree	Master's degree
	Mother	Bachelor's degree	Bachelor's degree	Master's degree	Junior college	Junior college
Monthly income	Father	5000–8000	>10000	>10000	>10000	5000–8000
	Mother	3000–5000	3000–5000	8000–10000	0	Less than 3000
Pedagogy background	Father	No	No	No	No	Yes
	Mother	No	No	Yes	No	No
The only-child or not	Father	Yes	Yes	Yes	No	Yes
	Mother	Yes	No	No	Yes	No

Table 11.3 Information of two-child families

	No. 1 family	No. 2 family	No. 3 family	No. 4 family	No. 5 family
Yearly household income	RMB 100,000–200,000	RMB 100,000–200,000	Over RMB 200,000	Over RMB 200,000	RMB 100,000–200,000
With or without nanny or the elders	With the nanny and the elders	With the elders	With the elders	With the elders	With the elders
Main caregivers before the first child is aged 3	The elders	The elders	The elders	The elders before the child was 1 year old; the mother when the child is aged 1–3	The elders
Main caregivers of the second child now	The elders	The elders	The elders	The mother and the elders	The elders
Quarrel frequency	Seldom	Seldom	Seldom	Never	Seldom
Family atmosphere	Harmonious	Harmonious	Harmonious and democratic	Harmonious	Harmonious
Decider	By discussion	By discussion	Parents	By discussion	By discussion

11.2 Research Methods

from work at night, the mother takes care of children together with grandparents. The nanny usually cooks and cleans. At weekends, when the nanny is off, grandparents come to help as parents are busy caring about children. The first child is in the middle class in kindergarten, while the second child is in early education.

In No. 2 family, both father and mother are engaged in artistic designing. The mother is a graphic designer, while the father is an interior designer. The mother has two days off each week while the father has one day off on Sunday. They spend time with children when they are available. Usually, the grandma looks after the second child aged 1 at home. At night, parents and grandma look after children, as grandma lives with them. The mother's native place is Zibo. In that case, the grandma goes back to hometown on Tomb-Sweeping Day and May Day. The first child is in the middle class in a kindergarten.

In No. 3 family, the mother with a preschool education MA is a kindergarten principal in Beijing. The father is a professional who often go on a business trip. Before the second child was born, No. 3 family is a stem family composed of grandparents and parents. In the daytime, grandparents look after the first child. At night, the mother looks after the first child. After the birth of the second child, grandparents no longer live with parents and two children. In the daytime, grandparents look after the second child at their own home. At night, parents pick up the second child. The first child is in grade three of a primary school.

In No. 4 family, the mother is a housewife, while the father runs his own business. He works at home, in ways to look after children together with his wife. Besides, grandparents also look after children at home. The mother quit and became a housewife when the first child was 1 year old. Before the first child was 1 year old, grandparents looked after the child. As indulgence did harm to development of independence, the mother quit. The father also quit and started his business from then on. Now, the company is on the up-and-up, and the family sees a growth of household income. The first child is in preschool education.

In No. 5 family, the father is an astronomy teacher of a university, while the mother is a staff of a public institution. Now, the father works and lives in Beijing with the first child, while the mother looks after the second child at the hometown. The reunion in summer and winter vacations. In the big family at the hometown, there are grandparents, uncle, aunt, and elder brother. Looking ahead to kindergarten, the first child was also in such a big family. Now, the second child is in senior grade of kindergarten in Beijing.

11.2.2 Research Methods and Research Tools

Case study, a method of qualitative research, was utilized in the study. Interview and observation methods were also used in the study.

11.2.2.1 Interview Method

Parents interview includes semi-structured interview and unstructured interview. Semi-structured interview is about information of parents and families, parenting of the first child before the birth of the second child (including concept, attitude, and behaviors of parenting), parenting of the first and second child after the birth of the second child, problems of and solutions to parenting of the second child, and open questions. In unstructured interview after observation, parents are informally interviewed according to observation results.

Interview of the first child: Interview of the first child is on the basis of semi-structured interview. The interview is about attitude of the first child toward the second child, attitude of the first child toward parents, and mindset of the first child in the face of transition from "the-only-child family" to "two-child family".

In the study, outline of semi-structured interview on parents and the first child is prepared. Interview outline is on the basis of questionnaire and interview outline according to Child-Rearing Practices Report (CRPR) (Block 1981) and What's Wrong with the First Child? Analysis on Influences of the Second Child on Social Development of the First Child and Solutions (Zou 2015).

11.2.2.2 Observation

Nonparticipant observation is utilized in the study. The study delves into family environment, family atmosphere, parent–child relationship, sibship, ways in which children and parents get along, and ways in which two children get along. With event sampling and anecdotal recording method, the paper records how parents get along with children, how grandparents get along with parents, and how grandparents get along with children during parenting in two-child families.

11.3 Research Results and Analysis

11.3.1 Analysis on Features of Parenting Before and After the Birth of the Second Child

11.3.1.1 Transition from "Parents' Dedication of All Love to the First Child" to "Two Children's Sharing of Parents' Love and Care"

Before the birth of the second child, parents give all their love and care to the first child. After the birth of the second child, the first child and the second child share such attention and love, which frustrates the first child. After the birth of the second child, as the second child is much younger, the second child has more urgent needs such as physiological needs, that is, defecation and suckling. In this regard, parents give priority to the second child. Parents' attention is directed to the second child. Although the love for the first child is not affected, the first child feels upset, as parents spend less time with him and focus less on him, sometimes parents even have less patience on listening to the first child. It's a great challenge for the first child to actively accept and understand it. It is a problem for parents.

The mother in the No. 1 family said, "Actually, I care more about the first child. After the birth of the second child, I care more about the first child. I will never make her have feelings of loss after having the younger sister. But, I worry about her psychological gap. To this end, I will care more about the first child."

Although parents say they take two children into consideration, they admit that, after the birth of the second child, they spend less time with the first child. Most of the first children in some families understand their own mothers. They know younger sisters or brothers need their moms. They play with their father, grandpa, and toys, as their moms are not around.

11.3.1.2 Transition from Monotonous Relationship to Different Relations According to Personality and Age

Before the birth of the second child, the way parents interact with the first child is monotonous. After the birth of the second child, ways differ with the personality and age of two children. Before the birth of the second child, there is only a child, and the way parents interact with the first child is monotonous. After the birth of the second child, there are two children in a family, and the way parents get along with two children changes. Before the second child is 1 year old, as the second child is less developed in each aspect, the way parents get along with two children slightly changes. However, in a family with the second child aged over two, the ways parents interact with children differs with the personality and age of children. For example, in the No. 1 family, the way mother interacts with two children differs with personalities of two children. The mother encourages the elder sister, while being strict with the younger one, because the first child is somewhat introverted in public places, while the younger sister is outgoing, unruly and naughty.

Different ways to interact with children according to their personalities benefit development of children. However, it shall take into account ways, methods, and feelings of children. Compared to encouragement, strictness may cause psychological harm to children. Parents are suggested to actively encourage their children to create rules, and supervise the abidance of rules. Parents need to encourage children to make progress, communicate with children, and have rule consciousness.

11.3.1.3 Transition from Peace of Parenting to Peace of Experience

Before the birth of the second child, parents are worried due to lack of material needs and emergency response experience. Parents in their 20s have few savings when they are raising the older child. They are worried and anxious in emergency, as they become the first-time parents. They learn to bathe children and make complementary food. They are at a loss when children have a fever. They stay calm in terms of growth and acceptance of the first child. Without comparison, No matter at what level your child is, parents never have ideas of delayed development of their children, nor are they worried about the temporary backwardness of children in some aspects.

After the birth of the second child, parents stay calm in terms of material needs and emergency response experience. At that time, parents have savings after years of work. With experience in raising the older child and emergency response, they are calm. To the contrary, in terms of development level, parents are worried about backwardness in level and speed of growth of the second child, compared to the first child. With experience of raising the first child at each level, parents will be worried about developmental retardation of the second child at a certain age. For example, in the No. 3 family, the second child expresses his ideas through body language when he is 1 year and 8 months old, parents become worried about language development retardation.

11.3.1.4 Transition from Intensive Feeding to Extensive Feeding

Before the birth of the second child, feeding was more intensive, as it was the first time to be parents. Parents at that time paid more attention and were willing to explore something new. After the birth of the second child, feeding was more extensive, with experience of feeding of the older child. In such extensive feeding, parents simplify feeding, without referring to books and experienced staff. They are skilled in feeding, without leaving children alone.

According to the No. 3 family, with the same feeding method, two children differ in eating. The second child like eating, while the first child is picky and never eats meat. Due to indulgence of the elders, children were fed until they were 5–6 years old. The second child aged 1 year and 8 months eats alone. According to the mother of the No. 4 family, two children eat different complementary food. The first child is ok after eating apple purees, while the second child has loose bowels after eating apple purees. Parents are suggested to make different feeding methods according to appetite and digestive absorption.

11.3.2 *Influences of Parenting on the First Child in a Family with Two Children*

Parenting in two-child families has no influence on the younger child who has an elder brother and sister. However, the first child saw transition from one-child family to two-child family in which he no longer has all of love from parents, but shares love with his younger sister or brother. It is a great challenge for him, especially for impressionable child.

11.3 Research Results and Analysis

11.3.2.1 Regression of Development of the First Child

In some families, the first child shows significant regression. For example, in the No. 4 family, the first child eats complementary food of the younger sister, and imitate how the baby speaks, and behaves in a spoiled manner to ask grandparents to zip. Possible reasons behind the phenomena are that parents care too much about the second child, while neglecting the first child. The first child behaves like a baby in ways to draw attentions from parents and prove parents' love for him. Besides, the unresolved problem cannot do without timely and appropriate guidance by parents. If parents may guide in an appropriate way, such regression will be reduced. When the first child wants to eat as what the second child eats (puree), parents are suggested to guide in such way. Parents can ask the first child to eat a little bit, and tell him "Your younger sister or brother has to eat like this because he/she has no teeth. After having teeth, your sister/brother will eat as we eat". The first child must be taught that his younger sister/brother eats the same with us, and parents care the first child the same with the second child. When the first child imitates how the baby speaks, parents are suggested to talk to the first child that parents used to be babies, and everyone sees a transition from inability to speak to ability to speak. Parents are suggested to talk to the elder child that, they prefer his previous ways of speaking, and encourage the elder child to teach the younger sister/brother to talk like them. Besides, the fundamental reason for such regression of the first child must be found, that is, parents care less about the first child. Therefore, parents shall rethink their behaviors, and care more about what the first child thinks. Parents shall not neglect the first child after the birth of the second child.

11.3.2.2 Emotional and Character Changes of the First Child

As parents care less about the first child and grandparents guide in inappropriate manners, the first child has some emotional and personality changes, such as emotional instability, short temper, introversion and lack of self-confidence. In families with two children, as the second child splits the mother's focus, parents sometimes care less about the first child. For example, parents interrupt the first child who is talking about his ideas, which upsets the first child; grandparents ask the first child to give into the second child, which leads to introversion and regression of the first child; the first child competes for privilege and love through crying. According to analysis, emotions and personality of the first girl will be more influenced by parenting of the second child, compared to the first boy. When raising the second child, if parents fail to timely take into account feelings of the first child, the first child will oppose through emotional changes, which requires parents to reasonably guide moods of the first child, and to pay more attention to the first child during parenting.

Positive emotions of the mother contribute to the development of children's emotional comprehension. At the same time, the development of children's emotions is affected to a large extent by parents' timely response to children's emotional cues (Zhang 2013). In a family environment of positive emotions, pro-social behaviors in which emotional expression rules are used will be promoted. However, a family environment of negative emotions does harm to emotional understanding and expression (Jones et al. 2004). Changes in moods and emotions of the first child, such as emotional instability and excitement, mean that parents have biases in treating two children. The first child wants the same love with his younger sister or brother by blowing up. Parents should be aware of injustice and bias do harm to two children. In many cases, a small or casual action of parents cause mood swings of the first child. Therefore, parents should pay reasonable attention to the mental state of two children and treat them fairly. It plays an important role in children's emotional and social development.

Reasons for introversion and lack of confidence of the first child are: first, failure of parents to guide the first child to develop an active consciousness when two children interact with each other; second, unreasonality of grandparents such as "obligation of the first child to give into the second child", which frustrates the first child, goes against development of interpersonal skill and sociability of the first child. Parents shall realize active roles of the first child when interacting with the second child, and guide in an appropriate manner, in ways to help the first child build confidence.

11.3.2.3 Influence of Crying of the Second Child on Study of the First Child

After the birth of the second child, all the family members focus on the second child. The first child has plenty of distraction from crying and laughing of the second child, which has an impact on learning of the first child. It always happens when the first child is about to attend primary school. At that time, the first child is in a critical period to develop good learning habits and have a sense of time. With poor immunity from interference, the first child is liable to be influenced by surrounding environment. It's important for parents to help children increase self-control, develop good living habits, and train self-control in learning.

11.3.3 Parents' Difficulties in Raising the Second Children

11.3.3.1 Parents and Grandparents Have Differences in Raising the Second Children

Grandparents and parents have great differences in the concept of family nurturing, in aspects of concept and behavior of development of children's independence and indulgence of children, solutions to disputes between the first child the second child, and development of their abilities and qualities. In terms of independence and indulgence, the first children turn to grandparents because they could not get the expected demand and satisfaction from their parents. They often ask their grandparents to pull their zippers, fasten shoelaces and pour water. While parents insist that their children do these things on their own, grandparents have already helped their children. In this regard, the first children are gratified in another way, and become more lazy and dependent. Therefore, children are weak in independence and self-care. When it comes to solutions to disputes between the first children and the second children, grandparents and parents have different attitudes. Grandparents hold that the first children shall act magnanimously, while parents argue it shall be on a case by case basis. According to causes, process, and results, parents determine the responsibility and communicate with them in a patient and active way. Two children will understand problems in so doing, and solve problems in case of inconsistency. As far as grandparents are concerned, the first children shall act magnificently, which is not conducive to establish prestige and confidence, and develop self-esteem for the first children and principles for the second children (Gulay 2011). In so doing, the first children make concessions without reasons. Factors such as consistency and coordination of concepts and behaviors during co-parenting, have a significant impact on the development of children's personality (He 2015). There is a big difference between grandparents and parents in terms of developing children's abilities, habits and qualities. Parents consciously develop their abilities, habits, and qualities, while grandparents think it is enough to take good care of children's diets and activities. In other words, in the process of parenting, parents play the role of raising and education, while grandparents play a role of caregiving.

Xiaowei et al. (2016) found that active co-parenting has a positive role in alleviating parenting pressure and reducing young children's problems. However, In real life, parents and grandparents conflict in the way of parenting. Therefore, it is of great significance to help grandparents to change the concept of education. At present, in the society, there is lack of channels and means for providing knowledge to parents and grandparents. Kindergartens and educational institutions can give more lectures on parenting to grandparents and parents, and more access to childcare knowledge. In addition, parents should guide children to respect and honor their elders, to help to do more than they can within their reach, instead of troubling their grandparents. Parents should communicate more with their elders and help them to learn some ideas of early childhood education to lead to parenting synergy for children's development.

11.3.3.2 The Mother's Physical Overdraft

Some mothers hold that parents need to be cautious to have a second child. Having a second child sometimes causes family disputes and postpartum depression. Worse still, elder mothers have difficulties in recovery compared to delivery of the older child. After talks with several mothers, as for mothers aged over 30, it's a great challenge to have a second child psychologically and physically. Parents shall take all into account before having the second child. Health of the mother shall be ensured. Family members need to care about and look after the mother after delivery, in ways to prevent postpartum depression.

11.3.3.3 Distracting Parenting Influences Learning and Career Development of Parents

Looking after the second child is too distracting, which influences career development of parents. A mother failed to write a thesis and get a translation certificate, as she had to look after the second child. As the elder child grows up, parents gradually make a career in their golden 30s. However, with the birth of the younger child, career of parents, especially the mother, is effected. Parents are back on the horns of that dilemma. How children grow up from 1 year old to 6 years old has its critical role in the years ahead. Parents need to realize that it's a once-in-a-lifetime opportunity to have early education. To the contrary, they have many opportunities to move up.

11.4 Suggestions

11.4.1 More Care About the First Child

As the first child gives into the younger one, parents need to give priorities to the first child appropriately, and take his ideas into account. When it comes to regression of the first child, parents need to prevent it from happening by giving special treatments to the first child, such as caring more about psychology of the first child, communicating with the first child, paying attention to needs of the first child, guiding the second child to respect the first child and encouraging and praising the first child, in ways to give the first child confidence and pride. At the same time, parents need to create a good learning environment and opportunities for the first child. Influence of the second child on the first child shall be minimized by having acoustic insulation equipment and silencers.

11.4.2 Fair Treatment of Two Children and Care About Emotional Changes of the First Child

With the transition from the one-child family to two-child family, parents must recognize the change in parenting environment of the first child. The first child has to share love and care with the second child. Parents are suggested to put themselves in the first child's shoes, and fairly treat two children. After the birth of the second child, mindset of the first child cannot be neglected. Emotional changes of the first child cannot be ignored. Parents are suggested to talk with the first child and give hugs to him as before. Negative response of children due to lack of love shall be prevented (Becker 1998). A sense of competition with the younger sister or brother shall be prevented, which lays a solid foundation for them to get along in the future. In case of disputes between them, bias must be prevented. Parents shall not just ask the first child to give into the second child. Instead, parents need to solve problems on a case by case basis. Reasons must be pinpointed. By talking with two children, faults of two children are found. Parents need to tell them that, disputes shall be prevented, as disputes only lead to escalation of contradictions. Next time in a similar case, two children shall bring out the facts and reasons in a calm way, or find a satisfactory solutions. If such disputes fail to be resolved by themselves, they can turn to their parents. Parents need to tell them that parents dislike unfriendly quarrels. After children understand it, two children need to apologize to each other.

11.4.3 Emphasis on Guidance of the First Child and Development of Interpersonal Skills

In two-child families, two children interact on the basis of peer relations and sense of trust, which lays a foundation for language competence, interpersonal skills and social adaptation ability. The first child is elder than the second child, and shall be active in interaction with his younger brother/sister. Parents need to actively guide the first child to help, share and communicate. Parents need to encourage the first child to build positive peer relations, which lays a solid foundation for interpersonal skills, understanding, and caring when he is in school age and get into the workforce, in ways to be highly competent with emotional intelligence.

11.4.4 Build Parenting Synergy Through Reasonable Communications

When parents find a difference in concept and behaviors of parenting with grandparents, they shall prevent confrontations with grandparents. Instead, parents need to talk with grandparents appropriately. First, parents need to appreciate grandparents for looking after children. If grandparents challenge parenting of the mother and the father, parents are suggested to learn some parenting knowledge to persuade grandparents. In such way, grandparents will know childhood education plays a critical role in lifetime development, and scientific parenting helps to develop healthy personality. Besides, it's important to develop good habits, characters and skills. If grandparents fail to prevent spoiling children in a short term, parents shall timely prompt grandparents to have correct concepts and behaviors of parenting. By communicating with grandparents in a reasonable way, parents and grandparents synergize childhood education for children's development.

11.4.5 Mother's Age and Health Shall Be Taken into Account Before Having a Second Child

Before you want a second child, you should fully consider various factors and do not blindly follow the policy. If economic conditions permit, in addition to considering the first child's opinions and making proper guidance, objective factors such as mother's age, mother's health, and family environment need to be considered. In addition, family members must be prepared to take good care of the postnatal mother. The father shall prevent business travels during pregnancy and production. He shall stay with his wife at home, and help his wife recover through scientific diet. At the same time, it is necessary to consider whether parents can take care of their children after birth of the second child. It shall be prevented that parents take care of a child in two places. Parents play an important role in the early nursery. Lack of exchange and interaction with their parents is not conducive to the development of children's healthy and personality.

11.4.6 Parents Take into Account Development of Children and Themselves

To have the second child is to assume more responsibility. Parents shall clearly know the main contradiction at present is to meet the needs of children, take good care of children and promote the healthy development of children. Parents should recognize that their own development and professional learning should temporarily give way to the growth and development of children. Parents should improve their overall planning ability and learning efficiency. As a saying goes, "you can't have your cake and eat it", parents shall take into account their career development and the growth and development of children. Health and good characters of children are a wealth and a great cause of parents.

11.5 Conclusion

With the advent of the universal two-child policy, two-child family rearing has a great impact on early childhood development. It not only has a significant role in early emotional and social development of young children, but also makes difference in the development of early childhood habits, abilities, and quality, which deserves the attention of educators and parents in two-child families.

Family rearing changes after the birth of the second children: (1) Attention and love change. Before the second children are born, parents give all their love and care to their first children. However, after the second children are born, the first children share the parents' attention and love, which frustrates the first children. (2) The way parents and children get along has changed. Parents and children get along in a monotonous way before the second children are born. After the second children are born, the way differs with age and personality of the second children. (3) Parenting mindset changes. Due to inadequate material needs and lack of experience in emergency response, they are more anxious about the second children, but less anxious about the first children because of development and acceptance of the first children. After the birth of the second children, parents are less anxious about material demands and emergency response. They are anxious about the second children, as development level and speed of the second children lag behind. (4) The way of feeding changes. Before the second children are born, the feeding style is more intensive; however, after the birth, the feeding is more extensive and experienced in an easy way.

Parenting in two-child families causes problems of the first child: (1) Regression of the first child. In some families, the first child imitates the way the baby talks, and eats what the baby eats, which reflects less care and love for the first child. (2) The first child changes in terms of personality and emotions, that is, emotional instability, short temper, introversion and lack of confidence. In this regard, parents fail to give fair treatment to two children and encourage the first child to dominate in peer relations. (3) What the second child behaves intervenes learning of the first child. The first child has plenty of distraction from crying of the second child, which influences his study.

Parents have challenges and problems when they are raising the second child: (1) Parents have disputes with grandparents in terms of concepts and behaviors of parenting, such as independence training and indulgence, solutions to disputes between the first child and the second child; (2) The mother is likely to have postpartum depression due to the age; (3) Raising the second child influences learning and career development of parents.

On this very note, suggestions are given: (1) Parents are suggested to give special treatment to the first child; (2) Parents need to treat two children fairly, and care about emotional changes of the first child; (3) Parents need to guide the first child and develop his interpersonal skills; (4) Parents are advised to build educational synergy by communicating with grandparents to minimize disputes; (5) Before having a second child, parents shall take into account age and health of the mother; (6) Parents need to take into account career development and children's growth.

References

Becker, A. J. (1998). Self-reports of mathematics self-concept and educational outcomes: The roles of ego-dimensions and self-consciousness. *British Journal of Educational Psychology*.

Block, J. H. (1981). *The child-rearing practices report (CRPR): A set of Q items for the description of parental socialization attitudes and values*. Berkeley, CA: University of California, Institute of Human Development.

Fengling, Z., & Shiwei, M. (2003). Influence of parenting on behaviors of preschoolers. *Journal of Clinical Pediatrics, 06*, 365–367.

Gulay, H. (2011). Assessment of the pro-social behaviors of young children with regard to social development, social skills, parental acceptance-rejection and peer relationships. *Journal of Instructional Psychology, 38*(3–4), 164.

He, M. (2015). *Comprehensive model of influences on personality development of children aged 3–6*. Liaoning Normal University.

Jones, N. A., Mc Fall, B. A., & Diego, M. A. (2004). Patterns of brain electrical activity in infants of depressed mothers who breastfeed and bottle feed: the mediating role of infant temperament. *Biological Psychology, 67*(1), 103–124.

Le, M., Bin, Z., & Yang, L. (2016). Misunderstanding of family education and solutions amid the universal-two-child policy. *Journal of Educational Development (Monthly Edition), 06*, 89–92.

Pei, L. (2015). Influence on and measures of the pre-school education amid the universal two-child policy. *Journal of Xingyi Normal University for Nationalities, 04*, 83–87.

Sulian, Ruan. (2014). Pro-social behaviors of children and influences. *Studies in Preschool Education, 11*, 47–54.

Xiaowei, L., Juan, X., & Yating, S. (2016). Features of co-parenting of grandparents and parents and relations with parenting pressure and children's problems. *Chinese Journal of Special Education, 04*, 71–78.

Zhang, Y. (2013). *Influence of family parenting environment on dependence and social emotion development*. Shandong University.

Zou, L. (2015). *What's wrong with the first child? Analysis on influences of the second child on social development of the first child in a family and solutions*. Sichuan Normal University.

Chapter 12
A Case Study on Sibling Relationship Characteristics for Urban Families with Two Children

12.1 Introduction

Troubled by low birth, labor shortage, and pension overdraft, China changed its policy winds from one-child policy in 1980 to selective two-child policy in 2013 and universal two-child policy in 2016. The population policy has profound implications for Chinese families. According to All-China Women's Federation, in a report on the influence of the universal two-child policy on family education in 2016, 43.2% of the first children have developed behavioral problems after having the younger child, such as heavy dependency on parents, temper tantrums, violent temper, easy mood changes, unavailability, worry, moodiness, unfriendliness, unwillingness to share, cooperate, and help others. At the same time, there is lack of research on the younger child in education field, which is mostly a comparative study between one-child and non-only children. Parenthood and sibling relationship is at stake, with revolution of family structure and complicated family relations.

Sibling relationship refers to relationship among children of the same parents. It also refers to psychological relations arising from influences and roles of siblings in a core family (Zhang 2015). Faced with a newborn, ways to deal with the sibling have a significant impact on infant education.

Foreign research about sibling relationship has been deeply discussed in the 1970s. Influenced by China's population policy and family structure, most of the concerns are to compare the differences between only children and non-only children, comparing domestic research on sibling relationship is scarce. Upon the analysis of the existing research, the research of sibling relationship usually focuses on three aspects: the Forms, influencing factors, and role of sibling relationship.

This study is divided into two parts. First, characteristics of the sibling as single-child families shift to families with two children in China in terms of sibling intimacy, conflict, rivalry, and right contrast. Second, influences and roles of sibling. The study adds some muscle to a growing body of educational research for the younger child, and explores sibling and influences of two children. The study provides reference for related preschool teachers and parents in raising younger children.

12.2 Research Methods

12.2.1 Target Groups

The study is targeted at urban families with elder children aged less than 6 and younger children aged less than 3. Through observation and interviews, examples of sibling relationship were collected for further analysis. To find objects of study, convenience sampling method was utilized. Families with children having different gender orders and age difference (brothers, elder brother and younger sister, sisters, elder sister and younger brother) were chosen for the study. Five objects of the study are listed below:

Object of study	The first child			The second child		
	Gender	Age	Nickname	Gender	Age	Nickname
A	Male	4-year old	Bao Bao	Female	2 and a half years old	Niu Niu
B	Male	6-year old	Yong Yong	Male	1-year old	Ji Ji
C	Male	5-year old	Shi Tou	Male	2-year old	Man Tou
D	Female	2-year old	Qian Qian	Male	3 months	An An
E	Female	4-year old	Hua Hua	Female	1 and a half years old	Duo Duo

12.2.2 Research Methods

The study is in line with case study in qualitative study, interviewing method, and observational method.

12.2.2.1 Observational Method

The study prepares a summary sheet with observational method. During a month, each family was observed for 2–3 times a week and for 3 h each time. For infant interactions in many cases, parents of kids were trained to observe behaviors of their kids at other times. With narrative research method, how two kids get along with was recorded in terms of intimacy, conflict, and rivalry. Behavioral frequency and how they get along with were recorded in different aspects for sibling analysis.

12.2.2.2 Interviewing Method

After the observation, parents were semi-structurally interviewed. Parenting styles were known through interviews to analyze correlation between such styles and infant sibling; interview helps to look back upon how two kids get along with before observation, know timing of transition of infant attitudes, collect cases of how two kids get along with in the memory, and add more stories of two-child sibling.

12.3 Research Results and Analysis

12.3.1 Beginning of Sibling: Sibling Willingness

Now, most of Chinese families are single-child families, and there are growing families with two children. Some of Chinese families whose first children are old enough choose to have a younger child, when they are more capable economically. That also means the only children have developed some capacity for thought for a long time. They usually express willingness and have options of a second baby. Usually, parents will ask their opinions, provide a stepping stone and relevant psychological counseling; however, part of families had the younger child when the first child was yet to develop capacity for thought and language. During pregnancy of the younger child, most of the first children failed to understand parents who failed to ask their willingness. Parents during pregnancy subtly influenced their first children who had interactions among peers, in a way to develop care for their younger sister or brother.

Before the birth of the second baby, we tried to persuade our first child. One day, he was fed up and said, "Got it! Stop saying! I agree on that. But I don't want a younger brother. I like a younger sister, as a brother will take my toy cars." (Yong Yong and Ji Ji)

During pregnancy of the second child, the elder child was just 1-year old. At that time, he had no idea about it, so we didn't ask his opinions. Before the birth of the No. 2 baby, we asked him, "Do you want a younger brother or sister who can play with you?" The elder child said yes. Usually, when we hung up with the elder child, we encouraged him to play with sisters and brothers, so that he would be more involved in a group (Qian Qian and An An).

Sibling willingness represents psychological transition as only-child families transit to families with two children. Sibling willingness exists in two families where parents dominate and the first child passively accepts and where the first child independently chooses whether to have the second newborn. It is closely related to age of the first child. Different sibling willingness leads to different traces of sibling.

12.3.2 Sibling Performance

Sibling performance consists of cognitive performance and behavioral performance. Sibling cognition of a child is revealed in sibling interactions. The study describes sibling in families with two children through sibling interactions. According to Howe et al. (2011), sibling performance is divided into four parts, that is, sibling intimacy, conflict, rivalry, and relative status.

12.3.2.1 Sibling Intimacy in Terms of Companion, Sharing, Help, Taking Good Care, Education, and Protection

The paper finds after observation and interviews, sibling intimacy of the first child is on the basis of taking good care of and protecting the second child; sibling intimacy of the younger child is on the basis of following and imitating the elder child's behaviors during games. The initiator differs when it comes to sharing and companion. Friendly and amiable interaction between brothers and sisters is one of sibling intimacies at the lowest level, also known as the amiable sibling relationship in a family. Sibling education and assistance are explicit and implicit, such as following examples during games.

I usually asked my elder child to watch nappies changing. She would get nappies and unwrapped them as soon as I wiped arse of the second child. She had the conditioned response after watching nappies changing for several times. After each nappies changing, I would say, "Baby, thank you for getting nappies. Your younger sister is so happy!" (Qian Qian and An An).

Even if a conflict happens, sibling protection is rooted in nature. Though they express their frustration and repugnance for their sibling in front of their parents, they would stand up to protect their sibling from any physical attack.

One day the elder child was playing a top with his classmates in the neighborhood, and the second child squatted nearby. The second child tried to pick at the spinning top. One of the classmates pushed the second child. The elder child was angry about it. He stood up and pushed his classmate down on the floor, said, "you can't bully him" (Shi Tou and Man Tou).

12.3.2.2 Sibling Conflict in Terms of Resource Occupancy

Parents are worried about common sibling conflict during the preschool years. Sibling conflict mainly occurs in case of language, behavioral, or intentional conflicts that may be intensified. Usually, such conflicts consist of resource occupancy, physical conflicts, disagreement, or rule maintenance.

Sharing is one of sibling intimacies. Declining to share toys and food is also a major factor that causes sibling conflict. Such resource occupancy conflict usually occurs as kids are too self-conscious to lose their "territories and goods". In families with two children, as many toys are jointly owned, conflicts over ownership and rights to use occur.

They quarreled and competed with toys all the time. It was perfectly normal. They seldom fought but quarreled. Conflicts occurred when they competed with toys or the younger kid ate up what was for his elder brother (Shi Tou and Man Tou).

The paper finds after investigation, though kids have a short temper, sibling relations will not be influenced by such conflicts. How parents resolve sibling conflicts influences sibling relationship, parenthood, and even mental health of kids. If parents are biased, such conflicts may be intensified. With open wounds in the little heart, the second child may be timid, less confident, and even unwilling to interact with his/her sibling to prevent from punishment by parents due to possible conflicts. So, it's essential to resolving sibling conflicts in a just and fair way.

As preschool-age children, especially younger children, are yet to develop their language capacity, most of the conflicts are because of behaviors. As such conflicts escalate, children during this period are more likely to compete and fight with each other. As each year goes by, conflicts are less seen; as kids have stronger self-control, language conflicts have gradually displaced physical conflicts; meanwhile, as parent education, self-consciousness, and social development interact, the elder child is more likely to make a concession.

12.3.2.3 Sibling Rivalry Due to a Third Party

Sibling rivalry refers to behaviors of sibling comparison and jealousy. It usually involves contending for parents' attention and care, in terms of sibling behaviors in a family. Sibling rivalry is broadly defined. In a narrow sense, more conflicts happen to siblings, especially in a family with two children; rivalry requires a third party that may be person, thing, or status. Rivalry refers to that two children compete with a third party.

Fight between two children also occurs. Usually, the dad shielded the younger sister, as lady is first. The dad ordered the brother to the small dark room to reflect on his misdeeds. He was upset every time. One day, he said, "Grandma, turn me into Niu Niu Niu and turn Niu into me. Dad likes her, but doesn't like me. Grandma, you can be grandpa, and change grandpa into you" (Bao Bao and Niu Niu).

The elder child feels upset when seeing her mom staying with her younger brother. She wished her mom gave her hugs. She was sad when seeing her mom staying with her brother in the bed every day. The elder child was more dependent and needy on her papa, grandpa, and grandma (Qian Qian and An An).

After the birth of the younger child, sibling rivalry starts. The elder child feels left out and has an attitude of exclusion, as parents freed up their energy and time to take care of the second child. What the elder child desire are more attention and love. In this regard, the first child may do something intentionally to get more attention. Such behaviors are divided into implicit behaviors such as depression, behavioral regression, and discomfort for no reason as well as explicit behaviors such as short temper, bullying siblings, and peers, declining to go to kindergarten. Meanwhile, the child may seek exclusive safety from other supporters, and refuse previous caregivers. Such sibling rivalry is fierce in families with elder brother and younger sister. In such families, to be lady first, the young sister wins more favor, while the elder brother who shall be strong and brave has an "unfair" distinction. He feels wronged, and even doubt whether parents love him. How he wishes to change his gender and birth order, and become the favored sister.

In the preschool years, sibling rivalry results from psychological disturbance arising from the birth of the sibling. The elder child gets his/her security by competing for parents' attention. In this regard, sibling rivalry is fierce when sibling relationship starts. As the first child is more adapted, when he knows parents also love him, sibling rivalry initiated by him reduces. At that time, the younger child develops his self-awareness, and there is more sibling rivalry initiated by the younger child. When two children are mature enough, as they establish a stable attachment, sibling rivalry reduces generally. Therefore, psychological problems need to highlighted so as to reduce sibling rivalry.

12.3.2.4 Sibling Right Comparison Requires Admiration

Sibling right comparison is divided into positive admiration and negative dominance. Admiration refers to admiration and behavioral imitation; dominance is one the basis of status. It refers to having sibling do something. There is a leader in group activities. Others try to imitate what he behaves and do what he advises. When others accept from their inner hearts, they are obedient, which means they admire their leader; however, if such acceptance is affected by power and violence, they are passive. That is dominance.

For sibling right comparison in two dimensions, on the one hand, one child sets the other child as his example. He imitates whatever the other child does in an active and happy way. As the first child has higher level of cognition and more life experience, the leader is usually the first child who is more likely to acquire admiration of the younger child. During the process, sibling relationship is enhanced. The younger child develops due to imitated learning, while the first child improves his confidence due to admiration of the younger child, and works to challenge himself due to a driving force of admiration of the younger child. Such one-way admiration is questionable. However, as the first child is the only leader and role model, he is likely to refuse interactions with the younger child that is weak and of lower level. A sound sibling relationship requires mutual admiration.

When it comes to the second dominance, the leader is not fixed. One child who is stubborn and short-tempered tends to be the leader. He meddles in affairs of the other child. The imbalance of the right comparison reveals parents' partiality, violence, or concession of the other one. This is a passive interaction.

The second child has a significant characteristic. He desires whatever his elder brother has, play, and eat. He wants the shoes his brother wears. All in all, he takes his brother as his role model to fight for rights and interests (Shi Tou and Man Tou).

When the second kid grows up, parents find that the second kid is particularly interested in the elder child. He always looked at his little brother with all his eyes. Sometimes, when the elder child played with balls or toy cars, he felt proud of tickling the second kid (Yong Yong and Ji Ji).

12.3.2.5 Intricacy and Mutability of Sibling Relationship

Sibling intimacy, conflict, and rivalry are not so contradictory. Conflict and rivalry also help to enhance relations and interactions among children. Appropriate sibling conflict promotes acquisition of social emotion of children, in a way to improve sibling intimacy. The reduction in conflicts will not spontaneously lead to increase in positive sibling interactions. On the contrary, it may lead to activities alone. In life, parents focus more on sibling conflict and rivalry. However, compared to obvious parts that require changes, changes in sibling intimacy are more difficult.

Sibling relationship differs in different cases and situations and in four dimensions. To compare sibling relationship, it's more appropriate to divide it into positive and negative behavioral interactions. Ratios and frequency shall be measured, so as to estimate quality of sibling relationship. High-quality sibling relationship is featured by intimacy, conflicts and rivalry, and relative status (Howe et al. 2011).

12.3.3 Influences and Roles of Sibling Relationship

Influences on sibling relationship consist of family structure, family relations, parental rearing, and child's traits. The study focuses on family structure. Family structure refers to gender, gender order, age, and age difference. Therefore, sex characteristics, sex preferences, and development level of ages differ. All that in the family structure influences sibling relationship.

12.3.3.1 Gender and Gender Order

Gender and gender order have an impact on sibling relationship. When it comes to gender, gender characteristics of different children determine to some extent performance. For example, as women's cognitive development generally precedes that of men, during social learning, they are more likely to accept the younger child. Women have higher level of sibling intimacy, while men have higher level of sibling conflict. Compared to elder brothers, elder sisters are more likely to act as teachers and caregivers during childhood, while providing more emotional support as adults.

Families with two children have four gender structures of children: elder brother and younger sister, elder and younger brothers, elder and younger sisters, and elder sister and younger brother. Difference of gender structure also influences sibling relationship. Sibling of the same gender shows higher level of intimacy and lower level of conflict than that of different genders. This is related to gender stereotypes. Children prefer those of their own sex. Children of the same gender can become their own playmates. However, it is not so absolute. Some children think it is the because of same sex that rivalry easily occurs. Children of the same sex are more excluded. Tolerance of the opposite sex also exists. Men, in this sense, are seen to be strong protectors, while women are so weak that they require to be well protected. In that case, women love men because they feel protected, while men love women because they play their roles.

Before the birth of the second baby, we tried to persuade our first child. One day, he was fed up and said, "Got it! Stop saying! I agree on that. But I don't want a younger brother. I like a younger sister, as a brother will take my toy cars." (Yong Yong and Ji Ji)

One day, we asked the elder child about whether she liked a younger brother or sister. She said, "A sister", as sister can hang out with me (Qian Qian and An An).

Now they are more independent. They sleep in canopy beds. The elder brother would say, "Sister, as you are a girl, you sleep in the lower canopy bed. I'm your elder brother. I sleep in the higher berth (Bao Bao and Niu Niu).

It's ideal to have a family with a son and a daughter. To have a sound sibling relationship, children are required to be well educated and prepared for their second brother/sister according to gender and gender order.

12.3.3.2 Ages and Age Interval

Age is closely related to sibling relationship. When my elder child was 2-year old, he refuses to have a baby sister and would like to throw Niu Niu away. When he was over 3 years, though he was angry with his little sister, he knew his responsibility to protect his sister. Children grow mature as each year goes by. They are more socialized and know more. They start to understand sibling and empathy.

When it comes to age intervals, Nadelman and Begun (1982), in his study, expressed that the first children are more likely to adapt to their newborn sibling if their parents have their second child before they are aged less than 2. However, they are also more prone to immature behaviors such as degeneration. In the study, we found that the smaller age difference, the more intimacy because of psychological and behavioral similarities, but more conflict rivalry; however, the bigger age difference, the more authoritative the first child is. The first child becomes a role model and educational protector of the younger child. In that case, the less the sibling conflict and rivalry, the less the sibling intimacy of higher levels.

After the birth of the second kid, the elder child had no idea about life difference. He did whatever he liked. He reacts violently when it comes to sleeping with his mom (Yong Yong and Ji Ji).

Yesterday, dad played hide-and-seek with them at home. The second child followed her brother. She hided wherever her brother hid. However, the second child was not a good hider. Every time, she made a sound or ran out, revealing his elder brother. So, her elder brother was unhappy, and asked me to take the second child

12.3 Research Results and Analysis

away. I asked the second child to find her brother with her dad (Shi Tou and Man Tou).

Niu Niu wanted to be a doctor, so grandma bought a stethoscope syringe and other medical equipment. One day, the younger sister said, "Brother, now I'm a doctor. I can handle your cases. The elder brother sat at a chair and said, "I'm not ill." The younger sister said, "You have a cold. Now prepare shot. The elder brother pretended to be coughing and said, "I need medicine. Prescribe drugs." Then with a medicine bottle, she said, "you will be ok after taking medicine" (Bao Bao and Niu Niu).

Children's age influences their behaviors, which influences sibling relationship. The ideal age interval of sibling is about 3 years.

12.3.3.3 Roles

Sibling relationship difference, positive and negative interactions have different effects on siblings. Generally speaking, sibling relationship promotes the development of their conflict management, management of negative emotions, helps to shape social understanding, provides a test ground for the development of partnership, improves a sense of cooperation, and has a collective sense.

As for the first child, the downside of sibling relationship is that unsafe dependency caused by it leads to behavioral and emotional reactions, including negative emotions such as anxiety and depression, sleep disorders, and behavioral regression. Advantages are reduced dependency on parents, increased independence, development of skills for self-care and caring for others, and increased cooperation. From the case, we found that because of the insecurity the newborn child gives, they turn to other caregivers, and compete with their sibling. "The elder child felt unhappy as her mom stayed with her little brother everyday. So, she relies more on her dad, grandpa and grandma."

As for the younger child, sibling relationship's flaw is that the younger child may be bullied and mocked, which may develop personality of timidity and psychological disorders. On the upside, the elder child may be a good protector, caregiver, bosom friend, and role model, and the elder child feels less lonely than the only child. During interactions, the younger child sometimes develops more capacity for language and cognition compared to the only child. "Niu Niu is smarter now. When she hangs out with other friends, she says more words than her peers."

Sibling relationship is the long-lasting compulsory blood relationship in life and is the result of the mutual influences and roles of siblings in the family (Kramer 2010). As Chinese society evolves, against the background of the only-child policy, sibling relationship is rare in urban families. Practically or academically, sibling relationship is easily overlooked. As China promotes the universal two-child policy, family relationships become complicated. With recent return of sibling relationship problems, sibling relationship becomes a whole new challenge for young parents, the first child and education.

For parents, sibling relationship influences parenthood, while parents need to pay attention to how parental rearing influences sibling relationship. After delivery and recovery, the mom has more time to hang out with the elder child, while the dad subconsciously plays with the elder child everyday. In that case, every time when the elder child is asked about his attitude toward his younger brother, he would say, "I love my brother". Parents subconsciously help their children to get their stable security, in a way to avoid negative impacts of sibling rivalry.

As for the first child, a major challenge is psychological change. In a world that is not full of families with two children, most family structure is on the basis of the only child. When families keep the focus on the only children, they have an innate sense of superiority. Then, after the birth of the younger child, the elder child has to learn to face a new family member who draw attention of parents, and learn to get along with the newborn, which is a great challenge for the first child.

12.4 Educational Suggestions

12.4.1 Create More Opportunities for Positive Sibling Interactions

Development of sibling relationship is based on wider interactions. Especially for the first child aged 0–3 who is yet to have more playmates in kindergarten, the younger child becomes his main playmate. Such sibling interactions establish the basis for his interactions with other classmates, which helps his sociability; as for the younger child who grows day by day, the first child is his role model. The younger child learns by observation, which promotes his capacity in language, sociability, and operation. In families with two children, great efforts must be made in promoting games and communications between sibling, finding common interests and hobbies, triggering active interactions, in ways to increase frequency and quality of interactions. Sibling interactions shall be positive and cohesive. During interactions, children learn to cooperate, share, trust, help, and support with each other, which promotes sibling development and sibling intimacy.

12.4.2 Help Children Learn to Resolve Sibling Conflict and Rivalry, Sibling Right Comparison

Sibling relationship changes in different dimensions. Sometimes, it is positive or negative. By measuring ratio and frequency of positive interactions, sibling relationship quality can be estimated. It proves sibling relationship can be improved in different dimensions.

Sibling intimacy is often overlooked by parents. It does not pose obvious negative impacts in another axis. Sibling intimacy of low level is more difficult to be improved than sibling conflict of higher level. Increase in sibling intimacy as children grow requires parents' involvement in shaping and active caring about and helping by themselves.

Sibling conflict and rivalry are unavoidable and transformable. Problem-solving helps children to acquire skills and enhance sibling intimacy. China, especially, is seeing a structural transition from single-child families to families with two children. Sibling rivalry exists as the first child feels anxious and stressed. Bullying shall be avoided. Sibling rights shall be well compared in two-child families with high level of admiration and low level of instigation.

Solutions to sibling problems require the following four skills: (1) respecting opinions and demands of sibling, learning empathy and putting themselves in sibling's shoes, (2) emotional adjustment: emotions can be well managed in negative and challenging cases, (3) behavioral control: wrongness of sibling harm shall be avoided, such as competing for goods and instigating the other one. In situations of conflict, behaviors shall be well controlled to prevent conflicts from escalating. Violence shall not be resorted to solve problems, (4) positive or neutral attribution: positive attribution of sibling behaviors shall be organized to avoid hostility (Kramer 2010).

12.4.3 *Manage Influence Factors to Enhance Sibling Relationship*

Influences on sibling relationship consist of family structure, family relations, parental rearing, and child's traits. To enhance sibling relationship, the best time to give birth to the second child is when the first child has well developed and prepared psychologically. Great efforts must be made in introducing more friends to the first child, acquiring skills to get along with friends. Acceptance of the second child shall be improved by turning to picture books, in ways to establish role awareness. Parenting differs with genders of sibling. Parenthood and family atmosphere of high level shall be established. Differential treatment shall be avoided. Safety dependency shall be established. Timely problem finding and solving help to improve sibling relationship quality.

12.5 Conclusion

In an era of the universal two-child families, sibling relationship, undoubtedly, is an important part of family relations, and influences children's development and parenthood. Sibling relationship consists of sibling intimacy, sibling conflict, sibling rivalry, and sibling right comparison. Sibling intimacy related to human nature consists of sibling companion, sharing, assistance, caring, education, and protection; sibling conflict results from resource occupancy conflicts in childhood. It means poor sociability; sibling rivalry is a hot topic for families with two children. During transition from single-child families to families with two children, the first child especially has to avoid sibling rivalry, care about his little sister or brother, and establish safe and stable attachment; sibling right comparison in terms of positive admiration and negative administration has a positive and negative impact on children's development.

Changeable sibling relationship consists of family structure, family relations, parental rearing, and child's traits. It is affected by a number of factors. The study focuses on family structure that consists of gender, gender order, age, and age interval. According to the study, sibling of the same gender shows higher level of intimacy and lower level of conflict than that of different genders. However, as tolerance of the opposite sex exists, sibling rivalry is fiercer in some families with children of the same sex. Boys tend to protect girls, while girls tend to take good care of boys. The study also finds, development of cognition and sociability as child grow up helps children to acquire ways to get along with, in ways to promote sibling relationship. The smaller the age interval, the higher the intimacy because of psychological and behavioral similarities, and more conflicts and rivalries due to similarities in demands and thinking; the bigger the age interval, the more authoritative the first child is, the higher admiration level in sibling right comparison, the less sibling conflict and rivalry, the less sibling intimacy of high level.

In the course of this study, we find that the relationship between compatriots is very complex, and we also find some contradictory explanations in specific cases. Therefore, the sibling relationship theories need to be further improved, especially focusing on the impression of Chinese local culture and environment. At the same time, based on the research conclusions, we can carry out relevant intervention of sibling relationship.

References

Baby.sina.com. Report on Influence of Universal Two-Child Policy on Family Education by All-China Women's Federation [EB/OL]. http://baby.sina.com.cn/news/2016-12-22/doc.
Howe, N., Karos, L. K. & Aquan-Assee, J. (2011). Sibling relationship quality in early adolescence: Child and maternal perceptions and daily interactions. *Infant and Child Development, 20*, 227–245.
Kramer, L. (2010). The essential ingredients of successful sibling relationships: An emerging framework for advancing theory and practice. *Child Development Perspectives, 4*, 80–86.
Nadelman, L., & Begun, A. (1982). The effect of the newborn on the older sibling: Mothers' questionnaires. *Sibling relationships: Their nature and significance across the lifespan*, 13–37.
Zhang, X. (2015). *Research on children's sibling relationship and relevant factors in selective two-child policy*. Sichuan: Southwest Medical University.

Printed in the United States
By Bookmasters